Balancing Pressures

Balancing Pressures analyzes how the economy, national politics, and supranational politics shape economic policymaking in the European Union. Economic theories alert policymakers of the problems associated with policy initiatives. Economic uncertainties shape political positioning during negotiations, while actual economic conditions affect both negotiations and implementation. National pressures to win office and pursue policies systematically influence negotiating positions, implementation patterns, and outcomes. Supranational pressures are associated with membership in the euro area, the expected and actual patterns of compliance, or the context of negotiations.

Spanning the period from 1994 to 2019, this book analyzes how these pressures shaped the definition of the policy problems, the controversies surrounding policy reforms, the outcome, timing, and direction of reforms, the negotiations over preventive surveillance, the compliance with recommendations, and the use and effectiveness of the procedure to correct excessive fiscal deficits. It concludes by assessing the effectiveness, fairness, and responsiveness of the policy.

FABIO FRANCHINO is Professor of Political Science at the University of Milan. He has published extensively on legislative and executive politics, especially in the European Union. He is the author of *The Powers of the Union: Delegation in the EU* (2007) that won the EUSA Prize. He has been the president of the European Political Science Association and co-editor of the *Italian Political Science Review*. He is currently an associate editor of *European Union Politics*.

CAMILLA MARIOTTO is Assistant Professor of European Politics at the University of Innsbruck. She has published several academic articles on the politics and policies of the European Union, and European legislative and executive politics, with emphasis on policy implications. She was the managing editor of the *Italian Political Science Review* between 2014 and 2018.

Balancing Pressures

The Politics of Governing the European Economy

FABIO FRANCHINO
University of Milan

CAMILLA MARIOTTO
University of Innsbruck

CAMBRIDGE
UNIVERSITY PRESS

CAMBRIDGE
UNIVERSITY PRESS

Shaftesbury Road, Cambridge CB2 8EA, United Kingdom

One Liberty Plaza, 20th Floor, New York, NY 10006, USA

477 Williamstown Road, Port Melbourne, VIC 3207, Australia

314–321, 3rd Floor, Plot 3, Splendor Forum, Jasola District Centre,
New Delhi – 110025, India

103 Penang Road, #05–06/07, Visioncrest Commercial, Singapore 238467

Cambridge University Press is part of Cambridge University Press & Assessment,
a department of the University of Cambridge.

We share the University's mission to contribute to society through the pursuit of education, learning and research at the highest international levels of excellence.

www.cambridge.org
Information on this title: www.cambridge.org/9781009595810

DOI: 10.1017/9781009595834

When citing this work, please include a reference to the
DOI 10.1017/9781009595834

First published 2025

A catalogue record for this publication is available from the British Library

A Cataloging-in-Publication data record for this book is available from the Library of Congress

ISBN 978-1-009-59581-0 Hardback
ISBN 978-1-009-59586-5 Paperback

Additional resources for this publication at http://cambridge.org/Franchino_Mariotto

To Matteo, Elsa, and Enea
To Eliana, Mathias, and Thomas
who help us find balance under pressure

Contents

Figures

Tables

Acknowledgements

We began working on this book in 2014 when the European economy was still hesitantly recovering from the double whammy of the global financial crisis and the sovereign debt crisis in the euro area. The two-pack regulations of May 2013 concluded an extraordinary period of reform that began soon after the Greek authorities drastically revised their forecasts for the budget deficit in October 2009. For the first time in six years, the Greek economy started to expand, but there were still widespread concerns about the momentum of the recovery of the European economy. As political scientists, we wanted to understand what shaped the economic policy of the European Union, employing the extraordinary set of analytical tools that the discipline has developed over the past forty years. At that time raged the debate about the role of ideas, epitomized by the recently published book of Mark Blyth titled *Austerity: The History of a Dangerous Idea*. But ideas are only one set of factors that shape policies: preferences are formed, negotiations take place, laws are adopted, executive decisions are taken, and policy outputs are produced. Lacking intellectual restraint for our own good, we embarked on an ambitious multiannual project to investigate the politics of governing the European economy.

This book is the result of that scholarly journey. The final product would not have been anywhere near completed without the insightful, thought-provoking, and, sometimes, frustrating comments we have received from our colleagues along the way. We have to thank them all: Michael Becher, Edoardo Bressanelli, Philipp Broniecki, Carlos Closa, Nicolò Conti, Valerie D'Erman, Catherine E. De Vries, Livio Di Lonardo, Fabrizio Di Mascio, Andreas Dür, Zoltán Fazekas, Tullia Galanti, Philipp Genschel, Daniela Giannetti, Mario Gilli, Igor Guardiancich, Markus Haverland, Lore Hayek, Simon Hix, Madeleine Hosli, Marcelo Jenny, Erik Jones, Christel Koop, Lisa Lechner, David Levine, Riccarda Longaretti, Lanny Martin, Andreas

Maurer, Massimo Morelli, Monika Mühlböck, Gianluca Passarelli, Simona Piattoni, Emanuela Pistoia, Christian Rauh, Christine Reh, Thomas Sattler, Frank Schimmelfenning, Daniel Schulz, Jonathan Slapin, Reinout A. van der Veer, Amy Verdun, David Willumsen, and Jonathan Zeitlin. We are particularly indebted to Bjørn Høyland who read the book in one day and not only provided excellent comments but was also instrumental in the choice of the title, to John Haslam from Cambridge University Press for supporting our project, and to the two anonymous reviewers for their precious insights. We also thank Luca Cabras, Nicolò Cremona, Matteo Mandelli, Johannes Marco Oberhofer, and Angelo Parnofiello for their invaluable assistance that eased considerably the research burden. The comments from the editors and the anonymous reviewers of the journals where the articles, on which this book builds and extends, have been published (*European Journal of Political Research*, *European Union Politics*, *Political Science Research and Methods*, *Rivista Italiana di Politiche Pubbliche*, *Journal of Common Market Studies*, *Journal of European Integration*, and *Journal of European Public Policy*) have played an indirect, albeit crucial, role in improving our manuscript. And we are grateful for the many useful comments we have received from participants at seminars and conferences where we presented parts of this book and to the institutions that hosted us (Bocconi University, Collegio Carlo Alberto, Erasmus University Rotterdam, European University Institute, King's College London, Sciences Po Paris, Sapienza University, University of Innsbruck, University of Mannheim, University of Milan, University of Milano-Bicocca, University of Oslo, University of Pisa, and University of Turin), as well as the organizing associations (CefES Center for European Studies, ECPR. Standing Group on the European Union, European Political Science Association, and Italian Political Science Association). We also thank the Jean Monnet Network for its financial support.

The last, most heartfelt gratitude goes to our families for their unflinching support, despite the annoying features of academic life they have to put up with.

1 *Governing the European Economy as Balancing Pressures*

The first lesson of economics is scarcity: there is never enough of anything to fully satisfy all those who want it. The first lesson of politics is to disregard the first lesson of economics.

Thomas Sowell on economic and political pressures

We all know what to do, but we don't know how to get re-elected once we have done it.

Jean-Claude Juncker on national pressures

The pact will work better if intervention by European institutions in the budgetary sovereignty of national parliaments is only permitted under very limited conditions.

Gerhard Schröder on supranational pressures

On 7 February 1992, twelve heads of state or government and their foreign ministers gathered in a large conference room of a modern building that was inaugurated just a few years prior and hosted the government offices of the southernmost Dutch Province of Limburg. The building sits on a greenish triangular islet of the river Meuse in the provincial capital Maastricht – a small city that since the sixteenth century has been routinely sieged, captured, and freed by Spanish, French, Dutch, German, and, more recently, American forces. Sitting on two rows of sturdy light-brown desks and facing a hemicycle of spectators, they took their turn at a centrally located desk to sign a treaty that the European Council finalized the preceding December. Aníbal Cavaco Silva, the Prime Minister of Portugal, gave the introductory speech to the ceremony, claiming that they were 'making another historic step' in the process of European integration. This often-repeated assertion may not have been so hyperbolic this time. Thirty years on, millions of Europeans still live under the shadow of this thick document – its provisions, protocols, agreements, and declarations.

Its adoption attracted noticeable opposition for the first time: from the minuscule butterfly-like effect of a young British stockbroker by the name of Nigel Farage leaving, in protest, the Conservative party that same year, to the rejection in the Danish referendum of June 1992 – the first time ever a European treaty was rebuffed by the citizens of a member state[1] – and the *petit oui* in the French referendum on the following September, where approvals exceeded rejections by just a bit more than half a million votes. With the benefit of hindsight, we know now that the ambitious Treaty on European Union (EU) punctured the balloon of public permissiveness towards integration (Inglehart 1970a, 1970b), planted the seeds of more assertive public scrutiny – a constraining dissensus, to use Hooghe and Marks's (2009) felicitous choice of terms – and, where conditions allowed, gave rise to Eurosceptic parties.

This book is about one crucial chapter of that momentous treaty: Chapter 1 on Economic Policy of Title IV on Economic and Monetary Policy – seven articles, and a protocol, that have constituted the basis for steering national fiscal policies and governing the European (macro)economy in the past thirty years or so. Between 1994 and 2019, European legislators agreed on a set of regulations, directives, and an ancillary international treaty designed to put into effect the provisions of this treaty chapter. And they adopted a large number of recommendations, decisions, and national measures that implement this primary and secondary legislation. These measures are the result of a complex balancing act that European politicians perform in order to manage the pressures coming from the economy, national politics, and supranational politics.

1.1 Balancing Economic, National, and Supranational Pressures

This book addresses the most fundamental questions for understanding the politics of European economic policy (below we provide an overview of the whole policy). These are listed in Table 1.1: Which economic ideas explain its design? What explains the main cleavages characterizing this policy? What explains the outcome, timing, and direction of reforms? What explains the adoption of its

[1] Bar Greenland.

Table 1.1 *Research questions*

Chapter	Research question
Defining the policy problem	
2	Which economic *ideas* explain its design?
Negotiating and designing economic governance	
3	What are the main *cleavages* and what are the *sources* of these controversies?
4	What explains the *outcomes* of the negotiations?
5	What explains the *timing* and *direction* of the reforms?
Implementing economic governance	
6	What explains the *adoption* of the country-specific recommendations?
7	What explains national *compliance* with the country-specific recommendations?
8	What explains corrective oversight and does it engender *fiscal discipline*?

implementation instruments, the so-called country-specific recommendations? Why does compliance vary? What explains the use of the corrective procedure and is it effective?

To tackle these questions and understand the politics of EU economic policymaking, it is useful to see European politicians as actors balancing pressures arising from (the understanding of) the economy, national politics, and supranational politics. These pressures and how they operate are summarized in Table 1.2. Economic theories alert policymakers of the possible problems that may be associated with policy initiatives, such as the creation of a monetary union. Uncertainties about economic developments shape the positions politicians take at the negotiating table, while the actual realization of economic conditions shapes the efficacy of implementation. National pressures can be exemplified by the standard objectives of winning office and pursuing policies, which systematically influence government positions, implementation patterns, and policy outcomes. Last, supranational pressures represent all those factors that are associated with politics at the EU level. They can be contextual, such as being a member of the euro area; related to policy, such as the patterns of compliance; or related to the bargaining

Table 1.2 *Types of pressures*

Type	Subtype	How it operates	Selected main factors
Economic	Ideational	Economic theories point to possible policy problems and solutions	Economic theories
	Informational	Uncertainty and expectations about economic trends shape policy design and executive decisions	Forecasting errors; expected economic conditions
	Factual	Actual economic conditions force to act, constrain public finances, and shape outcomes	Realized economic conditions; economic shocks and crises
National	Office	Need to win and remain in office	Proximity to elections; public support for the EU; politicization
	Policy	Need to implement preferred policies, targeted to their constituencies	Government left–right position; government anti–pro EU position
Supranational	Euro area	Euro area countries face greater exposure to externalities	Euro area membership
	Compliance	Noncompliance expectations shape positions and decisions; pervasive noncompliance undermines policy credibility and triggers reform	Noncompliance risk; noncompliance cost; noncompliance record
	Bargaining	EU-level bargaining shapes legislative and executive decisions	Voting power; veto and exclusion threats; legislative procedures; pivotal preferences

over the adoption of laws or executive measures. We unpack these pressures in greater detail below, highlighting the stages of the policy process where they display their effects.

1.1.1 Economic Pressures: Ideas, Uncertainty, and Conditions

The economy put pressure on politicians in three different ways: *ideationally*, *informationally*, and *factually*. First, the theoretical understanding of how the economy works informs policymakers of the challenges associated with the creation of a monetary union, the contour of the potential problems, and the measures that could be adopted to address them. These problems, which we discuss concisely in Section 1.2.1, originate from standard applications of macroeconomic theories to the creation of a monetary union and not, as we argue in Chapter 2, from unorthodox austerity-based models or ideas. As such, they pressure policymakers to act.

Second, theories, no matter how robustly corroborated, are simplified pictures of the world. They offer an incomplete understanding of how the economy operates. At most, they are imperfect predictive tools. John Kenneth Galbraith was renowned for his disparaging comments about economic predictions. He would put forecasters in two categories: those who do not know and those who do not know they do not know. The implications are twofold. First, policymakers are cognizant of the arbitrariness of some policy provisions. For instance, as we argue in Chapters 2 and 4, standard bargaining models of supranational politics shed more light on the specific determination of the Maastricht fiscal reference values than sophisticated applications of economic theories. Second, policymakers operate under significant uncertainty over the trajectory of the economic indicators this policy aims to oversee. For instance, the forecasting error of the ratio between government balance and gross domestic product (GDP) is well above 1 per cent of GDP – more than a third of the deficit reference value of 3 per cent (for details, see Chapter 5). Arbitrariness and uncertainty loom large over policymakers' heads and inform policy positions. For instance, they caution finance ministers in the Council against excessive reliance on supranational bureaucrats in policy implementation (see Chapter 5).

Last, actual economic conditions shape policy developments. For instance, during the euro area crisis, ministerial positions shifted towards tighter national constraints (see Chapter 3). When the economic prospects of a given country worsen, ministers intervene more actively in the design of recommendations addressed to it (see Chapter 6), and its government is more inclined to implement the recommended measures (see Chapter 7). Economic conditions also determine the revenue, spending, and open-economy shocks that public finances experience (see Chapter 8).

1.1.2 National Pressures: Policy and Office

Winning *office* and adopting *policy* are the core objectives of politicians (Müller and Strøm 1999). Politicians may care about them to different degrees, but the nature of domestic political competition forces them to act *as if* they care about both. Politicians who care only about policy must win office to be in a position to change policy, while politicians who care only about office are aware that voters will not support them if they were to run for office without a policy platform.

The implications of these national pressures are numerous. For instance, governments are likely to take positions during policy reforms that are shaped by their economic left–right and pro-European orientations, in order to cater for their support constituencies. Euroscepticism among the domestic public or politicization of the reforms may also affect their positions, as we see in Chapters 3 and 5. In Chapter 8, we show that governments' pro-European inclinations are associated with shorter corrective oversight. Similarly, the proximity to elections is likely to induce governments to delay the implementation of unpopular measures and to run looser fiscal policies (see Chapters 7 and 8).

1.1.3 Supranational Pressures: Euro Area, Compliance, and Bargaining

Supranational pressures can be grouped into three broad categories: *euro area membership*, *compliance issues*, and *bargaining dynamics*. As we elaborate in greater detail below, the EU economic policy has been primarily designed to address new or more severe negative externalities arising from fiscal profligacy that countries of a monetary union may be exposed to. This consideration suggests that euro area governments are likely to face common pressures and, therefore, to share (1) common positions during the negotiations over policy design and (2) common incentives to comply with preventive and corrective executive decisions, as we see in Chapters 3, 7, and 8.

Compliance looms large over policymaking since it lends credibility to a policy. Noncompliance tends to engender costs for individual governments and, if pervasive, it risks undermining the whole policy. The risk of noncompliance, therefore, shapes bargaining positions during the negotiations over policy reforms (see Chapter 3), while past noncompliance affects the timing and direction of reforms, as emerges in Chapter 5. At the implementation stage, the compliance record features prominently when Council ministers issue a recommendation or open a corrective procedure against a given country (see Chapters 6 and 8). A recommended measure that is associated with a higher cost for noncompliance is more likely to be adopted by governments (see Chapter 7), while supranational oversight engenders fiscal discipline (see Chapter 8).

The third type of supranational pressure originates from the bargaining dynamic operating at the EU level. Legal provisions and executive measures, such as issuing a recommendation or opening a corrective procedure, result from a bargaining process where preferences, procedures, decision-making rules, threats of exclusion and veto, and linkages across issues play key roles, as we show in Chapters 4–6 and 8. For instance, factors, such as the divisiveness within the Council, the position of the so-called Council pivotal minister whose support is necessary to adopt a measure, and the position of the Commission, are associated with the nature of the recommendations, the probability of opening a corrective procedure and the duration of the procedure. Supranational roles, such as holding the Council presidency, and a country's voting power within the Council shape governments' negotiating positions (see Chapter 3).

1.2 A Theoretical Framework for Analyzing Economic Policymaking in the European Union

In line with the established conceptualization of the EU as a political system where outputs, social demands, and decisions interact on an ongoing basis (Hix and Høyland 2022: 2–4), we use the policy cycle, pioneered by Lasswell (1956), as an organizing principle of our theoretical framework, although policymaking hardly proceeds in an ordered and circular manner. According to this perspective, an issue is first recognized as a public problem demanding attention. Policymakers then form preferences on how best to address it and negotiate over the measures that need to be taken. Once agreed upon, the policy is implemented and its performance may (or may not) trigger a reform. The three sets of pressures we introduced earlier affect policymaking throughout the entire cycle. They shape the definition of the policy problem, the formulation of policy alternatives, the choice of the policy option, and the implementation of the policy and its efficacy. To give the reader an idea about the overall structure of the book, Figure 1.1 maps its chapters onto the cycle of economic policymaking.

The objects of study differ across the cycle (and the chapters). We study preference formation in Chapter 3, bargaining outcomes in Chapters 4–6 and 8, and compliance in Chapters 7 and 8. Our theoretical framework, therefore, builds upon phase-specific explanatory mechanisms to flesh out the precise relations between pressure factors and policy features. We use macroeconomic theories to evaluate the influence of ideas; liberal intergovernmentalism and the international relations literature on the design of dispute settlement mechanisms to explain the formation of preferences; a comprehensive set of models of EU bargaining to explain the adoption of laws and executive measures; the three most prominent theories of European integration to explain the direction and timing of reforms; theories of compliance and political economy theories of economic reform to explain the adoption and implementation of recommended measures; and last, the extensive array of political economy theories of public spending to assess the efficacy of corrective oversight.

The common analytical thread is that each phase of the policy cycle is influenced to a more or lesser extent by the pressures originating from the economy, national politics, and supranational politics. The positions policymakers take, the measures they adopt, and the consequences of their actions result from balancing these pressures. Phase-specific theories laid out their relative importance. Supranational factors may be more salient when studying bargaining over laws and executive measures, while national factors and economic conditions may be more important when analyzing implementation and its consequences. We begin with the ideational pressures: how the theoretical understanding of the economy defines the contour of the problem European economic governance is meant to address.

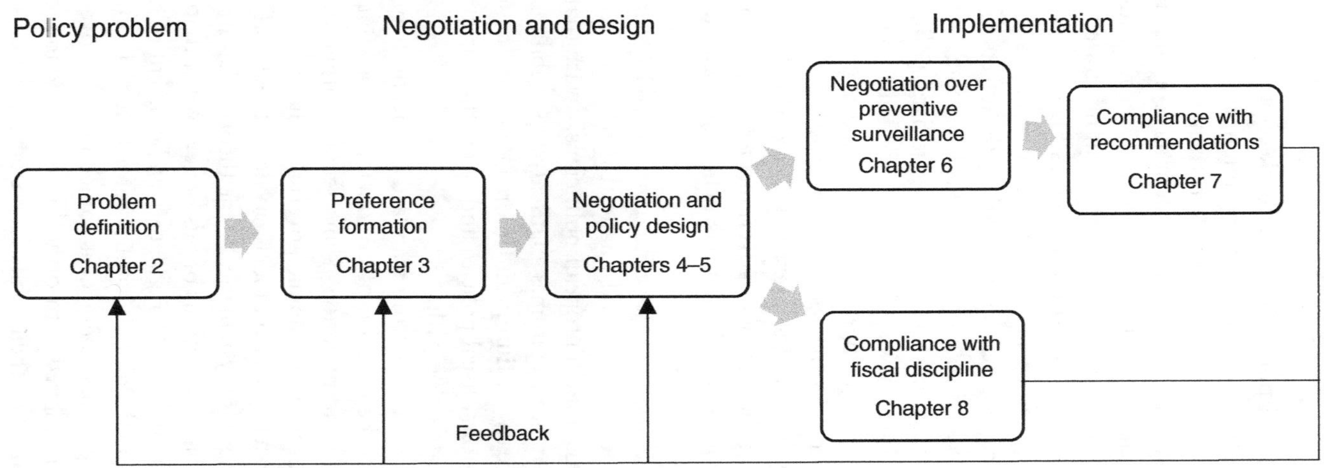

Figure 1.1 The cycle of economic policymaking of the European Union

1.2.1 The Contour of the Policy Problem

When politicians and policymakers embark on a new economic policy, such as the creation of a monetary union, the theoretical understanding of how the economy works alerts them to the challenges they face. The basic rationale for the adoption of an economic policy flanking a monetary union is apparently simple (Beetsma and Giuliodori 2010; Faini, Duranton, and Hau 2006). In an integrated capital market, the effects of a fiscal expansion, such as higher interest rates and lower investment, tend to spill over to other countries. If a monetary union promotes capital market integration, the effects of a *unilateral* fiscal expansion would be attenuated, thus loosening ever further the restraints for expansion. Moreover, profligate fiscal policies in a monetary union give rise to new spillovers, such as higher average inflation and (common) currency appreciation, thus undermining price stability and external competitiveness. And the possibility that a common central bank may be forced to prevent a sovereign debt default may in itself lead to moral hazard with governments adopting profligate fiscal policies. Of course, any bailout via debt monetization would have inflationary consequences.

In sum, because price stability can be threatened by fiscal profligacy in a single member country and financial markets do a poor job at deterring this behaviour, European politicians, aware that some governments had not been epitomes of fiscal responsibility, decided to include in the Treaty on European Union a common economic policy that oversees national fiscal policies and steers the European (macro) economy on a sustainable path.

This description derives from standard applications of macroeconomic theories to the creation of a monetary union. But there is no consensus on this interpretation. Some scholars argue that the rules that underpin European economic governance have been inspired by less orthodox austerity-based models or ideas. In Chapter 2, we take on this issue and peruse systematically the theories that may have provided the ideational foundations of this policy. We find no compelling evidence that this policy is the regulatory embodiment of modern austerity thinking. And the direction policy reforms took is opposite to the one we would expect had these ideas gained influence over time. That these rules appear aligned with orthodox macroeconomic theories is perhaps reassuring, but their limits in predicting the development of complex economies underlay the significant economic uncertainties pressuring policymakers. As we shall see, these informational pressures have important consequences for policymaking.

1.2.2 Negotiating and Designing Economic Governance

Defining the policy problem is just a starting point – a lightly sketched canvas that offers no explanation of the design of the policy, its reforms, implementation, and efficacy. To do this, we need to employ more phase-specific theories that flesh out how pressures operate throughout the whole economic policy cycle. We begin with those concerning preference formation, bargaining, and policy design.

Preference formation: We said that at the core of the policy problem lies the need to oversee national fiscal policies, two are, therefore, the most important design issues that have fuelled controversies during the negotiations: How intrusive and constraining should the policy be? Who should be primarily involved in its enforcement, the European Commission or the Council of the EU? In Chapter 3, we combine the insights from liberal intergovernmentalism – the most renowned approach to the study of the EU – with the international relations scholarship on the design of dispute settlement mechanisms to put forward several expectations on the supranational, national, and economic sources of these conflicts. The main argument is that governments at greater risk of noncompliance demand a less intrusive policy and prefer the enforcement procedures in which they can exercise more influence.

We indeed find that these governments push for more room for national manoeuvre and tend to prefer more Council involvement in enforcement *if* they enjoy higher voting power within this institution. On the other hand, governments with lower voting power in the Council do not necessarily prefer greater Commission involvement, even if they enjoy relatively more influence within this institution. This is primarily because of the uncertainty about the behaviour of the supranational executive during enforcement. And it is perhaps because of this that we find evidence of national factors, such as public Euroscepticism, shaping governmental positions. Other significant correlates of positions are supranational pressures related to holding the Council presidency and euro area membership and national ones such as the government's ideological inclinations. Economic circumstances too, such as the European sovereign debt crisis, and benefiting from EU financial assistance, shape positions.

Bargaining outcomes: Once the stage of opposing positions is set, what explains the outcomes of the negotiations? Here, supranational factors dominate the explanatory landscape. In Chapter 4, we rely on the array of procedural and bargaining models offered by the EU literature and compare and contrast their predictive accuracy. Despite some claims to the contrary, we show that compromise is the most robust *modus operandi* in dealing with these controversies (as long as the costs of failure are accounted for), that preference centrality is core to bargaining success, and that there is hardly evidence of a systematic advantage to one state or a set of states. Yet, supranational procedures matter too, as the next most accurate is a model that accounts for the sequential features of the legislative process and the differing prerogatives and preferences of the legislative actors (so long as we assume a high cost of no agreement). Indeed, proximity to the position of the European Parliament is important for a country's bargaining success when this institution is non-trivially involved in the adoption of these measures.

Timing and direction of reforms: The reforms occurred at specific points in time and took specific directions. Some provisions were tightened, and others were loosened. Some prerogatives were pooled within the Council, and others were delegated to the Commission. What explains the timing and direction of these reforms? Here, economic uncertainties and supranational pressures take centre stage. In Chapter 5, we derive four contending expectations from the three most prominent theories of European integration and policy design (i.e. liberal intergovernmentalism, neofunctionalism, and postfunctionalism) to address these questions. None of these theories is fully corroborated or falsified. For instance, the heavily Council-centred enforcement design is hardly in line with liberal intergovernmentalist expectations. The unavoidable arbitrariness of fiscal rules and the significant uncertainty in predicting fiscal performance explain the reluctance of Council ministers to delegate prerogatives to the Commission or to tie their own arms too tightly, despite significant noncompliance. On the other hand, the domestic politicization of negotiations does not seem to shape policy design as postfunctionalist theories expect. Yet, supranational factors, such as noncompliance patterns, commitment problems, exclusion and veto threats, issue linkages, and path dependencies – mechanisms emphasized by liberal intergovernmentalism and neofunctionalism – are valuable for explaining the overall timing and direction of these reforms.

1.2.3 *Implementing Economic Governance*

The implementation of economic governance takes a two-pronged approach, depicted in the right portion of Figure 1.1. The first part centres on country-specific recommendations, while the second on the supranational oversight of excessive deficits.

Bargaining over implementation: Implementation begins with the issuance by the Council of the EU of country-specific recommendations whose primary purpose is to prevent economic situations that would undermine the functioning of the economic and monetary union. Ministers clearly care about them since they modify half of the recommendations proposed by the Commission and, unlike the results reported in some studies, they tend to strengthen them. What explains these actions? In Chapter 6, we employ the bargaining models already introduced in Chapter 4 and complement them with theories of compliance to develop a set of testable expectations.

The extent to which recommendations are modified and strengthened is associated predominantly with supranational and economic factors. For instance, when the Council is divided and the position of the Commission (i.e. the median commissioner) is an outlier, the proposed measures are changed more extensively. The recommendations addressed to countries with a history of noncompliance and worsening economic conditions are also modified more. Governments of larger countries, which can rely on more resources for vote trading within the Council because of their greater voting power, have been slightly more successful at weakening the recommendations addressed to them, but this advantage has lasted only until 2010. Moreover, the Council has tightened the proposed policy actions addressed to highly indebted, hence noncompliant, countries. Tightening also occurred when the Council acceptance pivot, that is, the government whose support is necessary for the adoption of a recommendation under qualified majority voting, has moved to the right of the policy spectrum.

Compliance with recommendations: Eight months after adoption, countries implement fully or partially about 60 per cent of the recommended measures, but the figure could be as low as 25 per cent and as high as 80 per cent. Plausibly, governments are reluctant to adopt precisely these measures, possibly because of the costs they impose on their supporters. Measures that are beneficial to government support constituencies would not appear among the recommendations as they would be adopted without supranational nudging. So, what explains the differences in performance? To address this question, in Chapter 7 we employ, again, theories of compliance, together with political economy theories that see reforms as the silver lining of difficult economic conditions.

We show that factors related to economic, national, and supranational pressures influence compliance. Worsening economic conditions tend to act as triggers for action. On the other hand, the proximity to an electoral contest engenders pressure to procrastinate as governments show less enthusiasm to take costly decisions. Last, the recommendations that are associated with a more institutionalized supranational sanctioning system (i.e. higher noncompliance costs), such as those related to budgetary positions, are more extensively followed through.

Correction of excessive deficits: The excessive deficit procedure (EDP) is at the core of the second path to implementing economic governance: a last resort corrective mechanism that is designed to ensure compliance with the fiscal reference values of the Treaty of Maastricht after the Council has determined that a country is running an excessive deficit. In Chapter 8, we address the use, duration, and efficacy of this procedure relying on the bargaining models of Chapter 4, theories of compliance, and the extensive literature on the political economy of public spending. Here as well, the three pressure factors we have discussed earlier exercise their influence.

Consider first the use and duration of the procedure. As one would expect, the history and the expectation of noncompliance of a country affect the probability of using the procedure and its duration. Supranational bargaining also plays a non-trivial role. For instance, the positions on the left–right dimension of the Council minister, who is pivotal for opening and closing a procedure, and of the Commissioners for Economic and Financial Affairs shape both the reliance on and duration of the procedure. At the national level, governments with pro-European orientations and countries with a more pro-European public are associated with shorter oversight durations.

Last, do governments reduce their deficits when they are under the oversight of the EDP? This second part builds on the encompassing seminal study of Franzese (2002: 126–95) and the more recent analysis of Fortunato and Loftis (2018). The three sets of economic, national, and supranational pressures come particularly to light in this context. As basic tax-smoothing theory suggests, spending, revenue, and open-economic shocks are the core economic conditions that determine the performance of public finances. Then, a long list of national political factors that are associated with office and policy motives, such as the expected proximity to new elections, the fractionalization, polarization, and ideological inclinations of national executives, contributes to explaining a significant proportion of the remaining observed variation in deficit. Importantly though, supranational oversight during budget drafting leads a government to significantly reduce its deficit, especially if the country is a member of the euro area.[2] In other words, the procedure has been quite effective.

1.3 The Scope of the Inquiry: European Economic Governance

Before delving into the detailed analyses of each stage of the policy cycle, we provide a brief overview of the policy to help the readers familiarize themselves with its technicalities. Throughout the book, we will use the term 'European economic governance' to describe the collection of primary and secondary laws that regulate the economic policy of the EU. Usually, the term 'economic policy' covers a wide range of measures that governments employ to manage their economy, from setting the levels of taxation and spending to controlling the supply of money, promoting the creation of jobs, redistributing income, and regulating economic activities. In the EU, the array of measures that falls under this term is, however, much narrower. Economic policy consists of the acts adopted on the basis of the Chapter on Economic Policy of the Treaty on the Functioning of the European Union (TFEU, Articles 120 to 126). They primarily deal with multilateral preventive surveillance and correction of

[2] Regardless of whether governments have been negotiating or benefiting from assistance.

excessive deficits.[3] Like employment and social policy, economic policy is a coordinating competence, meaning that the EU has the primary function of coordinating national measures, but this activity may occasionally lead to the harmonization of national laws.[4]

1.3.1 Preventive Surveillance

As we said, European economic governance employs a two-pronged approach. The first carries out preventive surveillance as set out in Article 121 of the TFEU. This is the upper branch of the implementation step illustrated in Figure 1.1. Its purpose is to coordinate national economic policies to ensure that they contribute to the achievement of common policy objectives. Procedurally, the Council adopts, on a proposal from the Commission, recommendations that set out the broad guidelines of the economic policies of the member states. The Council is then expected to monitor and assess national policies on the basis of reports submitted by the Commission. Further recommendations could be issued following a warning from the Commission that some national measures are jeopardizing the proper functioning of the economic and monetary union.

[3] We will not cover the measures that have been adopted on the basis of Article 122 TFEU and are designed to address severe economic difficulties. Between 1994 and 2019, the Council adopted four directives to safeguard the oil and natural gas supply and three regulations to provide financial assistance to countries experiencing financial difficulties, such as the European financial stabilization mechanism and natural disasters. We also disregard two 1993 Council regulations that just specified the definitions for the application of the bailout prohibitions in Articles 123–125 TFEU and a 2004 Council regulation that simply extended to government debt the obligation to compile and transmit quarterly data (unlike earlier measures, this regulation was based on Article 126 TFEU rather than on Article 338 TFEU on the production of statistics that falls under the general and final provisions of the treaty).

[4] In terms of 'the *relative degree of responsibility of* [supranational and national] *public authorities* within a material policy field' (Schütze 2018: 236), coordinating competences fall in between shared competences, where the harmonization of national laws is a characterizing feature, and complementary competences, which do not entail harmonization. The category of coordinating competences was created by the Presidium of the Convention on the Future of the European Union in the first half of the 2000s because its members could not agree on which category some policies belonged to. The classification was then adopted by the drafters of the Treaty of Lisbon. However, according to Schütze (2018: 242), the constitutional character of this competence category remains largely undefined.

Over time, the process has become significantly more structured. Following the adoption of a 1997 preventive regulation, part of the so-called Stability and Growth Pact (SGP), member states submit an annual stability or convergence programme[5] for evaluation by the Commission. The programmes must be conducive to price stability, strong sustainable growth, and employment creation. They must include information on the national economic and budgetary situation, the main assumptions behind these data, a description of budgetary and economic policy measures, an assessment of their impact, a medium-term objective (MTO) of a close-to-balance or surplus budget,[6] and the related deficit and debt paths.

The following reforms refined these objectives and asked for more information. A 2005 measure established *revisable country-specific* MTOs that could diverge by no more than 1 per cent of GDP from a balance or surplus position, allowing room for budgetary manoeuvre, particularly for public investment. It also set out an adjustment path if the structural balance was off the MTO. In this situation, countries have to improve the balance by 0.5 per cent of GDP per year as a baseline.[7] Programmes must now include quantitative assessments of the budgetary and economic policy measures taken or proposed and accurate cost–benefit analyses of major structural reforms.

In 2007, the Treaty of Lisbon allowed for the possibility of the Commission to address a warning to member states that adopt measures inconsistent with the broad economic guidelines or the functioning of the monetary union. In 2011, a new preventive regulation established an expenditure benchmark: the net annual growth rate of real government expenditure should not exceed the medium-term potential economic growth if the structural balance is at the MTO. If the balance is not at the MTO, expenditure growth should be lower. In this circumstance, the Council may demand improvements of the balance that exceed 0.5 per cent of GDP when countries have high debt or face a severe risk of debt sustainability. A significant deviation

[5] Euro area countries submit stability programmes, while the others submit convergence programmes.

[6] This so-called structural budget balance excludes the impact of the economic cycle and one-off fiscal measures.

[7] Taking into consideration periods of high or low economic growth and major structural reforms, such as on pensions.

from the MTO or the adjustment path of at least 0.5 per cent (or 0.25 per cent for two years) of GDP may lead to sanctions.

Later on, an international treaty, the so-called fiscal compact, narrowed further the room-of-manoeuvre for countries with high debt or risk of fiscal sustainability: their MTOs can diverge by no more than 0.5 per cent of GDP from a balance or surplus position. The new 2011 preventive regulation also required programmes to include additional information, for instance, on implicit liabilities related to ageing and on the consistency with the broad economic policy guidelines. As part of the European Semester[8] for economic policy coordination, member states also had to submit national reform programmes on economic growth and job creation. The surveillance prerogatives of the Commission have been strengthened and the warning mechanism has been beefed up with a possible Council decision of noncompliance where the Commission enjoys enhanced proposal power (its proposals become easier to adopt than to reject). As we have outlined in the preceding section, these reforms are the objects of our analysis in the second part of the book (Chapters 3–5).

Programmes must be submitted every year by the end of April. The Council delivers an opinion on them, based on a recommendation from the Commission, within two or three months. As we said earlier, the negotiations over the content of these country-specific recommendations are the object of investigation in Chapter 6. In the second half of the year, national governments are supposed to incorporate these recommendations into their reform plans and national budgets for the following year. We study the determinants of national compliance in Chapter 7.

1.3.2 Correction of Excessive Deficits

The second pillar of the European economic governance concerns the correction of excessive deficits as set out in Article 126 of the TFEU, the Protocol on the EDP, and, initially, a 1993 EDP regulation laying out the reporting requirements about public finances (this is the

[8] Operationally, the European and national semesters are associated with respectively the first and second halves of a calendar year. The European Semester actually begins in November of year $t-1$, with the Commission setting the priorities and guidelines for the following year, and concludes in May–July of year t with countries receiving tailored policy recommendations.

lower branch of the implementation step illustrated in Figure 1.1). The system rotates around two reference values set in the protocol: the 3 per cent and 60 per cent ratios of the planned or actual general government deficit and debt to GDP, respectively. Importantly, actual numerical noncompliance with these thresholds is neither a necessary nor a sufficient condition to start a procedure for correcting a deficit. If the Commission thinks that a member state is running the *risk* of an excessive deficit as a result of, for instance, some planned measures, it can recommend to the Council a decision to establish the existence of an excessive deficit even if a country's actual public finances are in compliance with these reference values. Similarly, extenuating circumstances may be present that would advise against taking such a decision notwithstanding the numerical noncompliance with these thresholds.

Once the Council has determined the existence of an excessive deficit, it issues recommendations to the member state concerned with a view to reducing the deficit within a given period. Failure to act leads to a ratcheting up of the pressure with further recommendations, notices, and possible sanctions, such as non-interest-bearing deposits and fines. The procedure terminates with an abrogation of the decision that initiated the supranational oversight when the Council thinks that the situation has been corrected.

The following reforms have refined (and redefined) the procedures and criteria for determining compliance with these rules and the adjustment path for its attainment. For instance, the 1997 corrective regulation of the SGP established that a deficit would not be considered excessive if a country experienced an annual decline in real GDP of at least two per cent.[9] A 2005 reform loosened this definition of 'severe economic downturn': countries could be exempted from an EDP even in case of a protracted period of very low growth, with due consideration to the business cycle, debt sustainability, public investment, and major reforms. The reform shifted the attention to the minimum improvements of the structural balance to correct an excessive deficit. Countries under surveillance had to improve this budget balance by at least 0.5 per cent of GDP a year, allowing for revisions in

[9] A contraction of less than two per cent required *further supporting evidence* for exempting a state from the procedure. A resolution adopted at the Amsterdam European Council summit in 1997 further narrowed the possibility to exempt noncompliant countries to cases when the reduction was more than 0.75 per cent.

case of unexpected events. In 2005, the 1993 EDP regulation was also amended with a view to improving the quality of national statistical data, followed by another reform in 2010, which laid out further obligations for member states and strengthened the inspection powers of the Commission. Finally, the new corrective regulation, part of the so-called 2011 six-pack, added an adjustment benchmark for countries with a debt-GDP ratio exceeding 60 per cent: the differential with respect to this reference value should decrease at a rate of one-twentieth per year. These reforms are also the objects of our analysis in Chapters 3–5, while Chapter 8 assesses the use, duration, and effectiveness of supranational oversight of national budget deficits.

1.3.3 Ancillary Measures

These two pillars have been complemented by four sets of ancillary measures concerning budgetary procedures, surveillance, sanctions, and macroeconomic imbalances. First, in 2011, a directive set out a list of obligations concerning the procedures, rules, and institutions underlying the conduct of national budgetary policies. Second, the already mentioned fiscal compact established that countries that are subject to an EDP had to put in place a budgetary and economic partnership programme with a detailed description of the reforms to correct the deficit. Two 2013 regulations, applicable only to euro area countries, added further provisions concerning these programmes, the monitoring and assessment of draft budgets, and the surveillance when countries experience serious financial difficulties. Third, a 2011 regulation set out the sanctions for not complying with the various provisions of the governance framework, including those on the budgetary process, data quality, and corrections of excessive deficits or deviations from MTOs. Many penalties require only a blocking minority in the Council for approval, therefore significantly enhancing the proposal powers of the Commission. Finally, a regulation to prevent and correct macroeconomic imbalances and a sister regulation concerning the enforcement of the related corrective measures have also been adopted in 2011.

These measures are not at the core of our inquiry. However, the conflicts underlying their adoption are included in Chapter 4 on the predictive accuracy of procedural and bargaining models, and their provisions are included in Chapter 5 on the determinants of the policy design.

1.4 Conclusion

Since 2019, major events such as the Covid-19 pandemic and the Russian invasion of Ukraine have profoundly shaken the European economy. On 23 March 2020, ten days after the number of new Covid-19 cases in Europe exceeded the one in China, the finance ministers in the Council agreed with an assessment of the Commission that the general escape clause of the SGP should be activated because of the severe downturn that the European economy was likely to face. The clause allows for temporary departures of the adjustment paths towards the MTOs and revisions of the fiscal trajectories recommended to countries with excessive deficits. Then, on 24 February 2022, as the pandemic-related challenges were receding, the Russian invasion of Ukraine plunged the continent into one of the most severe security and refugee crises since the Second World War, causing extensive disruptions to energy and food markets. In May of that year, the general escape clause was extended for another year.

This respite provided an opportunity to further tinker with the policy design in spring 2024, but the path to implementation remains fraught and prolonged. It demands a measured, insightful evaluation of past performance and a keen awareness of the pressures confronting politicians. To take a step in this direction, we provide a theoretical framework for analyzing EU economic policymaking, relying on the extraordinarily rich literature offered by EU studies, international relations, and comparative political economy. We begin this journey by investigating in Chapter 2 the ideational pressures, that is, the economic theories that demarcate the contour of the problem this policy is meant to address.

PART I

Defining the Policy Problem

2 The Subtle Influence of Ideas
Austerity Needs No Rules

The ideas of economists and political philosophers, both when they are right and when they are wrong are more powerful than is commonly understood. Indeed, the world is ruled by little else.

John Maynard Keynes (1936: 239)

Germany's focus on rules, obligations, a strong monetary authority, a weak parliament, and no spending to compensate for busts [is] the basic design of the EU.... From the Maastricht convergence criteria to the Stability and Growth Pact to the proposed new fiscal treaty – it's all about the economic constitution – the rules, the ordo ... the most recent German innovation of a constitutional debt brake (Schuldenbremse) for all EU countries regardless of their business cycles or structural positions, coupled with a new rules-based fiscal treaty as the solution to the crisis, is simply an ever-tighter ordo by another name.

Mark Blyth (2013: 141)

In 1815, at the end of the Napoleonic Wars, the British government debt exceeded 200 per cent of GDP. Concerned about the economic implications, David Ricardo wrote an *Essay on the Funding System* for the Encyclopaedia Britannica 'to consider the best mode of providing for our annual expenditure both in war and peace' (1820: 1). In comparing taxation with the issuance of bonds, he concluded that the two methods of financing had equivalent consequences for economic growth and capital accumulation because forward-looking consumers internalize the government's budget constraint and adjust their consumption accordingly. In other words, consumers realize that the choice is between paying taxes now or later since bonds are loans that eventually must be repaid. As Piketty (2017: 187) observes, the increase in private savings that occurred in Britain alongside the higher public debt must have prompted this observation, although Ricardo was not convinced about its empirical relevance. The conjecture was further elaborated by de Viti de Marco (1893) but became prominent with Barro (1974; 1979) as the Ricardian equivalence proposition.

According to some scholars, such as Blyth (2013), this proposition, along with its assumptions of rational expectations and perfect capital markets, constitutes the kernel of austerity thinking and has inspired the design of the EU economic governance. As asserted in one of the epigraphs of this chapter, its provisions are simply the regulatory counterpart of expansionary fiscal consolidation – the policy recommendation offshoot of austerity thinking (Blyth 2013: 140–41). In other words, these rules make fiscal policy quasi-illegal (Matthijs and Blyth 2018: 119) and commit countries to permanent austerity (Moschella 2017). Along similar lines, even if somewhat more tangentially, other scholars have interpreted these rules as expressions of neoliberal ideas in support of small governments and rejection of Keynesian demand management (Gamble 2013: 73; Schmidt 2017; Schmidt and Thatcher 2013: 5, 38).

In this chapter, we peruse the economic theories and models that may have provided the ideational foundations for this policy.[1] Sustainability apart, we explain how the cross-country distributive effects on the composition of output, caused by expansionary fiscal policies, offer the rationale for these rules, as suggested by the application of three standard macroeconomic models to a monetary union. The provisions are designed to prevent the negative cross-country externalities arising from expansionary fiscal policies adopted by authorities with short-term incentives to boost output at the expense of inflation. Apart from some misreading of the provisions, claims of influence by austerity thinking are unconvincing. And, perhaps surprisingly, we demonstrate that, had these ideas gained influence over time, we should have actually seen *looser* rather than *tighter* rules. This is because theories based on rational expectations, including even the Ricardian equivalence proposition, point towards *diminished* effectiveness of expansionary fiscal policies and would, therefore, recommend *looser* oversight. In light of the direction that the reforms have taken over the years, doubts must have existed about the mechanisms underpinning expansionary fiscal consolidation.

[1] The chapter builds on Franchino (2020).

Before delving into the analysis of the ideational foundations for the regime, we first discuss in the next section our methodology, which differs somewhat from other ideational approaches. We then evaluate the models and ideas about the workings of the economy that would recommend such rules, showing that standard macroeconomic theories work better than austerity-based variants. Finally, we conclude by highlighting how the disregard of alternative theories of the business cycle in the standard approaches may be associated, at least ideationally, with serious flaws in the initial design of the regime.

2.1 Economic Ideas and Models

Economists have been employing mathematical models to put down on paper their ideas on how the economy operates since at least Jevons's (1871) marginal revolution. Correspondingly, scholars from the ideational tradition frequently trace back the origin of such ideas to some formal models. Blyth (2013: 167–68) for instance sees expansionary fiscal consolidation originating from models on public spending published in the late 1980s and early 1990s. However, our procedure differs somewhat from most ideational approaches.[2] Most ideational endeavours attempt to investigate how ideas make their way into policy paradigms, political discourses, and eventually policy decisions (e.g. Heipertz and Verdun 2010: 85–109). One such example could be the letter on fiscal multipliers that Olli Rehn (2013), the commissioner for economic and monetary affairs, addressed to the economic and finance ministers in February 2013. This document can be construed as embracing expansionary fiscal contraction *and* tighter fiscal rules.[3] In a similar fashion, other scholars concentrate on the ideas of, and the use of ideas by, policymakers, such as those that are associated with the monetary union (Dyson and Maes 2016; McNamara 1998; Quaglia 2004; 2005) or the euro area crisis (Carstensen and Schmidt 2018; Crespy and Schmidt 2014; Matthijs 2016; Schmidt 2016a, 2017; Warren 2018).

[2] For overviews of this rich and multifarious tradition, see Hall (1989), Béland and Cox (2010), and Swinkels (2020).

[3] See also Princen and van Esch's (2016: 370) analysis of the European Commission communication leading up to the six-pack reform, Matthijs and Blyth's (2018) study on the consequences of the 2005 reform, and Jabko's (2019) work on ideational repertoires in the euro area crisis.

In this chapter, we limit our attention to the fiscal-legal provisions of the EU economic governance, leaving aside other documents and policymakers' positions, and we peruse economic models, applied to monetary unions, which put into practice different economic ideas, to determine which would recommend the rules we observe. To keep in line with the other chapters, we use the terms 'economic governance' even though it would perhaps be more accurate to use 'fiscal governance' or 'fiscal rules' since the economic literature distinguishes between fiscal and monetary policies. By economic governance, we primarily mean fiscal rules.

Blyth (2013) contends that models based on mechanisms that underpin expansionary fiscal consolidation provide the ideational foundations for these provisions. For Schmidt and Thatcher (2013: 37–38), these rules are the regulatory epitome of neoliberal ideas engendering a hard-to-reverse path of fiscal consolidation. We will show that this is not the case, but before addressing this point, we first analyze three standard macroeconomic theories that provide, in our view, a better ideational fit.

2.2 Standard Macroeconomic Theories and the Need for Economic Governance

The economics of economic governance in a monetary union can be analyzed by applying standard macroeconomic theories that are based on the relation between output, the interest rate, and the exchange rate in the short run; output and the level of prices in the medium run; and capital, labour, and technology in the long run (that is, Keynesianism for the short run, monetarism or the classic approach for the medium run, and the Solow-Swan growth model for the long run).[4]

Consider a set of countries with their own fiscal authority and a single monetary authority. Assume that output and employment are at their natural medium-run levels. What happens if one fiscal authority decides to increase spending unexpectedly and permanently? Let us first take a union-wide perspective. In the short run, more spending increases output (and income) directly and the

[4] Heipertz and Verdun (2010: 71–74) appear to take the influence of these theories for granted since they discuss them when analyzing the neofunctional logic, rather than the ideational logic, behind these rules.

higher disposable income leads to higher consumption, which further increases output. Increased spending may also lead to more investment (and, again, higher output) if investment responds more to higher sales than to higher interest rates (for a given money supply, a higher income increases the demand for money, leading to a higher interest rate).[5]

Higher economic activity lowers unemployment, putting upward pressure on the nominal wage and the level of prices. The output is now above its natural level and the price level exceeds expectations. Wage setters will therefore revise their expectations upwards, leading to upward pressure on prices. For a given money supply, higher prices decrease the real money stock, leading to higher interest rates and lower output, until the natural level is reached again. In sum, the increase in spending raises the level of prices and changes the composition, but not the level, of output in the medium run, as the investment is crowded out through higher interest rates. In the longer run, lower investment leads to lower capital stock and output.

These dynamics change if we consider a monetary authority with an inflation target at potential output.[6] Assume that both current inflation and the nominal interest rate are on target, prior to the spending initiative. Once the programme is announced, the central bank expects lower unemployment and above-target inflation. It will therefore increase the interest rate, which lowers economic activity and prevents excessive upward pressure on wages and prices until inflation is back on target and output is again at its natural level. In other words, the interest rate rises more rapidly, decelerating both economic expansion and price increases.

Spending also has important implications for trade. First, the programme may build up trade imbalances within the union. Depending on the trade links and the propensity to import, it may increase imports

[5] In other words, the size of these effects depends on the fiscal policy multiplier. Higher spending may have a particularly strong effect on output in the short run if the propensity to consume and the sensitivity of investment to sales and of money demand to interest rate are high, and, additionally, if the propensity to import, the sensitivity of investment to interest rate and of money demand to income are low.

[6] Such as the Taylor rule, whereby the central bank sets the nominal interest rate at time *t* as a function of the target nominal interest rate, the weighted differences between the rate at time *t* and the target rate of inflation, and between output at time *t* and potential output at medium run.

in the spending country and, consequently, increase exports in the non-spending countries. Second, a higher interest rate will lead to an appreciation of the single currency and a union-wide decrease in net exports. This further changes the composition of output.

Let us now take the perspective of the countries participating in the union. Despite the long-run consequences on output and a non-accommodating central bank, the incentives for spending are there. All it takes is a government that is ready to forsake higher inflation for higher growth and lower unemployment in the short run.[7] As shown in Chapter 8, this is actually how governments tend to behave in the proximity of parliamentary dissolution. The resulting combination of a contractionary monetary policy and an expansionary fiscal policy has cross-country distributive implications because the composition of output can change in important ways.

For non-spending countries, the specific consequences depend on a host of factors, such as the propensity to import (in the spending country), the sensitivity of net exports to currency appreciation, and the sensitivity of investment to sales and the interest rate (in the non-spending countries). The trade balance may improve if the increase in exports to the spending country is higher than the decrease in net exports outside the union following the currency appreciation. Assuming higher net exports, even investment could increase if it responds more to sales than the interest rate. More importantly, things can turn out bad for non-spending countries. The trade balance could worsen and the higher interest rate could lead to lower investment, lower capital accumulation, and lower output in the long run. The profligacy of one fiscal authority could produce a recession and lower long-run growth in a fiscally responsible member country.[8]

[7] As pointed out by Beetsma and Giuliodori (2010), the government may face even looser constraints for expanding the fiscal policy if the monetary union fosters capital market integration, since the upward pressure on interest rates would be attenuated.

[8] One could read standard macroeconomic theory as an argument for small government. Indeed, a cut in public spending increases investment in the medium run and output in the long run. Aside from whether all private investment is indeed beneficial to long-run growth, note that spending on infrastructure, education, or active labour market policies builds up physical and human capital and may as well lead to higher output in the long run without increasing prices. The theory is a cautionary tale about managing the

2.2.1 *Short-Run Games of Fiscal-Monetary Interactions in a Monetary Union*

These cross-country externalities are at the core of a few studies on the strategic interactions between a monetary authority and the fiscal authorities in a monetary union. Dixit and Lambertini (2001, 2003) propose a model where the output of each country in a monetary union is also a (positive or negative) function of the fiscal policies of other countries (see, also, Dixit 2001). As discussed earlier, these fiscal policy spillovers operate directly through demand or crowding-out effects, as well as indirectly through the real effects of unexpected inflation. Actors' utility is a weighted function of ideal levels of inflation and output, where the monetary authority is at least as conservative as fiscal authorities.

Dixit and Lambertini (2001) assume that fiscal authorities desire a higher than natural level of output and they investigate the implications for inflation and output under different regimes, that is, when fiscal and monetary authorities simultaneously decide and when either fiscal or monetary authorities act first (i.e. monetary or fiscal leadership). They limit the analysis to a situation where a country's expansionary fiscal policy increases both other countries' output and union-wide inflation. They show that the Nash equilibrium of a simultaneous game produces higher output and lower inflation than the ideal levels, with consequences for debt accumulation and higher interest rates. This expansionary fiscal policy and contractionary monetary policy mix worsens as the ideal positions of the authorities diverge.[9] Importantly, the commitment to a monetary policy rule is ineffective if the fiscal authorities are not subject to any constraint. Therefore, rules imposed on the fiscal authorities can preserve the credibility of commitment to a monetary rule that would be negated in the case of fiscal discretion (Dixit and Lambertini 2001). In conclusion, this model demonstrates that even fiscal authorities who

business cycle rather than public spending per se (aside from the distortionary effects of taxation). It has policy implications for the composition, rather than the size, of spending. Long-run growth would actually be better served if the return from public investment exceeds that from private investment and if public investment increases productivity of the private sector.

[9] Outcomes are somewhat improved upon under different regimes of either fiscal or monetary leadership.

unanimously prefer higher output and inflation than the central bank have incentives to establish fiscal rules if they desire to preserve the credibility of commitment to a monetary rule.[10]

2.3 Rational Expectations, Ricardian Equivalence, and the Lesser Need for Economic Governance

According to Blyth (2013: 140–41), standard macroeconomic theories do not offer the ideational foundations for the EU economic governance rules. He traces their origin to ordoliberalism, a school of economic thought originating in 1930s Germany that emphasized the regulatory role of the state. Its primary objective is to ensure competitive markets and stable prices through politically independent authorities, rather than public spending. As stated in the epigraph to this chapter, the EU economic governance, by being oblivious to the business cycle and the structural position of member countries, 'is simply an ever-tighter ordo by another name' (Blyth 2013: 141; see also Gamble 2013: 73). In a subsequent analysis, Matthijs and Blyth (2018: 119) reach the point of asserting that the last reform makes 'fiscal policy quasi-illegal'. In a related prominent work on the influence of neoliberalism in Europe, Schmidt and Thatcher (2013: 37–38) reach a similar conclusion. They argue that '[t]he successive pacts for stability in the Eurozone – beginning with the Stability and Growth Pact that consecrated the 1990s Maastricht criteria for monetary union and culminating with various pacts during the Eurozone crisis – ensure that neo-liberal ideas about fiscal consolidation [i.e. a small size of government and no Keynesian demand management], regardless of their failure to solve the crisis, have created path dependence for the rules of EU monetary policy that will be difficult to reverse' (Schmidt and Thatcher 2013: 37–38).

These are dubious claims. As outlined in Chapter 1, since 2005 these rules have accommodated business cycle fluctuations, major structural reforms, and public investments. According to Claeys, Darvas, and Leandro (2016: 4), they allow for an automatic stabilization of

[10] Fiscal rules would be unnecessary, or even counterproductive, only if monetary and fiscal authorities were to share the same ideal levels of output and inflation. In these circumstances, a credible monetary commitment or a conservative central bank would not be needed as well (Dixit and Lambertini 2003).

up to 2.5 per cent of GDP in the rare case of a 3.6 per cent negative output gap (and further spending would be probably granted in such an exceptional circumstance). If neoliberal ideas were so successful, we should wonder why we do not see reference values that are centred on the ratio of government expenditure over GDP. If they were so resilient, we should wonder why the expenditure benchmark that was adopted in the midst of the euro area crisis concerns the *net* growth rate of government spending – meaning that additional revenues must match increases in spending that exceed the medium-term potential economic growth rate. Similarly, the fiscal compact and the new corrective regulation established rules that discriminate according to the sustainability of the debt rather than the size of the government. Doubting these ideational influences, Jones (2013: 149) indeed observes that the design of this policy does not 'imply constraints on the scope of national-welfare states. Instead, it focuses much more tightly on the market distortions caused by government borrowing. In this sense, the prescriptions it contains are embedded in different national state–market traditions'. The policy demands a commitment to sound, rather than small, finances.[11]

Nevertheless, Blyth (2013) sees ordoliberal ideas further developed in formal works on the impact of government alternations on budget deficits (Alesina and Tabellini 1990; Persson and Svensson 1989) and in empirical analyses of fiscal contractions during recessions (Alesina, Ardagna, and Galí 1998; Alesina and Perotti 1995; Giavazzi and Pagano 1990; Hellwig et al. 1987). Following Lucas (1972), the central theme is the role of rational expectations in shaping macroeconomic dynamics. According to Blyth (2013), this important innovation to macroeconomic theory appears to have provided the theoretical basis for the limited fiscal response to the early 1990s recession in the United States. Hence, it is not far-fetched to say that it may have influenced European policy cycles during the

[11] A neoliberal consensus on monetarism underpinned the European Monetary System and shaped the design of the monetary union, as McNamara (1998) insightfully argues. However, given capital mobility, monetarism would recommend opting for flexible exchange rates to support the targeting of domestic money supply, rather than borrowing the credibility to fight inflation from a semi-fixed exchange rate regime (let alone a monetary union, McNamara 1998: 150). That external anchoring was seen as necessary speaks volumes about the shallowness of such consensus.

negotiations of the Maastricht Treaty and in the following period. However, is economic governance more or less needed in a world of rational expectations?

Take the case discussed earlier of a fiscal authority in a monetary union deciding to increase spending. What if consumers and firms fully anticipate the long-run consequences of this measure; that is, they anticipate lower output, a higher price level, and a higher interest rate in the future? How would macroeconomic aggregates be affected? The short-run increase in output expected by the standard theory would be offset by two dynamics. Rational expectations have an impact on consumption through a wealth effect. After the announcement of the programme, consumers expect lower after-tax labour income in the future. If current consumption is affected by the present value of these income streams, a negative wealth effect kicks in and the growth of consumption is attenuated.[12] Similarly, firms revise their expectations of future sales (and profits) downwards, lowering present values and, consequently, the growth in investment. Higher expected real interest rates would lower current investment as well. These countervailing effects suggest a lower sensitivity of current output to an increase in spending, that is, *diminished* effectiveness of an expansionary fiscal policy, and, therefore, weaker incentives for governments to entertain this policy.

One important caveat is that a government may be tempted to front-load a multi-annual spending programme to maximize the positive effect of current consumption and investment on current output, and thereby minimize the negative effect of expectations. Ricardian equivalence would suggest, however, that front-loading is not going to work. If consumers internalize the government's budget constraint, higher debt-financed current spending will result in higher taxes in the future and the increase in current disposable income will be equivalent to the decrease in the present value of after-tax labour income in the future. The net wealth effect will be zero and the timing of a spending programme will not affect consumption. Note that the current increase in private savings (i.e. consumers do not spend more as a result of higher current disposable income) offsets the current decrease in public savings, leaving investment, capital accumulation, and long-run growth unchanged.

[12] Current consumption can also be influenced by other wealth effects. Lower expected future dividends may lower financial wealth for instance.

Now, the key question is: Would the full consideration of rational expectations, even up to the Ricardian equivalence proposition, call for tighter economic governance rules? First, we must distinguish between governance rules and policies. Blyth (2013) argues that recent European fiscal policies have been (mis)guided by a modern rational-expectations version of austerity thinking, the so-called expansionary fiscal consolidation hypothesis, according to which a reduction in spending *during an economic contraction* can increase consumption and output through changes in future expectations about taxes and government spending.[13]

European fiscal policies operate, of course, within the EU economic governance. In Chapter 8, we assess the impact of oversight on national fiscal discipline, and in Chapter 9, we evaluate this policy in light of its objectives. Here, we concentrate on policy design. Blyth (2013: 332) argues that these same ideas have also shaped the design and development of EU economic governance towards an 'ever-tighter ordo'. This argument is problematic for two reasons. First, one may maintain that these provisions are not accommodating *enough*, but, as discussed earlier, no rule advocates fiscal tightening during recessions, let alone a small size of government.[14] Second, if these ideas have truly gained currency in European policy circles, we should actually see the opposite: a *loosening* of the rules. The full consideration of rational expectations offers an even more cautionary tale about managing the business cycle. Spending has a much more attenuated effect on output, the interest rate and the exchange rate in full rational-expectation models than in standard macroeconomic theories – a *diminished* expansionary fiscal policy, indeed. This means that the incentives to spend are weaker and, for any amount of additional spending, the potential negative implications for non-spending countries are smaller. The need for

[13] For Alesina, Favero, and Giavazzi (2019: 1), the 'term "austerity" indicates a policy of sizeable reduction of government deficits and stabilization of government debt achieved by means of spending cuts or tax increases, or both'. To test whether fiscal consolidation is expansionary, these scholars 'exclude cases of spending cuts or tax increases occurring to cool down the economy' (Alesina, Favero, and Giavazzi 2019: 6) that reflect standard Keynesian demand management.

[14] Even austerity proponents find it more reasonable for fiscal consolidation to take place during economic expansions (Alesina, Favero, and Giavazzi 2019: 6).

economic governance is *lessened* and the rules should be *laxer* in a world of rational expectations. Contra Blyth (2013), we should have seen a relaxation of the rules if these ideas had gained any traction over the years. For the most part, we have not. Therefore, the development of economic governance rules cannot be squared with a presumed ascendancy of full-blown rational-expectation macroeconomic theories.

The causes of austerity measures should therefore be searched elsewhere since they are not embedded into these economic governance provisions.[15] And the fact that policymakers, such as commissioner Olli Rehn (2013), instrumentally embraced tighter fiscal surveillance and expansionary fiscal contraction does not make the former a prescription of the latter (see, also, Mabbett and Schelkle 2016). Ironically, if the economy worked according to the full-blown rational-expectation framework, these rules would not have been necessary in the first place. In other words, Rehn supported provisions whose existence refuted the assumptions behind this understanding of the economy and the consequences of the fiscal measures he recommended.

2.3.1 Games of Fiscal-Monetary Interactions with Budget Constraints in a Monetary Union

Indeed, games of fiscal-monetary interactions that explicitly take into account the intertemporal implications of government budget constraints do not unequivocally support the need for fiscal rules, at least as they are codified in EU law. Beetsma and Bovenberg (1998) propose a model where fiscal authorities set the tax rates, subject to a budget constraint, and act as Stackelberg leaders against the monetary authority with an inflation target at potential output (see, also, Beetsma and Bovenberg 1997a). The utility of fiscal authorities is a

[15] For De Grauwe and Ji (2013a, 2013b), the measures introduced during 2011 represent a panic-driven reaction to a self-fulfilling liquidity crisis where market sentiments were disconnected from economic fundamentals, given non-trivial flaws in the monetary union design. These measures had such a negative impact on output that the situation almost morphed into a solvency crisis. However, interest rates did subside following austerity and non-conventional monetary measures. For Alesina, Favero, and Giavazzi (2019), austerity works when cuts in public expenditure reduce the expectation of future tax hikes and trigger a rise in private investment.

weighted function of ideal levels of inflation, output, and government spending, while the utility of the monetary authority is only a weighted function of ideal levels of inflation and output. The central bank is conservative if it attaches a larger weight to price stability than do fiscal authorities and society at large. The model demonstrates that fiscal authorities have an incentive to strategically raise taxes and induce the monetary authority to raise inflation to protect employment (note that, initially, the incentives are for a fiscal contraction – monetary expansion policy mix). They do so because higher inflation relaxes the budget constraint by generating seigniorage revenues and lowering the real servicing costs of government debt. Higher taxes then lead to a spending bias and lower output. These incentives increase as fiscal authorities attach less importance to inflation than does the monetary authority and they diminish if the tax of a single authority has a lower impact on union-wide employment (e.g. in a larger union or for smaller countries) or the monetary authority assigns more importance to price stability than employment. Beetsma and Bovenberg (1998) argue *against* coordination because, if fiscal authorities can coordinate tax policy, then they are even more likely to prompt a reaction by the monetary authority (see, also, van Aarle, Bovenberg, and Raith 1997).

The EU fiscal rules do not seem to be motivated by the short-run policy mix produced by this model. These scholars also focus on only one externality: that is, the role of *common* actual and expected inflation in relaxing the budget constraint for *each* fiscal authority. Other externalities in terms of the level and composition of output are ignored.[16]

In a related model, Beetsma and Bovenberg (1999) analyze the impact of a monetary union on the public debt (see, also, Beetsma and Bovenberg 1997b; Beetsma and Uhlig 1999). If the monetary authority is not conservative, the fiscal authorities are likely to *reduce* the debt, especially in a union with few members. Again, this

[16] The fiscal authorities that are more likely to engage in strategic tax setting are those that benefit more from lower servicing costs, attach less importance to inflation, and have a larger impact on union-wide employment (therefore inducing a reply from the monetary authority). This sets the ground for conflict between large, high-debt and inflation-accommodating countries and small, low-debt and inflation-averse countries – a scenario that is not unrealistic in the EU.

results in a fiscal contraction – monetary expansion policy mix.[17] On the other hand, debt accumulation occurs when the monetary authority becomes more conservative, the fiscal authorities assign greater importance to the short term than the long term (i.e. they are myopic) and the size of the union increases. This bias originates from the failure of each government to internalize the union-wide inflationary consequences of debt (Beetsma and Uhlig 1999). Therefore, Beetsma and Bovenberg (1999) and Beetsma and Uhlig (1999) argue that the combination of a conservative central bank and myopic fiscal authorities explains the establishment of debt ceilings and sanctions for exceeding the deficit-output threshold.[18] Without these rules, debt and inflation would be suboptimally high for each government of the union.

Consider, finally, the fiscal theory of the price level (e.g. Canzoneri, Cumby, and Diba 2001; Canzoneri and Diba 2001), to which Heipertz and Verdun (2010: 75) assign an important influence over EU fiscal rules. According to this theory, the price level is determined by the interaction of monetary and fiscal policies, with actors that are subject to intertemporal budget constraints. If fiscal authorities dominate the monetary authority in a union, Bergin (2000) demonstrates that the price level is jointly determined by the budget constraints of governments. Hence, an increase in a member country's debt that is not backed by future tax increases leads to higher prices across the union via the augmented inflation expectations of Ricardian households. Therefore, governments with large debts have strong incentives to pursue this policy because the inflation tax on bond-holders could be large, even if seigniorage revenues are

[17] Van Aarle, Bovenberg, and Raith (1997) reach a similar conclusion. If policymakers cannot commit to their announced strategies and fiscal authorities do not cooperate, a monetary union leads to lower inflation and deficit and quicker debt stabilization. Fiscal cooperation leads to higher inflation and deficit and slower debt stabilization.

[18] Levine and Brociner (1994) reach a similar conclusion, although through a different channel. Given a conservative central bank, governments have the incentive to improve their terms of trade inefficiently if they do not cooperate. Chari and Kehoe (2007) have instead shown that it is the inability of the monetary authority to commit to an inflation rate that leads to excessive debt and inflation in a monetary union. This implies that EU fiscal rules would be necessary if one believes that the European Central Bank cannot credibly commit to an inflation rate.

not. Note that solvency rules for countries would be sufficient, even though they are not necessary,[19] to maintain price stability. This condition 'is much less restrictive than the debt ceilings imposed in practice' (Bergin 2000: 48).

These models do not provide a solid theoretical background for the adoption of fiscal rules in a monetary union and certainly not in the form adopted by the EU. Some models produce a policy mix that is not even addressed by these rules. Other models advise either against or for less fiscal policy cooperation. Still, other models, along the lines of Dixit and Lambertini (2001), are more convincing. They show, for instance, how a conservative central bank interacting with fiscal authorities with short time horizons could indeed produce a combination of exceedingly high debt and inflation. In conclusion, however, these works do not provide a theoretical basis to argue that economic governance should be tighter than that recommended by theories and models analyzed earlier.

2.4 Conclusion: On Political Economy and Missing Minsky

EU economic governance rules have been criticized for being the regulatory embodiment of modern austerity thinking and neoliberal ideas. That these rules appear instead aligned with the recommendations of more orthodox macroeconomic theories is perhaps reassuring. For instance, a core concept of this policy – the structural government balance – is based on the output gap, which is a cornerstone of standard medium-run macroeconomic models.

It would not be prudent to design a policy relying heavily on rational expectation theories, which are built upon the heroic assumption that every economic actor shares the exact same beliefs about the workings of the economy.[20] Indeed, we show in Chapter 8 that patterns of deficit spending can be explained by political economy theories that emphasize its distributional consequences and are based on

[19] Fiscal solvency is not necessary for each fiscal authority if responsible fiscal authorities bail out profligate ones (Bergin 2000: 48–50).

[20] Apart from doubts about its empirical relevance (e.g. Meissner and Rostam-Afschar 2014; Poterba and Summers 1987), the Ricardian equivalence proposition and its assumptions should probably be better understood as necessary conditions for countercyclical fiscal policy to be ineffective (Galbács 2015).

some degree of fiscal illusion, that is, on voters that do not behave fully according to the Ricardian equivalence proposition. This result may please ideational scholars doubting the empirical support for expansionary fiscal consolidation upon which, they contend, the whole edifice of economic governance is built. Yet, this *same* finding – that distributional considerations and politicians' opportunistic exploitation of voters' fiscal illusion partially drive fiscal discipline – provides a justification for these rules. In other words, it is this more realistic world of policy- and office-seeking politicians and fiscally illuded voters that makes economic governance necessary.

On the other hand, these standard macroeconomic theories did a poor job of predicting the 2007–2008 great recession – a Minsky moment with global repercussions – and they may not have alerted policymakers of the limited credibility of the no-bailout commitment, which is now effectively reneged. From an ideational perspective, this neglect could be traced back to the inadequate incorporation of financial market behaviour into traditional macroeconomic theories (Smithers 2022; Wolf 2014) and a disregard for the negative externalities of trade surpluses (Stiglitz 2016). If Lucas did not pay a visit to Brussels, neither did Minsky.

This is not to say that policymakers were unaware of these issues (in Chapter 5, we show indeed that economic uncertainties affect greatly policy design). Like with the monetary union, policy discussions on banking supervision can be traced back to the 1960s. The issue was discussed by the members of the Delors Committee in the late 1980s, but opposition from the Bundesbank kept it off the agenda during the negotiations of the Treaty of Maastricht (Mourlon-Druol 2014: 1289–91; 2020: 32). The early neglect of financial stability was noted by Buiter (1999) and, later, he argued that the risk of contagion should be prevented by limiting the exposure of systemically relevant financial institutions to sovereign risk (Buiter 2006: 695). Self-fulfilling liquidity crises unrelated to economic fundamentals, which De Grauwe and Ji (2013a, 2013b) see in the European sovereign debt crisis, are not new to scholars of financial markets. But the fact that, in the words of Wray (2015), 'Minsky matters' is perhaps not enough for these issues to reach the political agenda, let alone for policies to be adopted. They may become useful only when a crisis strikes and the urgency of the situation requires prompt action, as with the creation of the banking union and the macroeconomic imbalances procedure.

In conclusion, identifying the ideational foundations of the EU economic governance is just a preliminary step towards understanding this policy. These ideational pressures, as well as their theoretical limits in grasping economic complexities, will resurface throughout the policy cycle. But economic theories only point to the potential problems associated with a monetary union. They offer practically no insights into explaining how the policy is designed and implemented. In Parts II and III of the book, we rely on a richer set of theoretical tools to address these issues. We begin with preference formation in Chapter 3. Here, we employ international relations theories to investigate the economic, national, and supranational sources of the main controversies that have characterized the adoption of the main secondary laws.

PART II

Negotiating and Designing Economic Governance

3 *The Battle Lines*
Noncompliance Risk, Asymmetric Power, and Enforcement

Precision is necessary when defining a serious recession.

Jürgen Stark, Secretary of State of Germany's Federal Ministry of Finance (1995–1998)

We support sanctions that are as automatic as possible.

Jan Kees de Jager, Minister for Finance of the Netherlands (2010–2012)

On 17 January 2005, German Chancellor Gerhard Schröder wrote a commentary piece in the *Financial Times* where he forcefully argued for a more flexible application of the excessive deficit procedure (EDP) that 'reflect[s] the fact that it is not just a stability pact, but also a growth pact'. To justify his position, he emphasized a presumable trade-off where 'the goal of consolidating public budgets may well conflict in the short term with the goal of enhancing the potential for economic growth'.

The article also contained a not-so-veiled criticism of the Commission. Mr Schröder decried that the 'mechanistic application of the pact has led the EU to recommend further restrictive measures, which have delayed recovery and thus put at risk long-term consolidation'. In pointing out that the triggering of the EDP is not automatic, he noted that provisions required the Commission to 'take into account all other relevant factors, including the medium-term economic and budgetary position of the member state'.

This commentary exemplifies the main battle lines underlying the reforms of the EU economic governance. More than half of the controversies that have emerged during these negotiations can be traced back to three overarching issues: (1) the degree to which provisions should constrain member states (i.e. the depth of cooperation), and the degree to which (2) the Council of the EU and (3) the Commission should be involved in the enforcement of the policy.

These are conflicts about the implementing discretion of an agreement and the design of its enforcement mechanism. In this chapter, we explain what shapes the attitudes of member state governments about such issues and how these positions are affected by the institutions that carry out the enforcement and by the properties of contracting states.[1] Our main argument is straightforward: governments at greater risk of noncompliance should push for a more discretionary application of the policy and should prefer enforcement procedures over which they can exercise more influence. In other words, supranational factors play centre stage in shaping preferences, but, as we shall see, other types of pressure come into the picture as well.

As scholars of international relations have frequently remarked, enforcement mechanisms come in many shapes and forms. Some treaties lack formal procedures and solely rely on reciprocity and reputation; others contain arbitration, prosecution, or dispute settlement procedures that increase ex-post costs of noncompliance, render commitments credible, and decrease transaction costs (Abbott et al. 2000; Keohane 1984; Koremenos, Lipson, and Snidal 2001: 763; Raustiala and Slaughter 2002; Simmons 2010). These scholars have also identified several factors that shape the design of international organizations, such as the extent of trade interdependence, the number of and power asymmetry among contracting states (Haftel 2013; Hooghe et al. 2013; Hooghe and Marks 2015; Koremenos 2008: 154; Koremenos, Lipson, and Snidal 2001; McCall Smith 2000). But they have paid no attention to whether and why states frequently do not share the same position over the design of an agreement's enforcement mechanism.

The EU has arguably the world's most advanced compliance system. It combines an international bureaucracy (the Commission), in charge of taking noncomplying member states to an international court, with a decentralized procedure, based on national courts referring cases to the international adjudicatory body (Tallberg 2002; Tallberg and McCall Smith 2014). Scholars have extensively investigated both the monitoring (e.g. Fjelstul and Carrubba 2018; König and Mäder 2014) and the adjudicatory (e.g. Alter 2001; Burley and Mattli 1993; Carrubba 2005; Carrubba, Gabel, and Hankla 2008; Stone Sweet and Brunell 1998) stages of this process. But this is only one aspect of this elaborate compliance system.

[1] This chapter extends the study of Franchino and Mariotto (2021).

As encapsulated by the epigraphs at the beginning of this chapter, the design of an enforcement mechanism begins upstream, when government ministers in the Council of the EU, sometimes together with members of the European Parliament, set the depth of a regulatory arrangement, establish the enforcement prerogatives and constraints of the supranational bureaucracy, and may reserve to themselves some involvement in enforcing the policy. Indeed, the negotiations over the reforms of the European economic governance revolved around the criteria to determine an excessive deficit (e.g. should spending on research be excluded? How should pension reforms be accounted for?), the procedure to follow (should a proposal sanctioning an excess require a Council-qualified majority for approval or rejection?), and the sanctions for noncompliance (should they amount to 0.2 per cent or 0.25 per cent of a country's GDP?). In this chapter, we explain why EU governments took different positions on these design features.

These attitudes have hardly received attention in the extensive literature that investigates the conflict dimensions structuring negotiations in the EU (c.f. Bailer, Mattila, and Schneider 2015; Hagemann and Høyland 2008; Thomson 2011; Thomson et al. 2006). In some studies, the depth of cooperation emerges as a salient divide. For instance, Thomson, Boerefijn, and Stokman (2004) suggest that one dominant conflict dimension represents the support for policy change, but it is unclear whether this implies deeper cooperation. Hagemann, Hobolt, and Wratil (2017) find that governments facing Eurosceptic publics are more likely to oppose measures that extend EU policy authority. In the narrower field of EU economic governance, the most systematic works report divides among countries opposing or supporting the recent euro area reforms (Armingeon and Cranmer 2018), fiscal transfer or fiscal discipline (Lehner and Wasserfallen 2019), or more integration (Târlea et al. 2019). Except for Schure and Verdun (2008), no other study systematically investigates positions on policy enforcement design.

Liberal intergovernmentalism, a prominent theory of European integration, sees the delegation of enforcement prerogatives to the Commission as the standard practice to ensure credible implementation of common policies, and it expects governments anticipating noncompliance to oppose these decisions. This perspective neglects that enforcement may be shared between the Commission, where power resources are equalized across states, and the Council, where they mostly vary according to country size. This raises the question of what explains attitudes towards different enforcement designs. Broader scholarship on international organizations suggests that less powerful (smaller) states should prefer greater centralization in order to secure more equality vis-à-vis powerful counterparts.

In this chapter, we take the lead from these works and put forward expectations of how size (power asymmetry) and risk of noncompliance shape attitudes about the room for manoeuvre member states should enjoy in this regime and about the involvement of the Council and the Commission in its enforcement. We subject these expectations to empirical corroboration with the use of an original dataset of the positions that governments took over the enforcement-relevant contested issues, which emerged during the negotiations on the design of the European economic governance from 1997 to 2012. The impact of correlates of governmental positions is estimated by employing a system of structural equations that accounts for the simultaneity with which governments express their views on these issues during a negotiation occurrence.

As expected, we find that governments with a greater risk of noncompliance prefer greater discretion (i.e. looser cooperation) and that governments with higher voting power prefer more Council involvement in enforcement as their risk of noncompliance increases. Voting power and risk of noncompliance also partially explain attitudes towards the involvement of the Commission, but, given their greater indeterminacy, public support for the EU at the national level emerges as the most relevant correlate of these positions. These are not the only influences though. In a way that best reflects the recurrent theme of the book, a host of other economic, supranational, and national pressure factors shape governmental positions.

3.1 Depth of Cooperation and Implementing Discretion

At the centre of most negotiations are the exact provisions that are to be enforced. These rules specify the depth of cooperation of an accord, in particular how far they tighten governmental action or grant discretion in implementation. That this issue could take centre stage was first recognized by Dimitrova and Steunenberg (2000) in the context of EU negotiations, and it has been an object of inquiry in studies on other international agreements (e.g. Rosendorff 2005; Rosendorff and Milner 2001).

The depth of cooperation is intrinsically linked to the risk of noncompliance: the greater the national discretion, the shallower the agreement and the less the states have to do to comply. So, what position on implementing discretion is a government at risk of noncompliance likely to take? That depends on whether a government sees the prospect of noncompliance as a cost or an incentive. If a government wants to avoid the costs associated with an infringement (such as pecuniary sanctions, audience, and reputational costs), it is likely to support provisions that expand discretion and reduce the risk of breaching such an agreement. In other words, *a government's preference for discretion should increase as its risk of noncompliance rises* (H3.1, we label the expectations to help the reader navigate throughout the book). But what if a government wants to use the agreed provisions as a tool to engender domestic reform, especially when fiscal adjustment is much needed but long delayed because of dysfunctional national politics? According to this external constraint argument, which has been employed particularly in the case of Italy (e.g. Dyson and Featherstone 1996; Quaglia 2004; Sbragia 2001), we should *not* expect governments that face greater risks of noncompliance to argue for looser provisions (H3.2).

3.2 Noncompliance Risk, Power Asymmetry, and Enforcement

Negotiations over implementing discretion do not occur in a vacuum. While discussing the depth of cooperation, governments negotiate over the procedures that should ensure the enforcement of an agreement. Indeed, the nature of the enforcement problem has implications for the terms of an agreement (Fearon 1998), and good compliance is often the result of agreements that require states to take negligible measures (Downs, Rocke, and Barsoom 1996). Where cooperation is shallow, states are probably hardly concerned about enforcement. But, if regulatory requirements are cogent, the enforcement mechanism matters.

Liberal intergovernmentalism expects governments that anticipate greater difficulties in complying to be more reluctant to delegate enforcement prerogatives to a supranational agency such as the Commission (Moravcsik 1998: 69, 73–77). After all, this so-called 'guardian of the treaties' has the mandate to ensure proper enforcement of EU law and, because of its independence, it should pursue this activity more credibly than a council of elected ministers would. Straightforwardly, *a government's preference for more Commission-based enforcement should decrease as its risk of noncompliance rises* (H3.3).

As we show in greater detail in Chapter 5, enforcement prerogatives are hardly delegated solely to the supranational executive in the context of the EU economic governance. The Council is heavily involved. And the use of such prerogatives can be the object of heated arguments, as Schröder's commentary piece suggests. This raises the question as to what explains governmental preferences for a more Commission-based rather than Council-based enforcement.

A plausible starting point is that governments should prefer an enforcement procedure over which they can exercise more influence. Indeed, Moravcsik (1998: 76, fn. 111) conjectures that smaller states may favour centralization (delegation) because equal treatment increases their influence. States are equally represented at the apex of this supranational institution, while the Council gives larger states more influence when it decides by qualified majority voting.

Students of the design of dispute settlement mechanisms make a similar point: less powerful (smaller) states should prefer more legalistic (centralized) procedures because they secure more equality and effective compliance by powerful states (McCall Smith 2000; Tallberg and McCall Smith 2014). However, these scholars do not investigate actual positions about enforcement mechanisms. Similarly, Moravcsik (1998) does not subject his conjecture to investigation since he focuses solely on the three largest European countries. Clearly, given the large differences across EU states, especially after the enlargement to several medium-to-small countries, size should not be ignored in the politics of enforcement design.

This latter perspective casts doubts on the independence of the Commission. It puts more emphasis on commissioners being possibly delegates, rather than arbiters, of national interests. In other words, this approach does not take at face value Article 245 of the Treaty on the Functioning of the European Union, which proscribes governments from influencing commissioners. Indeed, the possibility that commissioners may be tools of national influence should not be ignored. They are predominantly career politicians, frequently sharing the positions of their home country (Thomson 2008). An attempt at reducing the size of the College of Commissioners was successfully blocked by the Irish government during the ratification of the Treaty of Lisbon.

Indeed, the College, where each member state is entitled to one commissioner, is the primary channel through which a government can exert influence. And such influence should not be discarded, despite norms protecting the autonomy and agenda-setting prerogatives of individual commissioners and the first-among-equals role of the Commission President (Hartlapp, Metz, and Rauh 2014; Nugent and Rhinard 2005). The Penrose–Banzhaf voting power index of governments in the Council's qualified majority voting procedure ranges from 0.09 per cent for Malta to 16.01 per cent for Germany.[2] In a pre-Brexit College of 28 members who decide by absolute majority (Article 8 of the rules of procedure), the power index of each commissioner is 3.57 per cent. Accordingly, a formal model proposed by Schure and Verdun (2008) suggests that larger (higher Council-voting power) states should prefer more Council-centred enforcement, while smaller states should opt for greater Commission involvement in enforcement.

Lingering issues remain, however. The original argument for Commission-based enforcement rests on the higher probability of sanctioning noncompliance. Would small states that anticipate compliance problems therefore still prefer empowering the supranational agency rather than the Council? Would large states that expect to be compliant prefer retaining control over enforcement in the Council rather than diluting their influence in the Commission? How do size (power asymmetry) and risk of noncompliance concurrently shape attitudes towards enforcement design?

A more articulated view would contend that governments that expect to be more at risk of infringement display stronger preferences for enforcement procedures over which they can exercise more influence. Following Schure and Verdun (2008), let us equate this influence with the voting power governments have under the Council's qualified majority rule (more on this later). We should expect *a government with high voting power to prefer more Council-based enforcement as its risk of noncompliance rises* (H3.4), while *a*

[2] These values are calculated using the new procedure operating from 1 November 2014 (Article 16.4 of the Treaty on the European Union). The computation of this index is discussed later.

government with low voting power to prefer more Commission-based enforcement as such risk rises (H3.5). Larger states at risk of noncompliance should push for a Council-based procedure over which they have more sway, while smaller states in a similar position may find themselves in a conundrum. On the one hand, centralized enforcement could be more attractive as it bestows on them (via their commissioner) more influence than a Council-based procedure (H3.5). On the other hand, they may be reluctant to empower a Commission too zealous in enforcing the rules (H3.3). How this trade-off is solved is a matter of empirical investigation.

3.3 Controversies, Government Positions, and Their Explanans

These expectations are well suited for understanding the patterns of contestation behind the reforms of the economic governance regime for three main reasons. First, a majority of the controversies can be traced back to questions about the depth of cooperation and the design of enforcement. Government positions have differed with regard to the demands on national authorities and the involvement of the Council and Commission in enforcement. In other words, constraints over national policy autonomy are tightened enough to generate divergences among governments over their scope and enforcement. Second, as discussed in detail in Chapter 5 and Part III of the book, noncompliance has been pervasive and has varied across space and time. Between 1994 and 2011, the government deficit of every country, except for Estonia and Luxembourg, has been deemed excessive at least once, and in some cases twice or thrice. Every country, except for Hungary, Slovakia, and Sweden, has experienced a period where the rate of adjustment of its structural budget has not been in line with the objective established by these rules. Last, although the details of these controversies may appear highly technical sometimes, we should not underestimate the salience of this regime for policymakers, given the significance of government spending in European economies (Genschel 2013; Genschel and Jachtenfuchs 2016; 2018). In Chapters 7 and 8, we will show how it shapes the domestic policies and the budgetary decisions of governments. Some of its reforms have, therefore, been highly politicized. In a study of six countries, Kriesi and Grande (2016: 253) report that the revisions that were adopted during the sovereign debt crisis generated the most intense public debate on European issues since the 1970s. Politicization was on a par with that occurring during the ratification of the Treaty of Maastricht.

3.3.1 Divisive Issues and Government Positions

The twenty controversies that are relevant to our inquiry have emerged during the twelve negotiation occurrences that took place between 1997 and 2012 over the adoption and the following reforms of the EDP, the Stability and Growth Pact (SGP), and the fiscal compact.[3] Conflicts that cannot be associated with the implementing discretion or the design of enforcement have been dropped. These include inter-institutional issues that have divided Council ministers and parliamentarians, as well as the issues that have emerged during the negotiations of the ancillary and complementary measures of the six-pack in 2011 and the two-pack in 2013. Some controversies behind the adoption of the macroeconomic imbalance procedure can be associated with discretion and enforcement, but this measure requires a completely different operationalization of the risk of non-compliance. We have, therefore, disregarded it.

Recall that the regime's linchpins consist of three fiscal rules: two reference values – the 3 per cent and 60 per cent ratios of, respectively, government deficit and debt to GDP, established by the Treaty of Maastricht – and a close-to-balance structural budget, which was included in the SGP but was agreed-upon prior to formally tabling the proposal (Artis and Buti 2000: 564–65). These provisions are the cornerstone of European economic governance, and, once established, they have not been subject to subsequent negotiations. The reforms that we include in our analysis have progressively refined the procedures and criteria for determining compliance with these rules and the adjustment path for their attainment.

Our three dependent variables are the governmental preferences with regard to (1) the level of national discretion in implementing this regime and the level of involvement of (2) the Council and (3) the Commission in its enforcement. Four steps are taken to measure these positions. The first two consist of identifying and categorizing

[3] Please refer back to Chapter 1 for an overview of the whole regime.

the *relevant divisive issues*, and the next two of identifying and categorizing the *governmental positions* on such issues.

As a first step, we have selected the twenty relevant issues of intergovernmental conflict that emerged during these negotiations. Since these reforms cover a twenty-year timespan, we have employed several sources and strategies to identify and cross-validate divisive issues.[4] In the second step, we have assigned these issues to one of three categories: *National discretion, Council enforcement*, and *Commission enforcement*. Six divisive issues concern primarily demands on national authorities. For instance, during the adoption of the enforcement regulation, governments had different views about the obligations of, and the sanctions to impose on, member states for manipulating statistics. These positions reflected differences with regard to the discretion of national policymaking. Eight issues are about the Council's room of manoeuvre in decision-making. For instance, the mitigating factors the Council has to consider for establishing whether a deficit is excessive generated considerable animosity both in 1997 and 2005. Contrasting opinions reflected differences about the leeway the Council should have enjoyed – in other words, its involvement in policy enforcement. The statement of Jürgen Stark in this chapter's epigraph reveals a desire to set clear boundaries for its prerogatives.

The remaining six divisive issues concern the role of the Commission, such as the scope of application of reverse qualified majority for the adoption of recommendations for sanctions. Under this procedure, recommendations require only a blocking minority, rather than a qualified majority, in the Council for approval. Where applied, the supranational executive's involvement in policy enforcement is therefore strengthened. These latter conflicts emerged mostly during the 2011–2012 reforms. By using distinct categories for Council and Commission enforcement, we do not have to assume that they are mutually exclusive.

In the third step of the procedure, we have identified the governmental positions of EU member states at the beginning of the negotiations, that is, as close as possible to when the Commission tabled

[4] For a detailed description of these procedures, see Section 3.1 of the online appendix to this chapter, while Table A3.1 of the same appendix lists these controversies.

the proposals (for the fiscal compact, we followed Wasserfallen et al. 2019). These preferences can be more easily associated with the specific legal provisions under negotiation.[5] Moreover, at these early stages, they are less likely to have shifted in reaction to other governments' position-taking. Most scholars tend to consider these positions to be sincere and free from strategic considerations, given the information-rich environment of such deliberations (e.g. Bailer 2004; Moravcsik 1998: 61; Târlea et al. 2019). According to Lundgren and his colleagues (2019: 4), 'this assumption is particularly warranted in the financial domain, where state interests may be deduced from publicly available statistics'. In the fourth and last step, positions have been assigned to one of three levels of an ordered scale (see Figure A3.1 for an illustration). If the issue is about the discretion of national policymaking, a government may prefer a low, middle, or high level of discretion. If it is about Council or Commission enforcement, it may prefer a low, middle, or high level of policy involvement. Our three dependent variables are, therefore, measured on a three-level ordinal scale.

3.3.2 *Risk of Noncompliance and Voting Power*

The *Risk of noncompliance* is measured by the ratio of the general government's gross debt to the country's GDP during the negotiations of a given measure.[6] This ratio is a plausible indicator of past profligacy and it is reasonably linked to the propensity to overspend. Moreover, governments of more indebted countries pay higher servicing costs and have to operate in tighter fiscal environments when experiencing recessions. All other things being equal, including business cycle volatility, they are more likely to breach these rules. This ratio is also acceptably exogenous to governmental preferences and actions in the short term. For instance, von Hagen and Harden (1995) find that it correlates with a structural index of national budgetary institutions that are quite hard to modify in the short term. Franzese (2002: 188) shows that debt levels are affected by other political factors, but only in the long run.

[5] See Table A3.1 in the online appendix.

[6] Armingeon and Cranmer (2018) use a similar measure as a predictor of support for the fiscal compact. The variable has been rescaled (divided by 10) to take on more informative values.

The influence a government exercises over enforcement is measured by its Penrose–Banzhaf *Voting power index* in the Council's qualified majority voting procedure – the most frequently employed rule in the implementation of fiscal governance – at the time of adoption of a measure.[7] This index measures the probability a given government is pivotal in forming any winning coalition, out of the number of times any government is pivotal.[8]

This index ignores the positions of decision-makers. It can also be criticized because a government usually cannot vote if it is the addressee of an enforcement measure, such as an excessive deficit decision, and because it disregards changes resulting from EU enlargements that occurred after the adoption of the act. However, its purpose is to capture a government's *expectation* of executive influence at the time a measure is negotiated. The index is therefore appropriate in contexts where there is uncertainty about future preference configurations, noncompliance patterns, and possible enlargements.

We include several control variables that are plausible correlates of positions and reflect other economic, national, and supranational pressures facing politicians. We do not find strong reasons to consider them colliders or affected by the above covariates to justify their exclusion. First, governments that are more exposed to the negative spillover effects from noncompliance may be inclined to prefer lower national implementing discretion. As discussed in Chapters 1 and 2, fiscal governance is designed to prevent negative externalities arising from fiscal profligacy. Assuming an inflation-averse central bank, in a monetary union, these externalities range from higher interest rates, (common) currency appreciation, trade imbalances, up to default, financial contagion, and, in the long run, lower capital accumulation and output. Whether these exact fiscal rules are necessary, effective, or even deleterious is beside the point. Governments from euro area countries, which share a common monetary policy and cannot take advantage of currency fluctuations to soften the transmission of these effects, can plausibly expect to be more exposed. We, therefore, include an indicator variable *Euro area* that takes the value of one if the country has adopted the euro at the time of negotiations. This variable is also

[7] Since non-euro area governments did not have the right to vote in the 2011 SGP enforcement regulation, they have been dropped from the analysis.

[8] A player is pivotal if, by leaving, she turns a winning coalition into a losing one.

used as a control in the analyses of the attitudes towards Council or Commission-based enforcement because fiscal obligations differ between euro area and non-euro area countries.

Second, negative spillovers during the European sovereign debt crisis took the vivid form of contagion from Greece to Ireland and Portugal. With the risk of spreading to other countries, they prompted subsequent reform efforts. During this extraordinary period, some governmental positions, which may have otherwise remained unchanged, could have plausibly shifted towards tighter national control (lower discretion). We, therefore, include an indicator variable *Economic crisis* that takes the value of one for the negotiations that occurred during 2011 and 2012. There are no plausible reasons for the crisis to affect the attitudes towards Council- and Commission-based enforcement as well, but benefiting from EU financial support in this period may have shaped the positions on these issues, given the involvement of these institutions in granting and managing assistance. We, therefore, control for another indicator variable *Financial assistance* for countries that requested or were receiving assistance during the negotiations.[9]

Third, the government holding the Council presidency is in charge of setting the agenda, proposing compromises, and negotiating with other institutions, such as the European Parliament. These duties as well as the incentive to take credit for closing dossiers are likely to affect its position (e.g. Tallberg 2006; Warntjen 2008). Thus, we include an indicator variable (*Presidency*) that takes the value of one if a government is chairing Council meetings during negotiations. Fourth, fiscal governance regulates an important domestic economic policy tool and provides for a non-trivial involvement of EU institutions. Accordingly, governments' positions may differ along the economic left–right and anti–pro integration divides that underlay this policy (Mattila 2004; e.g. Hagemann and Høyland 2008). We control for governmental positions on the economic left–right dimension (*Left–right position*) by including the legislative seat-weighted average of governing parties' positions on a one-to-ten left–right scale. Similarly, a government's attitude towards the EU (*Anti–pro EU position*) is the weighted average of governing parties' positions on a one-to-seven

[9] Data come from https://economy-finance.ec.europa.eu/eu-financial-assistance_en

anti/pro-integration scale.[10] Fifth, governments are more likely to oppose the expansion of EU policy competences when facing public scepticism towards European integration (Hagemann, Hobolt, and Wratil 2017). We employ a commonly used Eurobarometer survey question asking respondents whether they think that their country's membership to the EU is a 'good thing', a 'bad thing', or neither. *Public support* is the share of respondents answering that membership is good, net of the share saying that it is bad, in the survey conducted before the negotiations.[11] Descriptive statistics are reported in Table A3.2 of the online appendix to this chapter.

3.4 The Sources of Controversies

We are now ready to analyze the sources of most controversies surrounding the reforms of economic governance. The unit of analysis is a position of a government on a relevant divisive issue during a negotiation occasion, such as the German government's view on the exceptional circumstances for avoiding an excessive deficit during the adoption of the SGP corrective regulation in 1997. These circumstances delineate the involvement of the Council – its decision-making discretion – in enforcement since this institution establishes whether an excessive deficit exists. In this case, the German and Dutch governments wanted precise conditions and, therefore, tighter control over the Council (i.e. *low* involvement in enforcement). The Belgian, French, and Italian governments preferred no conditions, hence looser control (*high* involvement). The remaining governments had an intermediate position, which became the final compromise.

Government positions are cross-classified by country. Each position is nested in a divisive issue, and each issue is nested in a measure under negotiation. To account for the simultaneity of bargaining

[10] We rely on Ray's 1999 dataset for party positions during the 1997 negotiations and on the Chapel Hill Expert Survey data in Polk et al. (2017) for positions in the remaining negotiations. For Cyprus, Luxembourg, and Malta, we used as national party positions those of the European Parliament party groups to which they are affiliated, using data from McElroy and Benoit (2012).

[11] Governments' positions on the EU correlate positively, albeit only moderately, with their publics' support for the EU (the correlation is 0.29, $p < 0.01$). This is in line with the literature (e.g. Hobolt, Spoon, and Tilley 2009). Governments are broadly representative but tend to be more pro-European. This limited collinearity is a good reason for including both variables in the analysis.

over discretion and enforcement in a given negotiation occurrence, we estimate a structural equation model.

The results are reported in Table 3.1. The columns list the coefficients estimated from three ordinal logistic regressions. The predictor variables are simultaneously regressed, as part of a single system of equations, on the three distinct dependent variables. These are the three-level (low, middle, and high) ordered governmental positions across the relevant divisive issues concerning discretion, the involvement of the Council, and the involvement of the Commission in enforcement, which emerged during the negotiations of the measures. The model also estimates equation-specific 'fixed' effects for these level variables (*Measure* and *Issue*) and common random effects for these variables, allowing, therefore, for their effects to vary across equations.[12] Among the benefits of structural equation models is the possibility of testing and evaluating complex theoretical expectations and different model structures through model-specific goodness-of-fit statistics.

We discuss the results starting with expectations H3.1 and H3.2 on governmental positions on national discretion. We then move on to positions on Council enforcement (H3.4) and leave the analysis of expectations H3.3 and H3.5 on Commission enforcement to the end as it requires a more detailed discussion. Section 3.3 of this chapter's online appendix reports robustness tests for the multilevel data structure and the miscategorization of divisive issues and governmental positions.

National discretion: As expected by hypothesis H3.1, governments with a higher risk of noncompliance support more discretion (second column in Table 3.1). If we keep all other covariates at their mean values, the probability that a government prefers more discretion increases by 16 percentage points[13] as the risk of noncompliance rises

[12] More specifically, the common variance components measure the deviation of a given observation/issue mean log-odd from the equation-specific issue/measure mean log-odd. The total effect (comprising a common random effect and an equation-specific fixed effect) of these level variables, therefore, differs across equations. In other words, we estimate the joint variability of the mean log-odds of these level variables *across* the three equations. Hence, we model their interdependence. This is one additional benefit of employing generalized structural equation modelling.

[13] This is the difference between the predicted probability of a government preferring more discretion holding every variable at their means (52.5 per cent)

Table 3.1 *Governmental positions on national discretion and enforcement mechanisms*

	National discretion	Council enforcement	Commission enforcement
Supranational factors			
Noncompliance risk	0.25**	-0.20*	0.02
	(0.058)	(0.085)	(0.127)
Voting power		-0.35	-0.60*
		(0.262)	(0.300)
Noncompliance risk × Voting power		0.08*	0.02
		(0.033)	(0.019)
Euro area	-1.21**	-0.77	-1.08
	(0.377)	(0.409)	(0.700)
Presidency	-0.86**	-0.37	-0.44
	(0.122)	(0.356)	(1.245)
Financial assistance	0.27	0.99*	-1.66**
	(0.203)	(0.411)	(0.408)
Economic factors			
Economic crisis	-2.36**		
	(0.675)		
National factors			
Left–right position	-0.32**	-0.21**	0.07
	(0.091)	(0.045)	(0.140)
Anti–pro EU position	0.33**	-0.13	-0.40
	(0.067)	(0.194)	(0.218)
Public support	2.01**	0.46	5.16**
	(0.444)	(0.761)	(1.211)
Measure	0.38**	0.46*	1.00[a]
	(0.142)	(0.185)	(0.000)
Issue	1.17**	1.06*	1.00[a]
	(0.282)	(0.423)	(0.000)
Constant (cut 1)	-2.27	-3.78	-2.73
	(1.437)	(0.774)	(2.032)
Constant (cut 2)	-0.52	-0.64	-2.67
	(0.799)	(0.965)	(2.023)
var(Measure)		3.14	
		(2.871)	
var(Issue)		0.84**	
		(0.301)	
Observations	439 (20 issues, 7 measures)		
Log-pseudolikelihood	-311.22		

Note: Generalized structural equation model of three ordinal logistic regressions. Robust standard errors in parentheses, adjusted for seven clusters of measures. **$p < 0.01$ *$p < 0.05$. [a]Constrained at 1.

by a standard deviation, that is to say, if the debt–GDP ratio moves from 65 per cent (the sample mean) to 100 per cent, approximately the difference between the Dutch and Belgian mean values. The average debt–GDP ratio of governments supporting more discretion is 18 percentage points higher than the average ratio of governments supporting less discretion. On no occasion did Italian governments, with an average debt–GDP ratio of 116 per cent during these negotiations, support more tightening than German governments, which averaged 75 per cent. Governmental positions, therefore, do not seem guided by a desire to establish external constraints for engendering national reforms (H3.2). In Section 3.4 of the online appendix, we test variants of this proposition, without success.

The remaining results indicate that several other factors shape attitudes towards national discretion. Euro area governments, being more exposed to the negative externalities of fiscal profligacy, display a systematic propensity towards tighter oversight of national policies. They are 18 percentage points less likely to take a high national discretion position than non-euro area governments. Governments presiding at Council meetings are 12 percentage points less likely to take a high discretion position.

As for economic factors, the crisis looms large over the process of preference formation. Governments are 36 percentage points more likely to prefer tighter oversight in this period. On the other hand, left-leaning governments have been more inclined towards loosening oversight, probably because of their greater proclivity towards public spending. A standard deviation leftward shift in government ideology increases by 10 percentage points the likelihood of preferring more discretion. Interestingly, governments that display a more critical attitude towards the EU and face a more sceptical public tend to favour tighter national oversight, but the size of these effects is small.[14]

and the same probability but with a standard deviation increased debt–GDP ratio (68.1 per cent). We discuss differences in predicted probabilities since they are easier to understand.

[14] A standard deviation anti-EU shift in government ideology or in public attitudes increases by 5 and 6 percentage points, respectively, the likelihood of preferring less discretion. Governments at low risk of noncompliance or with pro-EU orientation are more likely to adopt a tighter stance when facing a Eurosceptic shift in public opinion. Additionally, in countries with Eurosceptic publics, an anti-EU shift in government ideology is associated with tighter positions.

Council enforcement: The third column in Table 3.1 reports the results from the equation regressing governmental positions on Council involvement in policy enforcement on the interaction between noncompliance risk and voting power. Figure 3.1 shows the marginal effect of the risk of noncompliance on the likelihood of preferring more Council-based enforcement, for different values of the voting index. Expectation H3.4 is corroborated. Governments exceeding a voting power index of 4 per cent (i.e. approximately, the Dutch government's index in 2005) are more likely to prefer greater Council involvement as their risk of noncompliance increases. Above this threshold, governments supporting more involvement have a mean debt–GDP ratio that is 26 percentage points higher than that of governments supporting less involvement. Keeping all other covariates at their means, if a large country like Italy were to face an increase in noncompliance risk (specifically, a standard deviation increase in the debt–GDP ratio over the overall mean), the probability that its government would support more discretionary Council involvement increases by a very substantial 44 percentage points. If the Maltese government were in the same situation, such a probability would actually drop by 3 percentage points, but this figure is not significantly different from zero. On the other hand, governments negotiating or benefiting from financial assistance are 14 percentage points more likely to prefer greater Council involvement. We discuss this finding later, as it should be interpreted in light of the attitudes towards the Commission's empowerment.

As a national factor, the ideological composition of governments has a small but non-trivial impact. Keeping other variables at their means, a rightward shift by a standard deviation (approximately the difference between the 2005 Austrian centre-right government of Wolfgang Schüssel and the 2011 grand coalition of Werner Faymann) increases by 5.5 percentage points the probability of preferring less involvement. More concerned about fiscal probity, right-wing governments prefer subtracting fiscal oversight from the political manoeuvring that takes place within the Council.

Commission enforcement: The last column in Table 3.1 reports the results from the equation regressing governmental positions on Commission involvement in policy enforcement. There is no overall evidence either that governments oppose Commission involvement as they face higher noncompliance risk (H3.3) or that small voting-power

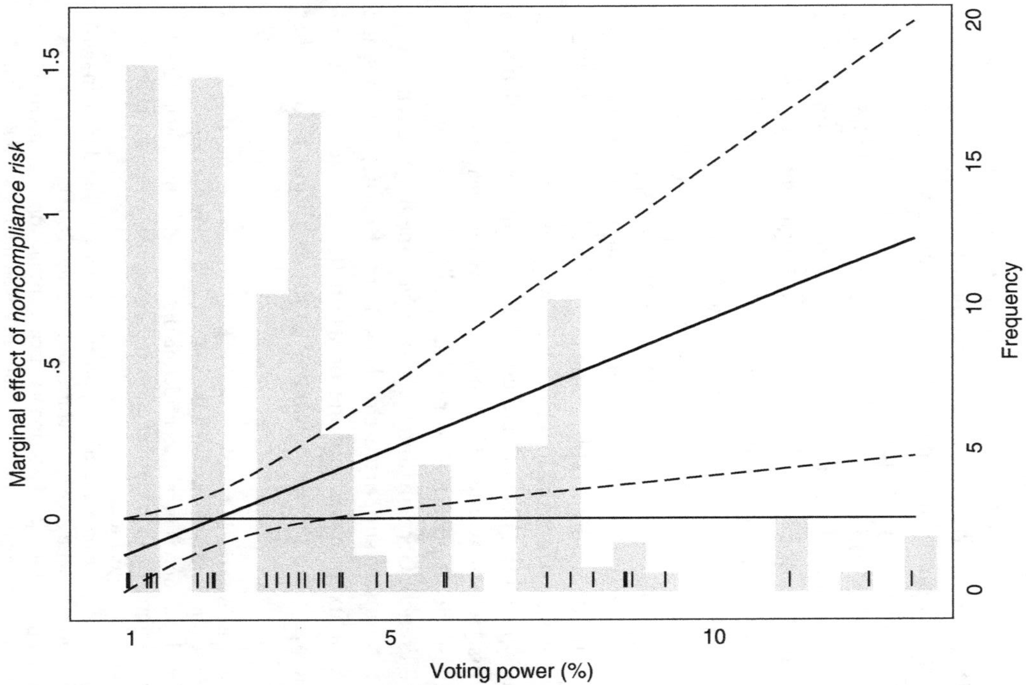

Figure 3.1 Marginal effect of noncompliance risk on preferring more Council involvement, over voting power
Source: Franchino and Mariotto (2021). Reprinted with permission.

governments support greater involvement as such risk increases (H3.5, see, especially, Figure A3.2 on the marginal effect of this covariate). We must delve deeper into our data to better understand these results.

Only one divisive issue about the Commission's prerogatives emerged before the euro area crisis. It occurred during the 2005 EDP regulation reform and concerned methodological inspections. Governments of the four largest countries opposed the regularity of the Commission's intrusive inspections of national public accounts as well as a first in-depth monitoring visit proposed by the Luxembourgish presidency and supported by other governments. As expected by H3.5, among countries at above-average risk of noncompliance, large voting power governments opposed the expansion of prerogatives; medium-to-small voting power governments supported it.[15] However, this divide extends to governments with below-average risk as well.[16]

Three relevant divisive issues surfaced in 2011, as the euro area crisis was intensifying and Olli Rehn, a staunch supporter of tight fiscal surveillance and presumably of expansionary fiscal consolidation (Hodson 2013: 306; Mabbett and Schelkle 2016; Schmidt 2020: 186–87),[17] was the Commissioner for economic and monetary affairs. These issues pitted the Belgian, Dutch, and Luxembourgish (Benelux) governments, which wanted to expand the Commission's influence by extending the application of reverse qualified majority voting,[18] against the French, German, and Spanish governments. The remaining governments mostly supported the Task Force Report, which sided with the Benelux proposal on one occasion (the enforcement regulation) and with the French–German–Spanish coalition in the other

[15] Malta, Cyprus, Austria, Portugal, Hungary, Belgium, Greece, and the Netherlands supported expansion; Italy, France, and Germany opposed it. The Greek position is notable considering that, in December 2004, the Commission initiated an infringement procedure against Greece for failing to comply with the regulation.

[16] The only exception here being the support from the Spanish and the non-euro area Polish governments, see also Schure and Verdun (2008).

[17] As discussed in Chapter 2, expansionary fiscal consolidation is a heterodox economic theory predicting that reductions in government spending during downturns may expand economic activity by changing expectations about future taxation and government spending, see also Alesina, Favero, and Giavazzi (2019).

[18] With this rule, only a qualified majority in the Council can block a Commission's recommendation, therefore significantly strengthening the supranational executive's influence.

two cases (the preventive and corrective regulations). The position of these latter three countries is in line with H3.5 as they had large voting power and above-average debt–GDP ratios.

Five small-to-medium voting power governments at high risk of noncompliance sided *against* Benelux in two of the three issues.[19] This is clearly more supportive of H3.3 than H3.5. Three of these countries (Ireland, Greece, and Portugal)[20] were receiving financial assistance during these negotiations. Their reluctance can be explained by a heightened sensitivity to the intransigence of the supranational executive, perhaps combined with the necessity to take sides with large countries, which were the main contributors to the funds. Indeed, governments of countries that requested or were receiving assistance during the negotiations are 31 percentage points *less* likely to prefer greater Commission involvement in enforcement and, as we reported earlier, are also more likely to prefer greater Council involvement.

However, if we accept H3.3, it is harder to justify the enthusiasm of Belgium for expanding the Commission's influence and the recalcitrance of several governments with below-average noncompliance risk.[21] A notable, yet partial, exception is the Italian and British governments' support for expanding the Commission's influence in one out of, respectively, three and two issues they were involved in. As expected, the Italian government was on average more recalcitrant and the British government was essentially indifferent.

Divergences over the extension of reverse qualified majority voting resurfaced during the 2012 fiscal compact negotiations, at the apex of the crisis, instigated on this occasion by five countries, including Germany, the Netherlands, and Austria. In line with H3.3, all the countries with public debt exceeding GDP – including Ireland, Greece, Italy, and Portugal – were not supportive, but several others with

[19] They were supportive only in the enforcement legislation, where they incidentally enjoyed higher voting power because non-euro area governments could not vote.

[20] The other two are Austria and Malta. Hungary was opposed in one issue and had an intermediate position on another. Its government also received financial assistance.

[21] All the 2004 and 2007 enlargement countries belonging to this group, from Estonia to Poland, were reluctant (note that Cyprus would soon need financial assistance). The Nordic and Scandinavian countries were more supportive.

solid public finances also shared this view. A second divisive issue concerned the prerogative of the Commission to bring noncompliant countries before the European Court of Justice. Here as well, we find greater support amongst more financially solid countries. The mean debt–GDP ratio of this group is more than 32 percentage points lower than the mean ratio of the opposing set of countries. There are however important exceptions, such as the support from the Italian government and the opposition from the financially solid Czech government, which eventually took seven years to ratify the treaty.

Table 3.1 helps to shed light on these discrepancies. Similar to the finding of Hagemann, Hobolt, and Wratil (2017), governments facing more sceptical public opinion were more reluctant to empower the Commission. All else kept at the mean values, a standard deviation decrease in public support decreases by 15 percentage points the probability of preferring greater involvement of the supranational executive. Among cases at low risk of noncompliance, public support in those countries whose governments opposed expanding the Commission's powers is almost 17 percentage points lower than in those whose governments supported such an expansion. On the other hand, public support in countries with shakier public finances and governments that favoured expanding the Commission's prerogatives was 10 percentage points higher than in countries in a similar financial situation, but with governments that opposed such empowerment. Public support in Belgium was among the highest and in Italy the highest among large countries.

In sum, the high-low voting power divide among governments at high risk of noncompliance (H3.5) was evident in 2005, but it was mirrored among governments at low risk of noncompliance. In 2011 and 2012, the perception of a tougher Commission had two plausible effects. The small-medium-sized countries under fiscal strain and dependent on financial assistance became more reluctant to empower the supranational executive, while the larger countries with less severe compliance problems appeared enticed to do so. A reasonable explanation of why we fall short in finding stronger evidence in support of expectation H3.3 is that governments at low risk of noncompliance confronted more Eurosceptic publics and were, therefore, less inclined to empower the Commission, while some governments at high risk were more accommodating since they faced a strong pro-European public opinion. That public opinion played an important role in shaping governments' positions is plausible given the salience of the policy and the mass politicization of these latter reforms (Genschel and Jachtenfuchs 2018; Kriesi and Grande 2016).

3.5 Conclusion

Most of the controversies surrounding the reforms of the European economic governance have been about the degree to which provisions should constrain states and the degree to which the Council and the Commission should be involved in enforcement.

These conflicts originate primarily from a desire to avoid the costs associated with noncompliance. Governments that perceive being at a greater risk of flaunting the regime's key provisions try to expand the room for national manoeuvre (H3.1), while there is no evidence of governments attempting to use the regime provisions as an external constraint to engender domestic reform (H3.2).

Similarly, governments facing greater risks of noncompliance should prefer enforcement procedures over which they can exercise more influence. How this plays out in practice is complicated, however. Governments at greater risk prefer more Council involvement in enforcement *if* they enjoy higher voting power within this institution (H3.4). However, as far as the supranational executive's prerogatives are concerned, in some cases, different power resources drive support for empowering this institution, with smaller state governments displaying greater enthusiasm and larger state ones more reluctance (H3.5). In other circumstances, expectations of compliance problems make governments more hesitant, especially when the Commission is perceived as a tough enforcer (H3.3). Thus, noncompliance risk and power resources may push positions in opposing directions in different circumstances. And it is perhaps because of these conflicting pressures, and the concomitant mass politicization of negotiations, that public support for the EU – an important national pressure factor for politicians – offers governments guidance for positioning on this issue: those facing more sceptical publics display more reluctance to empower the Commission.

But positions are also shaped by ideological inclinations and other contextual features related to supranational politics and economic conditions. Left-leaning governments prefer greater room for national manoeuvre and more Council involvement in enforcement.

A government presiding Council meetings takes a stricter stance on national discretion. Euro area governments display a propensity for tighter national control. The sovereign debt crisis may have shifted preferences towards more national tightening, while governments requesting or receiving assistance during this period had a strong preference for Council, rather than the Commission, involvement.

As we shall see, several of these themes will resurface throughout the book. Having identified the sources of the main controversies, we proceed now to investigate the determinants of the outcomes of these negotiations, the winners and the losers.

4 *Compromises, Procedures, and the Costs of Failure*

I say no to those who want to replace stability by a flexibility without limits, and I also say no to those who want to create an unchangeable dogma of the pact as it is.

Jean-Claude Juncker, Prime Minister of Luxembourg (1995–2013) and President of the Council of the European Union (January–June 2005)

Neither the European Council, the French and Germans at Deauville, nor Mr Van Rompuy's taskforce have the power to decide alone. No definitive decision can be taken without agreement from the Parliament.

Sylvie Goulard, Member of the European Parliament (2009–2017) and rapporteur of Regulation 1173/2011

On 8 November 2011, in a large conference room of the Justus Lipsius building in Brussels, ministers and ambassadors gathered around a set of solid wooden desks, laid out in a hexagonal shape, for the 3,122nd meeting of the Economic and Financial Affairs Council. Items four to eight on the agenda were the five regulations that made up the six-pack on economic governance. These were A items, meaning that ministers reached an agreement and were supposed to approve them without debate. All delegations voted in favour, although three statements were added to the minutes.

How best should we understand the outcomes of these negotiations? Which factors best explain bargaining success? The establishment of these rules has given rise to contrasting claims. Several analyses assign a dominant influence to the German government (e.g. Bernhard and Leblang 2016; Heipertz and Verdun 2010; Schimmelfennig 2015; Schmidt 2020: 26–35; Schoeller 2017; Steinberg and Vermeiren 2016), but other scholars doubt that this presumed pre-eminence has translated into bargaining success because of the counterbalancing clout of other governments and institutions (e.g. Bressanelli and Chelotti

2016; Camisão 2015; Degner and Leuffen 2019; Schild 2013; 2020; Schure and Verdun 2008; Segers and van Esch 2007).

In the first part of this chapter, we assess the accuracy of several procedural and bargaining models in predicting the outcomes we observe. In the second part, we investigate the determinants of success.[1] We consider only the EU secondary legislation that makes up its economic governance, while we disregard the fiscal compact because procedural models do not apply to international treaties. Compared to Chapter 3, the analysis is extended to the directive on national budgetary frameworks that is part of the six-pack, the two-pack measures, and the procedure for monitoring macroeconomic imbalances.[2]

Although no study has carried out such a longitudinal analysis of these negotiations, we share common ground with Finke and Bailer (2019) and Lundgren et al. (2019). These scholars have similar research questions but they limit their attention to the most recent reforms. For the set of measures that overlaps with our inquiry, Finke and Bailer (2019: 126–29) find that a procedural (agenda-setting) model that accounts for the status quo or reference point most accurately explains the reform outcomes. Lundgren et al. (2019) find no clear winners and losers across member states and show how preference centrality and proximity to the position of the European Commission significantly affect bargaining success, especially in the ordinary legislative procedure (OLP).

Following Thomson *et al.* (2006) and Thomson (2011), we outline in Section 4.1 the expectations of two procedural and five bargaining models. An important distinguishing feature is whether these models incorporate the reference point, that is, the outcome in case of failure. Despite the importance of this theoretical construct, its empirical relevance in the broader literature is not robust (e.g. Arregui 2016; Cross 2013; Thomson 2011: 229–51). Accordingly, these negotiations are of particular interest because they have been characterized by high costs of no-agreement. In 1997, failure to adopt the SGP would have most probably led to the exclusion of some countries from the euro area. In 2005, no reform meant continuing the abeyance of the excessive

[1] This chapter builds on Franchino and Mariotto (2022).

[2] Please refer back to Chapter 1 for an overview of the whole regime. For the full list of measures and their adoption procedure, see Table A4.1 in the online appendix to this chapter.

deficit procedure. And during the European sovereign debt crisis, lack of reform would have delayed the adoption of bailout measures, with the associated risk of breaking up the euro area (we discuss these features in greater detail in Chapter 5).

The empirical analysis is based on data on governmental and institutional positions over 35 controversial issues that emerged during these reforms.[3] Fifteen are the enforcement-related controversies discussed in Chapter 3 (excluding five fiscal compact ones), while the remaining twenty are either unrelated to enforcement or are related to the macroeconomic imbalances procedure.

Given the object of inquiry, only supranational factors are relevant here. In line with the literature, the results corroborate the accuracy and robustness of the compromise bargaining model. But they also show that a procedural model with a costly reference point performs well, especially in terms of point predictive accuracy. Misestimation of the cost of no agreement appears therefore to be a likely reason for the commonly reported poorer accuracy of procedural models. On the other hand, these models are more sensitive to measurement errors. The last section builds on these results and investigates the determinants of bargaining success. Results indicate that both models are useful in predicting success and that the conditional influence of the European Parliament should not be ignored.

4.1 Models of Legislative Politics

4.1.1 Procedural Models

The predictions of procedural models depend on the sequential features of the legislative process, the differing prerogatives and preferences of the actors that are entitled to propose, amend, and adopt a new measure, as well as the location of the reference point or status quo, that is, the outcome in case of no agreement (König and Proksch 2006; Steunenberg and Selck 2006).

Consider the procedure that has been employed for the SGP corrective regulation: consultation with unanimity voting in the Council. Here, the Commission proposes a measure that is amended and approved unanimously by the Council. Following Crombez (1996: 204), the

[3] See Table A4.2 in the online appendix.

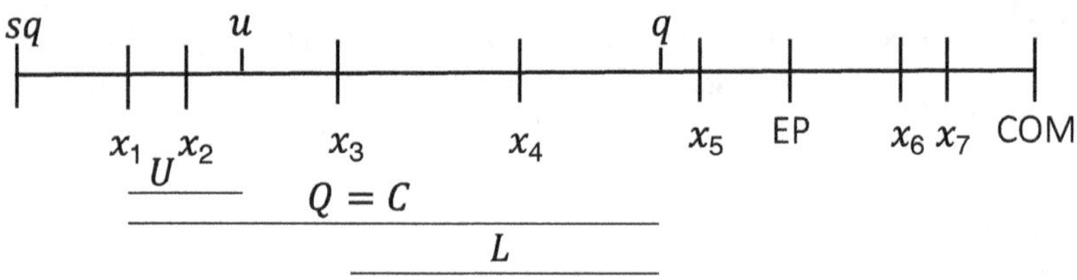

Figure 4.1 An illustration of procedural models
Note: $x_{1...7}$, EP and COM: ideal policies of governments, European Parliament, and Commission. *sq*: status quo or reference point. u, q: policies that are utility equivalent to *sq* for the pivotal government under unanimity and qualified majority voting in the Council. U, Q, C, L: sets of policies that can be adopted under unanimity and qualified majority consultation, cooperation, and ordinary legislative procedures.
Source: Franchino and Mariotto (2022). Reprinted with permission.

Commission enjoys the monopoly of making proposals, but it does not have the power of gatekeeping. Also, while the European Parliament issues an opinion on the proposal, ministers and the Commission are not bound by it. To establish the outcomes that are predicted by the procedural model, we follow Steunenberg (1994) and Crombez (1996). As an illustration, we employ Tsebelis and Garrett's (2000) stylized representation depicted in Figure 4.1.

Assume that the Council is composed of n governments with ideal positions x_i for $i = 1 \ldots n$ distributed on a unidimensional policy space $X = \mathbb{R}^1$. The governments have single-peaked Euclidean preferences, that is, the closer a measure to their ideal, the higher the utility. The Commission and the Parliament have similarly specified utility functions. Actors have complete information. The procedural model requires the identification of (1) the minimal winning coalition, comprising of the actors whose approval is necessary and sufficient for a policy change, and (2) the acceptance set of this coalition's most conservative actor(s), comprising of the policies this actor weakly prefers to the status quo *sq*. This so-called pivotal actor(s) can help to pinpoint the predicted outcome (it may be more than one, depending on the direction of the policy shift and the location of the status quo).

In the unanimity variant of the consultation procedure, the minimum winning coalition comprises all the governments, and the most conservative member is the government with the ideal position that is closest to the status quo (Crombez 1996: 209; Steunenberg 1994). In Figure 4.1, it is government 1. This government supports any policy p in its acceptance set $A_1 = \{p \mid sq \leq p \leq u\}$, where sq and u are equidistant to its ideal x_1. The government is indifferent between sq and u and opposes proposals outside $[sq, u]$, the line segment from sq to u inclusive. In Figure 4.1, proposals in A_1 are also preferred to sq by all the other governments. Finally, let $S = \{p \mid x_1 \leq p \leq x_n\}$ be the support set of policies p such that no policy is weakly preferred to an element of S by all governments. We can derive the intersection $U = A_1 \cap S$ as the set of proposals that can be adopted under the unanimity-based consultation procedure. In other words, a proposal must belong to the acceptance set A_1 *and* to the support set S to become law. If the status quo is an element of the support set, U is empty and no reform is possible.

One can generate a more precise prediction. Since the Commission is positioned at the right end of the policy spectrum in Figure 4.1, it will want to move the policy rightward as much as possible and propose a measure close to u. If we assume that governments support proposals that are utility equivalent to sq, the Commission's proposal and predicted outcome would be u. Clearly, such an outcome would change with different configurations of preferences.

The qualified majority voting (qmv) variant of the consultation procedure, employed for the adoption of the EDP regulations and the budgetary frameworks directive, differs only slightly. A qualified majority in the Council suffices for the adoption of the Commission's proposal. Consequently, the minimum winning coalition comprises the Commission and the governments that make up such a majority[4] (Crombez 1996: 209; Steunenberg 1994). The pivotal member(s) is the government that is closest to the status quo and can form a blocking minority. In Figure 4.1, it is government 3 if a qualified

[4] During the adoption of the 1997 SGP, a qualified majority required sixty-two of the eighty-seven votes held by the fifteen member states in relation to their population sizes. During the 2005 reform, a complex triple-majority system, introduced by the Treaty of Nice, was operating for the twenty-five member states. A qualified majority required 232 out of 321 votes. In addition, the states supporting a measure had to be at least thirteen and representing at least 62 per cent of the total population of the Union. During the 2011 six-pack and 2013 two-pack reforms, the supporting votes had to be 255 out of 345, with at least fourteen out of the twenty-seven states in favour and representing at least 62 per cent of the population.

majority requires, say, five out of seven votes. This government supports any policy p in its acceptance set $A_3 = \{p \mid sq \leq p \leq q\}$, where sq and q are equidistant to its ideal x_3. Proposals in A_3 are also preferred to the sq by the governments to its right. Its elements are therefore also proposals that are preferred to the status quo by a qualified majority. And $Q = A_3 \cap S$ is the set of proposals that can be adopted under the qualified majority-based consultation procedure, while a more precise predicted outcome would be q, given the preference configuration of Figure 4.1.

The preventive SGP measures of 1997 and 2005 have been adopted following the now-repealed cooperation procedure. Its key innovation was the opportunity for the Parliament to insert amendments to a draft text adopted by a qualified majority of the Council. If these changes were accepted by the Commission, the Council could either adopt them by a qualified majority or modify them unanimously (Tsebelis 1994). The Parliament, therefore, becomes a member of the minimum winning coalition (Crombez 1996: 214–18) and, with reference to Figure 4.1, the set of proposals that can be adopted under cooperation is $C = A_3 \cap (A_p \cup A_1) \cap S$, where A_p is the Parliament's acceptance set. C is a subset of Q, but they can be equal as in Figure 4.1. Here, the predicted outcome is q as well, but it may obviously differ under different preference configurations.

Last, the remaining six-pack and two-pack measures have been adopted following the OLP, as specified in the Treaty of Amsterdam. This procedure establishes that the Council and the Parliament have formally equal power as co-legislators. In case of protracted disagreement, a conciliation committee composed of ministers and parliamentary representatives is set up to produce a joint text that must be approved by the Council and Parliament to become law. The minimal winning coalition, therefore, comprises a qualified majority in the Council and a majority in the Parliament. Considering Figure 4.1, let $M = \{p \mid \min(x_3, EP) \leq p \leq \max(x_5, EP)\}$ be the support set of policies p such that no policy is weakly preferred to an element of M by a qualified majority of governments and the Parliament. The set of proposals that can be adopted is $L = A_3 \cap A_p \cap M$ (Crombez 1997: 107–9). Under this preference configuration, a proposal q would be approved.

In the empirical section, we will consider two variants of procedural models that differ with regard to the relevance given to the status quo, but first, we introduce the family of bargaining models.

4.1.2 Bargaining Models

Bargaining models offer alternative predictions, abstracting away the procedural features of a legislative process and the prerogatives of the actors involved. One way to put it is that these rules are endogenized, rather than ignored. Since they reflect political power, their application simply replicates the will of powerful actors (Achen 2006b: 91). Others characterize these models as offering predictions when procedural prerogatives are de facto widely dispersed across actors to have no impact on outcomes (e.g. Predtetchinski 2011).

We consider here a set of bargaining models that have been subject to empirical corroboration by Thomson *et al.* (2006) and Thomson (2011). We begin with the *Nash bargaining solution* (NBS), which is the dominant approach in cooperative bargaining games. Adapting the earlier setting, let x_i for $i = 1 \ldots n$ be the ideal positions of n actors involved in bargaining, distributed along a unidimensional policy space $X = \mathbb{R}^1$, with quadratic utility functions. In line with several studies (Achen 2006b: 100; Bailer and Schneider 2006: 162; Thomson 2011: 167), a specification of the NBS is the policy

$$\dot{p} = \underset{p \in \mathbb{R}^1}{\operatorname{argmax}} \prod_{i=1}^{n} s_i \left[(sq - x_i)^2 - (p - x_i)^2 \right] \tag{1}$$

In other words, NBS is the outcome $\dot{p}$ that maximizes the product of actors' utilities, where s_i is the salience attached to the issue by actor i. The first part of Equation (1) captures the utility originating from the status quo and the second part the utility loss from a given policy. The utility is maximized when a policy is located in an actor's ideal position, that is, $p = x_i$. If an actor were to prefer the status quo, any other measure would generate a loss.

In the case of a very high cost of no agreement, Achen (2006b: 94, 117) demonstrates that the NBS is approximated by the salience-weighted mean of actors' ideal policies. A quasi-utilitarian formulation is the following:

$$\dot{p} = \underset{p \in \mathbb{R}^1}{\operatorname{argmax}} \sum_{i=1}^{n} - s_i (p - x_i)^2 \tag{2}$$

NBS is the outcome $\dot{p}$ that maximizes the salience-weighted sum of actors' utilities. The *compromise model* of Van den Bos (1991) adds to Equation (2) a second weight parameter v_i measuring the power of actors, as follows:

$$\dot{p} = \underset{p \in \mathbb{R}^1}{\operatorname{argmax}} \sum_{i=1}^{n} - v_i s_i (p - x_i)^2 \tag{3}$$

If we set v_i and s_i in Equation (3) equal to one, the predicted outcome becomes the *mean position* that maximizes simply the sum of actors' utilities. This prediction bases its theoretical foundation on Caplin and Nalebuff's (1991) mean voter theorem according to which the mean position is an equilibrium outcome in a multidimensional setting with supermajority voting (Thomson 2011: 173).

The last model we consider is the *minimax solution*, which minimizes the maximum utility loss of any actor. With quadratic utility functions, this outcome can be formalized as follows:

$$\dot{p} = \min_{p \in \mathbb{R}^1} \underset{i \in n}{\operatorname{argmax}} \, s_i (p - x_i)^2 \tag{4}$$

This solution has its normative foundation in the Rawlsian theory of justice whereby outcomes should minimize the utility loss of the actor that is disadvantaged the most.[5]

4.2 Controversial Issues, Positions, and Research Design

Recall that the EDP has been modified thrice since 1993, while the 1997 SGP has been amended in 2005 and 2011. Five more measures make up part of the 2011 six-pack and the 2013 two-pack. We have

[5] Evidence of trading gains across issues is sparse in this policy area, so we will not consider more sophisticated models that account for issue linkages. Also, models that add this layer of sophistication do not necessarily perform better. Arregui, Stokman, and Thomson's (2006) position exchange model builds upon the compromise model, but it underperforms according to most accuracy measures (it only marginally improves the mean Euclidean error and hit rate, Achen 2006a: 275–93). König and Proksch's (2006) procedural exchange model is normally an improvement over the poorly accurate procedural model, but it does not reach the accuracy of bargaining models.

identified 35 controversial issues – including disagreements that produced no changes – emerging during these reforms. They are listed in Table A4.2 of the online appendix to this chapter, along with references to the specific provisions that were under negotiation. As we have discussed in Chapter 3, our analysis relies on information on the positions of government ministers and institutions at the beginning of negotiations since they are more plausibly free from strategic considerations.[6]

Figure 4.2 illustrates a controversy concerning the exceptional circumstances for preventing a deficit from being considered excessive. This issue emerged during the negotiations of the 1997 SGP corrective regulation. The German and Dutch governments argued for precise thresholds and proposed that automatic exemptions should apply only to countries experiencing an annual decline in real GDP of at least 2 per cent. The Belgian, French, and Italian governments preferred the status quo, thus leaving the Council free to determine country-specific exceptional circumstances. The Commission did not propose to modify this provision nor did the Parliament amend it at its first reading. The remaining governments held an intermediate position as outlined in an agreement adopted by the ministers of the Economic and Financial Affairs Council. Eventually, the 2 per cent threshold was included in Article 2.2 of the regulation, but the third comma stipulated that, *in light of further evidence*, circumstances could also be exceptional in case of a contraction of less than 2 per cent. In other words, it remained a matter of Council discretion to stipulate whether exceptional circumstances applied to milder recessions. Therefore, this was overall a modest amendment.

Differently from Chapter 3, positions on controversial issues are standardized on a scale from 0 to 100 where the status quo is set at 0 (on no occasion, it is centrally located) and 100 is the most reformist position (see Table A4.3 for summary statistics). In most cases, identifying the status quo is unproblematic, as in the issue depicted in Figure 4.2 where the left-most position is the outcome in case of no agreement. In other circumstances, it is harder. During the negotiations on the enforcement SGP regulation in 2011, some

[6] Recall that the sources and strategies employed to identify and cross-validate issues and positions are discussed in Section 3.1 of the online appendix to Chapter 3.

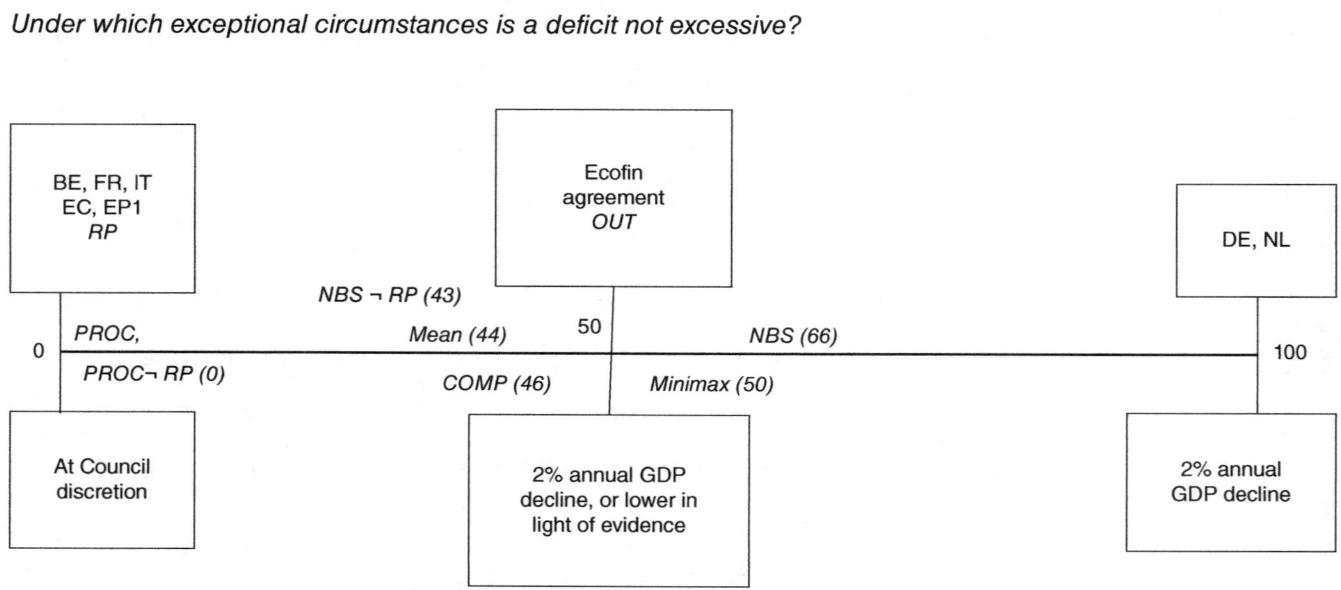

Figure 4.2 A controversial issue in the negotiations on the 1997 corrective SGP regulation
Note: OUT: Outcome, RP: Reference point, NBS: Nash bargaining solution, PROC: Procedural, COMP: Compromise, BE: Belgium, DE: Germany, EC: European Commission proposal, EP1: parliamentary position at first reading, FR: France, IT: Italy, NL: Netherlands. Other countries' positions are represented by the Ecofin (Economic and Financial Affairs) Council agreement. Procedure: Consultation with unanimity.

governments supported the Commission's proposal of redistributing the amounts collected from fines among euro area states with no excessive deficit. Others preferred transferring them to the European Stability Mechanism, thus expanding the EU's financial capacity. In this and similar situations, the most proximate to the status quo is usually the most conservative position, that is, the one that implies less capacity building, less pooling or delegation of policy prerogatives, or less tightening of national authorities. We, therefore, assign the status quo to this position. Note that by positioning the status quo in this manner, rather than at an arbitrary distance away from this position, we bias the research design in favour of the status quo influencing outcomes.

Careful legal analysis is paramount for identifying other positions as well, even for issues that seem unproblematic. For instance, the controversy in Figure 4.2 appears to be easily associated with a continuous scale of 0–2 per cent and the outcome should accordingly be located close to the right end of the scale, assigning a bargaining success to the Dutch and German governments over the Belgian, French, and Italian ones. In reality, considering the third comma of Article 2 of this regulation, we should doubt whether the initial situation had been significantly changed. Indeed, these provisions were eventually repealed in the 2005 reform. In light of this analysis, it seems appropriate to assign the outcome to the mid-point of 50. In our dataset, positions only take the values of 0, 25, 50, and 75. When there are minor differences, we opt for clustering positions rather than differentiating them further because these nuances are very hard to measure accurately.

Especially for older negotiations, we started from initial Council documents as the baseline position of governments, and then, using all the sources and validation strategies at our disposal, we systematically investigated which governments went their way to explicitly record different or similar stances. We assigned a higher salience s_i of 1.25, over the baseline of 1, in these circumstances, accounting for the fact that governments plausibly made an effort to signal their position when issues mattered more to them. We assign a similarly higher salience to the parliamentary position if significant and related amendments have been adopted at its readings or if the issue emerged in trilogues (informal meetings among parliamentary, Council, and Commission representatives). The Commission's salience is set at 1.

Last, Figure 4.2 displays also the outcomes that are predicted by the models. Recall that we consider two variants of procedural models. In the first one, the predicted outcome is the option, belonging to the relevant procedure-specific set (U,Q,C,L) of adoptable policies, that is most preferred by the Commission. The second procedural model instead accounts for the fact that our positioning of the status quo may underestimate the true cost of no agreement. As we argued in the introduction and will discuss further in Chapter 5, this is highly plausible in our context. The second variant, therefore, assumes that acceptance sets do not constrain any longer the set of adoptable measures (recall that the size of acceptance sets is determined by the status quo or reference point, associated with the cost of no agreement, and it expands with such cost). Thus, the predicted outcome is the option, belonging to the relevant procedure-specific support set (S,M), that is most preferred by the Commission. In the situation illustrated in Figure 4.2, both procedural models expect legislators to leave the Council's prerogatives intact.

The expected outcomes of the NBS, NBS without reference point ($\neg$ RP), and minimax models are computed employing gradient ascent-like procedures that implement respectively Equations (1), (2), and (4). The compromise and the mean models follow Equation (3), the former with the parameter v_i taking the Penrose–Banzhaf voting power index scores,[7] the latter with salience s_i and power v_i weights set equal to one. In the controversy of Figure 4.2, minimax predicts the actual outcome.

4.3 Predicting Negotiation Outcomes

Table 4.1 reports the mean average of the absolute differences between predictions and the actual outcome across each controversy, also known as the mean absolute error per issue. It is arguably the most comprehensible metric of accuracy since it measures the average size of the forecasting error of a model (Achen 2006a: 275). Table 4.1 also includes the mean absolute differences with the reference point.

The mean outcome is 59.29, which is fairly reformist, considering that the status quo is anchored at zero. On average, the compromise

[7] In unanimity, governments have equal voting power of 1, while we use voting weights for computing the index in qmv. The Commission has no voting power, while the voting power of the Parliament is set at 0.5 in the OLP and zero otherwise.

Table 4.1 *Means of absolute differences between reference points, outcomes, and model predictions*

	OUT	RP	PROC	PROC ¬ RP	NBS	NBS ¬ RP	COMP	Mean
RP	59.29**							
	(37.91)							
PROC	31.43*	33.57**						
	(38.51)	(42.85)						
PROC ¬ RP	20.00	50.71**	17.14**					
	(30.20)	(42.65)	(34.18)					
NBS	47.86	31.43**	44.66	50.49				
	(39.01)	(37.81)	(40.83)	(41.26)				
NBS ¬ RP	20.69	52.37**	26.06†	15.54	45.91			
	(22.02)	(30.02)	(25.40)	(14.09)	(32.53)			
COMP	18.46	55.51**	28.17†	18.57	43.23	7.54		
	(17.47)	(28.34)	(25.65)	(17.30)	(32.06)	(9.05)		
Mean	20.26	52.80**	25.80*	14.54	46.51	1.34	7.86	
	(22.56)	(31.03)	(26.51)	(13.92)	(33.32)	(1.19)	(9.60)	
Minimax	30.71†	49.83**	42.31	36.77	37.09*	24.71	22.54	25.77
	(23.05)	(1.77)	(16.69)	(21.08)	(18.21)	(17.01)	(17.35)	(17.31)

Note: OUT: Outcome. RP: Reference point. NBS: Nash bargaining solution. PROC: Procedural. COMP: Compromise. Standard deviation in parenthesis. In bargaining models, the Parliament is accounted for only in the OLP. The Commission has no voting power in the compromise model. †$p < 0.1$ *$p < 0.05$, **$p < 0.01$: two-sided sign test that the median of the differences is different from zero.

model expects an outcome of 55.51 and produces the most accurate predictions, with the lowest mean absolute error per issue of 18.46. The next best performing model, with a mean error of 20, is the procedural model that assumes a high cost of no agreement (i.e. ¬ RP). The mean model and the NBS (¬ RP) follow. The differences between the compromise, mean, and NBS (¬ RP) models range between 1.34 and 7.86, meaning that adding information about salience and voting power improves accuracy but does not change predictions drastically. On the other hand, the differences from the predictions of the procedural model (¬ RP) are more than twice as large on average (they range from 14.54 to 18.57), indicating that this model is based on substantively different premises.

The least accurate are the NBS and procedural models that account for the reference point. Although their predictions differ on average by a considerable 44.66 points, they both expect excessively conservative outcomes, averaging 31.43 and 33.57, respectively. NBS is the worst performer, with the highest mean absolute error of 47.86. In between this and the previous group of models stands the normative minimax model with a mean error of 30.63.

These results are mostly consistent with the existing literature. Achen (2006a: 276) finds the compromise and mean models to be the most accurate. In Thomson (2011: 180), the NBS (¬ RP) and the mean models produce the lowest errors. Procedural models generally perform poorly in these works as our first procedural model does (but cf. Finke and Bailer 2019: 126–29). Thomson (2011: 220–24) also finds that models employing equal or regressive (i.e. voting weight-related) power distributions in the Council are the most accurate, and so is our compromise model, which assigns equal power in unanimity and voting weight-related power in qmv procedures. Models using more equal distributions, such as NBS (¬ RP) and mean models, as well as those employing more unequal ones, are less accurate. In the online appendix, we report the accuracy of compromise models that include only the five or six largest countries or that employ Thomson's (2011: 204–9) derived voting power indexes of supranational institutions. These variants are systematically less accurate than the original (see Tables A3–A6). Giving credence to Schure and Verdun (2008) and Heipertz and Verdun (2010), small countries matter in economic governance reforms.

An interesting difference from the existing works is the low mean error of the second procedural model (PROC ¬ RP), which is not considered by Achen (2006a) and Thomson (2011). The summary statistics in Table A4.3 offer a rough-and-ready understanding of why this model does as well as the compromise model (at the cost of ignoring heterogeneity across issues). The mean outcome is in between the centrally located mean position of the Commission and the more reformist mean position of the Parliament. Its key feature lays in the treatment of the reference point, suggesting that issue-specific status quos, even when they can be easily identified from a legal standpoint, as in the example of Figure 4.2, underestimate the cost of no agreement. This cost is more probably associated with the entire measure rather than a single controversy. Indeed, a common thread of these findings is that models that do not consider issue-specific reference points perform better than those that do. The mean difference between the predictions of the two procedural models is 17.14 points (close to the differences between the procedural model [¬ RP] and the well-performing bargaining models). The predictions of the two NBS models differ by a considerable 45.91 points (Thomson [2011: 180] reports a similar result). Since the contexts of these negotiations suggest no agreement to be very costly, differences in model accuracy plausibly lie in the measurement error engendered by issue-specific status quos that underestimate such cost.[8]

It seems to us that here may lie also the reason for the prominence of the reference point in the findings of Finke and Bailer (2019: 126–29). These scholars identify, for the same measures, only a third as many divisive issues as we do and aggregate them into three higher-level conflict dimensions. It could be that the reference point loses salience if a divisive issue is identified at a fine-grained provision-specific level.

Lundgren et al. (2019) use the same dataset as Finke and Bailer (2019), but they disregard proximity to the status quo in their research, so unfortunately they cannot confirm Finke and Bailer's (2019) findings.

Interesting results also emerge from the analysis of accuracy across legislative procedures.[9] The compromise model is the most accurate

[8] The accuracy of the procedural model (¬ RP) worsens if we employ the mean Euclidean error (see Table A4.5). This method uses proposals, rather than issues, as units of prediction and it measures accuracy in a multi-issue Euclidean space, assuming continuous issue scales (for details, see Achen 2006a: 282). The pseudo-R^2 yields the same results.

[9] See Table A4.4 in the online appendix.

in the OLP and it is among the top three in the other two legislative procedures. No obvious patterns are emerging from the other bargaining models, with an interesting exception. NBS is the most accurate model in consultation with unanimity and the least accurate in qmv-based procedures. Underestimating the cost of no agreement appears particularly deleterious in these latter circumstances.

Procedural models perform well in consultation with qmv, less well in OLP, and poorly in consultation with unanimity. This should not be surprising since predictions in these models depend on the selection by the Commission of its most preferred measure among the set of adoptable policies in a given procedure. The Commission's agenda-setting power is at its strongest in qmv consultation. In unanimity, negotiations *within* the Council take centre stage and bargaining models appear better suited. In OLP, negotiations between the Council and the Parliament raise relevance.

Last, outcomes in OLP seem to be the hardest to predict overall. Across all models, the mean absolute error is 30.84 on average, compared to 24.08 in qmv consultation and 20.14 in unanimity. But given the limited number of observations, we should caution against any generalization. Achen (2006a: 278) and Thomson (2011: 181–12) do not find large differences or clear patterns in model accuracy across procedures.

One final aspect deserves attention. Models with the lowest mean average errors may not display the best point predictive accuracy. Schneider, Finke, and Bailer (2010) indeed find that symmetric NBS models, which disregard power resources such as voting power index scores, have lower errors *and* lower point accuracy than asymmetric resource-based NBS models. We, therefore, conclude this section by comparing the predictive accuracy of these models against each other. Table 4.2 reports the number of times that row model predictions improve, worsen, or are identical to column model predictions. The relative performance of bargaining models does not change. The compromise model wins most head-to-head contests, followed by the mean, NBS (¬ RP), and minimax models. NBS loses every comparison, most of the time by a statistically significant margin. Procedural models perform much better overall. For instance, the ¬ RP variant wins every contest. In contrast to Table 4.1, the comparisons in Table 4.2 are less dependent on the scale of the issue, but close and large victories are treated the same (Achen 2006a: 289).

Table 4.2 *Model performance comparison between row model predictions and column model predictions*

		PROC	PROC ¬ RP	NBS	NBS ¬ RP	COMP	Mean
PROC ¬ RP	Better	6†					
	Worse	1					
	Equal	28					
NBS	Better	9	7				
	Worse	14	20**				
	Equal	12	8				
NBS ¬ RP	Better	17	13	26**			
	Worse	17	19	9			
	Equal	1	3	0			
COMP	Better	15	11	26**	17		
	Worse	16	18	7	13		
	Equal	4	6	2	5		
Mean	Better	16	12	26**	18*	15	
	Worse	17	19	9	8	16	
	Equal	2	4	0	9	4	
Minimax	Better	16	11	27**	11	11	11
	Worse	16	18	8	22*	21†	22*
	Equal	3	6	0	2	3	2

Note: See Table 4.1. †$p < 0.1$ *$p < 0.05$, **$p < 0.01$: one-sided sign test.

Hence, considering both tables, results indicate that victories of procedural models are likely to be close, while mispredictions are likely to be by large margins. When accurate, the predictions of procedural models win contests because they are point precise since they are based on the existing distributions of positions. Bargaining models' predictions instead are derived from maximization algorithms and point accuracy is less likely (see also Achen 2006a: 292–93).

4.4 Determinants of Bargaining Success

Given the accuracy of the compromise model, high-voting-power actors with centrally located preferences should be more successful in these negotiations, especially if they attach high salience to the issues at stake. But the equally good performance of some procedural models invites caution. Preference centrality should still matter a great deal, but how voting rules shape the set of adoptable proposals does not suggest a direct relation between voting power and success. Procedural models also highlight the conditional influence of supranational institutions – parliamentary positions should make a difference under OLP – whilst they give less emphasis to salience (with few exceptions, e.g. König and Proksch 2006). Proximity to the issue-specific status quo may be less relevant in our circumstances.

In Table 4.3, we report the results from regressing *Bargaining success*, the opposite of the absolute difference between a governmental position on a given divisive issue and the negotiation outcome, on the covariates identified in the models earlier and on other commonly employed determinants (Aksoy 2012; Arregui 2016; Arregui and Thomson 2009; Bailer 2004; Cross 2013; Lundgren et al. 2019; Thomson 2011: 229–51). For any government, success, therefore, takes the value of zero if the outcome is located at the government's ideal point and negative values as it moves away from it. Descriptive statistics and further measurement information are available in the online appendix (Table A4.8).

Proximity to the status quo does not seem to provide a significant advantage, while centrality does. Governments with positions that are located 20 points (a standard deviation) closer to the mean position in the 0–100 scale attain outcomes that are on average 10 points closer to their position. Results instead do not corroborate the emphasis some bargaining models assign to salience and voting power, nor the importance given to the Commission by procedural models.[10] On the other hand, for measures that are adopted under the OLP, governments with positions that are located 41 points (a standard deviation) closer to the parliamentary position reach outcomes that are 27 points closer to their positions.

These results are acceptably in line with the existing literature. The importance of preference centrality and the irrelevance of voting power are the most robust results, while the effects of salience and the status quo are inconsistent across studies (e.g. Arregui and Thomson 2009; Bailer 2004; Cross 2013; Thomson 2011: 229–51;

[10] Results hold if the Commission's position is interacted with specific procedures and voting rules.

Table 4.3 ***Determinants of member states' bargaining success***

	Coefficient
Supranational factors	
Distance to the reference point	-0.130
	(0.090)
Distance to Commission position	-0.095
	(0.094)
Distance to Council President position	-0.055
	(0.093)
Distance to Parliament position	-0.008
	(0.193)
Ordinary legislative procedure (OLP)	18.21
	(11.25)
OLP × Distance to Parliament position	-0.651*
	(0.205)
Extremeness of position	-0.491*
	(0.144)
Voting power	-0.406
	(0.494)
Issue salience	0.216
	(0.339)
Economic and other factors	
Population	0.071
	(0.059)
GDP per capita	-0.005
	(0.024)
Constant	-2.257
	(11.31)
Var(Constant)	335.48
	(109.225)
Var(Issue)	146.920
	(37.171)
Observations	759
Number of issues	35
Log-pseudolikelihood	-3038.80

Note: Two-level linear regression with random intercepts by issue. Random intercepts by act are not included because they are not significant. Robust standard errors are in parentheses. $*p < 0.01$.

Arregui 2016). The clearest difference is perhaps the irrelevance of the Commission's position, despite good evidence to the contrary. Proximity to this institution's position is also the covariate Lundgren et al. (2019) chose to focus on in their study on bargaining success in the most recent economic governance reform. However, in the OLP, the effect of proximity to the Parliament's position – these scholars report in their supplemental material – is not only significant, but its size is actually larger than the size of the effect of proximity to the Commission's position. The two covariates are included in separate regressions because the positions of these institutions are co-located in 7 out of 10 of their issues (Lundgren et al. 2019: 85, supplemental material: 10). By including both covariates, we instead find the Parliament to matter more. As Table A4.3 suggests, its influence is unlikely to be inflated by proximity to powerful actors, while that of the Commission may be diluted because of its centrist positions (probably reflecting anticipatory behaviour, see Kreppel and Oztas 2017). Indeed, parliamentary amendments to the Commission's proposals of these measures are four times more likely to be adopted or partially adopted if an act is negotiated under OLP rather than under other procedures. And Levenshtein's (1966) minimum edit distance between the texts passed by the Parliament and the final acts divided by the length of an act (a measure of text dissimilarity) is on average 25 per cent lower. Although the informal trilogues that took place during the negotiations of the six-pack and two-pack measures may make it harder to identify the parliamentary position, their mere occurrence is an indication of parliamentary clout.

These results are not in contrast with Bressanelli and Chelotti (2018). These scholars argue that the Parliament has had a limited impact on the recent reform, but they do not compare parliamentary performance across time and procedures. The influence of the assembly may have been more symbolic than substantive; yet, its position mattered *more* under OLP, as it is indeed mostly corroborated in the broader literature (Arregui 2016; Arregui and Thomson 2009; Bailer 2004; Cross 2013; Thomson 2011: 229–51).

The relevance of preferences suggests that we should not expect any *specific* member state or institution to systematically outperform others. Figure A4.1 in the online appendix displays the mean bargaining success of member states, groups of states, and institutions, while Table A4.9 reports the significance of *t*-tests on the difference between these means. In the large majority of cases, results indicate no significant differences.[11] Keeping this in mind, Ireland, Austria, and Malta appear to do relatively well, while Germany, Spain, the Commission, and larger member states tend to underperform. Lundgren et al. (2019) report a similar rank order for Ireland, Malta, and Germany and this group of countries, but they too fail to identify clear winners and losers. No significant differences are found in the broader literature as well (Arregui and Thomson 2009; Bailer 2004; Thomson 2011: 229–51), although some small states may outperform larger ones in some circumstances (Arregui 2016; Cross 2013; Golub 2012).

The nature of the outcomes is a further indication of the explanatory power of both models. In 12 issues, outcomes are compromises (i.e. middle positions) among at least two opposing groups of governments, and in three more instances, they are interinstitutional compromises.[12] Two linchpins of EU economic governance appear to be direct applications of the mean bargaining model: The 3 per cent deficit-to-GDP reference value was presumably the average ratio of public investment to GDP for the 1974–1991 period, and the 60 per cent debt-to-GDP figure was the average ratio of government debt to GDP for 1991 (Buiter et al. 1993: 62–63).[13]

Evidence of trading gains across issues instead is sparser. If the mere existence of these rules plausibly accommodates the demands of Germany and other euro area governments, these countries had probably to give concessions on procedures and criteria for determining compliance, as Figures A4.2 and A4.3 indicate and the issue in Figure 4.2 illustrates. For Lundgren et al. (2019 supplemental material: 15), governments that avoided the suspension of Council voting rights as a penalty for noncompliance had to concede to the use of reverse qualified majority for blocking sanctions. We could similarly argue that the unsuccessful extension of this rule to more provisions of the SGP and macroeconomic imbalance procedure, as proposed by the Benelux governments and the Parliament, was counterbalanced by

[11] Figure A4.2 and Table A4.10 employ salience-weighted success with similar results.

[12] See Table A4.2 in the online appendix.

[13] For instance, if we use the data from Franzese (2002), the average gross debt of the twelve members of the European Economic Community in 1991 was around 62.8 per cent of GDP.

its application in the two related enforcement regulations. These are however unconvincing linkages because losing governments did not gain anything, they just lost less. Minimizing losses is not quite the same as trading gains for losses across issues.

4.5 Robustness to Positional Uncertainty

How robust are these results to measurement errors? We have employed Neumayer and Plümper's (2017: 127–28) re-categorization test to evaluate the consequences of the miscategorization of positions and a Gaussian noise test to assess the robustness to increasing perturbation of positions. Sections 4.5 and 4.6 of the online appendix explain these procedures in detail.

The relative performance is unaltered within the two groups of models, but error estimates of procedural models are more uncertain (except for NBS) and more sensitive to both reclassification and perturbation. The mean absolute errors of the original data differ from the (mean of the) same metric of the re-categorized samples by 5.5 points on average for procedural models, compared to 1.1 points for bargaining ones.[14]

Accuracy worsens almost across the board as models are increasingly perturbed, but procedural ones do particularly badly. Figure 4.3 maps the overall mean absolute errors as models are perturbed by increasingly dispersed Gaussian noise. As expected, performance ranking replicates Table 4.1 at low levels of disturbance. Errors then increase almost across the board as the noise is drawn from more dispersed distributions, but procedural models do particularly badly. From the second-best, PROC ¬ RP becomes the third-worst performing model.

Greater sensitivity to categorization errors and perturbation does not imply lower accuracy but may explain why procedural models are found to be comparatively less accurate. Indeed, if we set the outcomes equal to the respective predictions of the procedural model (¬ RP) and compromise model as if they were representing the true data-generating process, the re-categorization test would produce a mean absolute error of 3.3 (as central tendency) for the compromise model and 10.3 for the procedural one. Scholars would incorrectly infer that the latter is less accurate while it is only more sensitive to errors.

[14] Compare Table 4.1 with Figure A4.3 in the online appendix.

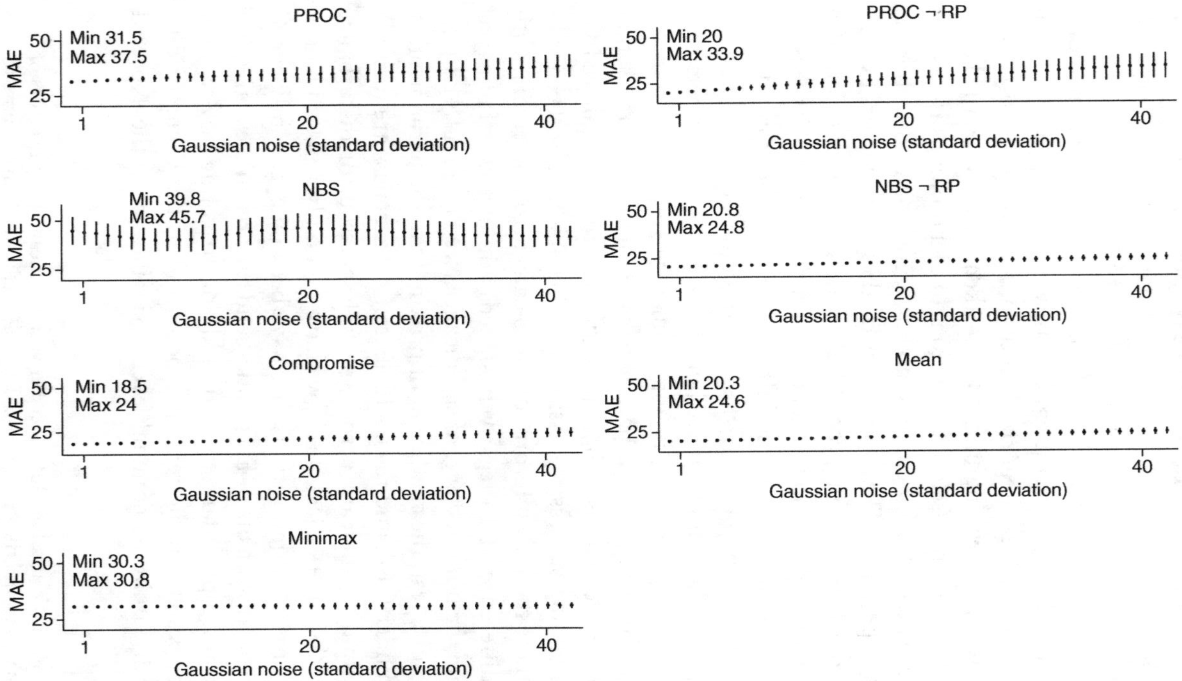

Figure 4.3 Overall mean absolute errors per issue, across levels of Gaussian noise
Note: The vertical lines represent the 95 per cent confidence intervals. MAE = mean absolute error
Source: Franchino and Mariotto (2022). Reprinted with permission.

Such sensitivity, already underscored by some scholars (Junge and König 2007; Slapin 2014), results from two interacting effects. First, the predictions of procedural models heavily depend on the positions of the actors in the minimal winning coalition. If these are modified, predictions may change substantially and produce larger errors. For instance, error estimates decrease if Parliament's and Commission's positions, which can nevertheless be easily established from official documents, are not re-categorized. Second, for the re-categorization test, the fewer the meaningful positions taken on an issue, the larger the shift of a randomly selected position. In dichotomous issues, for instance, re-categorization implies moving a position to the opposite end of the spectrum. The interaction of these two factors is particularly consequential for procedural models. If the position of a minimum winning coalition member over a dichotomous issue is re-categorized, predictions could shift from one to the opposite end of the spectrum. In this test, the re-categorization probability of positions on dichotomous or trichotomous issues of members of a minimum winning coalition is approximately 30 per cent. On the other hand, 90 per cent of the parameters in Equations (1) to (4) that underlain the predictions of bargaining models remain unaltered.[15]

The bargaining success regression of Table 4.3 has also been subjected to these tests. Results are robust to categorization errors, with the only difference of a (negatively signed) voting power falling, as well, within the nominal level of significance (see Figure A4.4). In the Gaussian noise test, the coefficient of proximity to the parliamentary position, under OLP, and the coefficient of extremeness are the only ones remaining significant across the full spectrum of disturbance (see Figure A4.5). As a last check, we have randomly replaced half of our observations with positions that have been independently coded by two doctoral students of EU politics, and then rerun the regression across the resampled datasets.[16] In addition to voting power, now also the proximity to the reference point and to the Commission's position fall within the nominal level of significance in the expected

[15] Note also that the absolute difference between the mean absolute errors of the original data and the re-categorized samples reduces relatively more for procedural than bargaining models if we were to shift the randomly selected positions to more proximate fictitious locations.

[16] See Section 4.6 of the online appendix for details.

direction. Nevertheless, the impact of extremeness and proximity to the Parliament remains significant and much larger (see Figure A4.6).

4.6 Conclusion

Three are the main takeaway points from this chapter. First, negotiations over EU economic governance have followed a well-trodden path. Compromise is the most robust *modus operandi*, based on country-based raw influence and exemplified by the accuracy of bargaining models and the significance of preference centrality for bargaining success. No single member state has outperformed others in these negotiations, and these results are in line with Lundgren et al. (2019) and the broader literature.

Second, the cost of failure casts a long shadow on bargaining outcomes. Correctly accounting for it is key to the accuracy of predictions, especially for the commonly underperforming procedural models. In these reforms, models that consider such costs to be uniformly high are more accurate than those that rely on the mere legal status quo ante of the issues under negotiations. And the latter is irrelevant also for bargaining success. This result differs from that reported by Finke and Bailer (2019: 126–29). Because of the lower level of aggregation of positions, our provision-specific status quos may underestimate the true cost of disagreement. If legislators have decided on most issues of a given proposal, no-agreement outcomes may not capture the full consequences of negotiation failure. We suspect that our level of analysis is closer to that used in broader studies, which indeed report similar results to ours (Achen 2006a: 276; Thomson 2011: 180). Yet, this does not mean that the reference point would begin to matter with more aggregation because, as will be shown in Chapter 5, these negotiations were indeed characterized by high disagreement costs. Unfortunately, Finke and Bailer's (2019) results are not replicated by Lundgren et al. (2019). Also, since these negotiations are embedded within a repeatedly interactive political system, future benefits of cooperation tend to weigh in against decisions to block proposals.

Third, procedures matter, *conditionally*. One such condition is, needless to say, procedural: Proximity to the parliamentary position increases success, *under* the OLP. Unlike both Finke and Bailer (2019: 126–29) and Lundgren et al. (2019), we find proximity to the Parliament's position to matter more than proximity to the Commission's position. But this is also what appears to emerge from the supplemental material of Lundgren et al. (2019). A second condition is, less obviously, methodological. The robustness analysis indicates that taking procedural features seriously improves our precision in estimating outcomes *if* we are confident about actors' preferences. In this circumstance, the point predictive accuracy of procedural models is notable. Where no such certainty exists, predictions from bargaining models are a safer bet.

We have now analyzed the *sources* of the controversies that have emerged during the reforms of the EU economic governance, and we have established the *modus operandi* to settle these disputes. We move now on to Chapter 5 and investigate *how* policymakers address the challenges of *designing* the policy, that is, the actual outputs of these processes. This will allow us to understand the specific bargaining *dynamics* of these reforms, as well as their *direction* and *timing*.

5 *Governance Design under Uncertainty, Threats, and Politicization*

We need rules for a common finance policy that will be observed by member countries and, if need be, enforced [...] That's why we need a treaty change, so that we are no longer reliant on promises.

Wolfgang Schäuble, German Finance Minister (2009–2017)

Prediction is very difficult, especially about the future.

Uncertain author

Legislators often repeat a quotation (mis)attributed to the German Chancellor Otto von Bismarck that 'If you like laws and sausages, you should never watch either one being made' to point out how the chaotic and sometimes unpalatable process of adopting laws can produce good outcomes. Sausage makers would object to this characterization and a visit to a modern sausage factory would probably convince any observer that they are right. Likewise, a large scholarly literature indicates that the process of EU lawmaking has far more structure than we give credit to. When legislators adopt a policy, they take three key design decisions. First, they establish common rules. Second, they determine the modality and extent to which they are involved in policymaking. Third, they determine the prerogatives and constraints of the authorities in charge of implementation. In the context of the European Union, the *design* of a policy can accordingly be conceived as a set of provisions with specific and, occasionally, multiple properties. *Tightening* provisions impose requirements and obligations on national authorities, whereas *loosening* ones relax such demands or offer them leeway. For instance, the deficit and debt reference values in the treaty protocol on excessive deficit procedure (EDP) tightened control over national fiscal policies, while the adoption in 2005 of country-specific (rather than common) medium-term budgetary objectives (MTOs), which can diverge from a balanced position, loosened control. In Chapter 3, we saw that these provisions have been the object of several controversies during the negotiations of these reforms. *Pooling* provisions are those where the Council takes decisions by voting procedures other than unanimity and *delegating* ones are those where policy prerogatives are conferred upon the European Commission. Both pooling and delegation can be subject to *constraints*. For instance, the decision to establish the existence of an excessive deficit is pooled within the Council, but until 2005, exceptional circumstances could be granted only in case of an annual fall of real GDP of at least 2 per cent. Since 2005, the Commission can amend poor-quality data on public finances, subject to prompt communication to the relevant member state and the Economic and Financial Committee. Again, in Chapter 3, we have seen how the involvement of these two institutions in policy enforcement has been highly controversial.

In this chapter, we explain how the overall design of the EU economic governance came to be.[1] In so doing, we compare and contrast expectations about the determinants of policy design derived from traditional theories of European integration, that is, liberal intergovernmentalism and neofunctionalism, with those arising from a new wave of theorizing, which originates from postfunctionalism and falls under the general rubric of new intergovernmentalism. These new theories argue that politicization has consequences for policy design that are unaccounted for by traditional approaches. We conceptualize *politicization* as an expansion of the scope of conflict within national political systems, which translates into bottom-up pressures on EU-level actors, that is, a national pressure factor in the context of the typology introduced in Chapter 1. To test the new expectations, we leverage the documented observation that, unlike earlier reforms that attracted the interest of only the specialized press, the most recent one was characterized by significantly broader and more polarized involvement of public actors (Kriesi and Grande 2016: 253) – two key dimensions of politicization –, making such reform a most-likely case for politicization to shape policy design.

Studies of economic governance design take mainly one theoretical perspective, such as liberal intergovernmentalism (Biermann

[1] The chapter extends the work published in Franchino and Mariotto (2020).

et al. 2019; Schimmelfennig 2015), neofunctionalism and its variants (Niemann and Ioannou 2015; Pan, Hosli, and Lantmeeters 2023; Verdun 2015), or postfunctionalist-based approaches (e.g. Börzel and Risse 2018; Fabbrini 2016; Genschel and Jachtenfuchs 2018; Puetter 2012). We follow Heipertz and Verdun (2005; 2010) and Schimmelfennig (2014) and consider all the most relevant theories of policy design (see also Vilpišauskas 2013). Additionally, most works concentrate solely on the most recent reform. We instead analyze economic governance since its inception, building on the extant analyses of the 1997 and 2005 reforms (Heipertz and Verdun 2005; 2010; Schure and Verdun 2008; Segers and van Esch 2007). But unlike these studies, we subject expectations to empirical corroboration through a systematic analysis of the bargaining dynamics and the provision-specific patterns of governance design adopted between 1993 and 2013. This allows us to document clearly the direction of the changes in policy design as well as to understand the timing of these reforms.

We will show that the Council-centred enforcement of economic governance – a dominant feature, despite noncompliance, until the sovereign debt crisis – does not sit comfortably with traditional theories, but it can be explained by policy salience and economic uncertainties. On the other hand, the emphasis that traditional approaches assign to supranational pressures such as noncompliance, problems of credible commitment, threats of exclusion and veto, issue linkages, path dependencies, and supranational decision-making allows to adequately account for the overall direction of reforms towards more tightening and delegation, notwithstanding the pooled enforcement in recent ancillary measures. Instead, postfunctionalist theories overall fall short in highly politicized contexts, exactly where they should do most of the explaining.

We begin our investigation by introducing the theoretical predictions.

5.1 Expectations and Driving Mechanisms of Policy Design

We limit our attention to integration theories, or variants therein, that offer clear expectations about policy design. We leave aside the full richness of these approaches and concentrate only on the predictions concerning tightening, loosening, pooling, and delegation. These are summarized in Table 5.1.

Table 5.1 *Expectations and driving mechanisms of policy design*

Integration theory	Expectations	Driving mechanisms
Liberal intergovernmentalism	H5.1: Pooling for additional measures, delegation for enforcement and implementation. H5.2: Noncompliance leads to more delegation and plausibly tightening	Veto threats, exclusion threats, and issue linkages shape outcomes
Neofunctionalism (institutionalist variant)	H5.3: Delegation also to benefit from centralized expertise	Exit costs, supranational institutions, and decision-making also shape outcomes
Postfunctionalism/New intergovernmentalism	H5.4: Less pooling and delegation, and plausibly loosening in salient policies and politicized contexts[†]	Governments object to pooling and delegation and try to loosen obligations

Note: [†]Loosening and *more* delegation for Hooghe and Marks (2009).

For liberal intergovernmentalism, pooling and delegation are driven by the need to bolster the *credibility of policy commitments*, when incomplete contracting and incentives to renege on agreements create problems of time consistency (Moravcsik 1998: 73–77). Pooling and delegation occur when future decisions are *uncertain*, joint gains are high, and distributional conflicts are moderate. Pooling entails less loss of governmental control than delegation. It is preferred when policies require additional measures because it undermines unilateral vetoes of secondary legislation. In addition to reducing legislative workload, delegation addresses concerns about domestic compliance and it is more likely in the case of enforcement since a supranational bureaucracy pursues this activity more credibly than a Council of elected ministers does (H5.1). A higher risk of noncompliance should therefore tilt policy design towards delegation (i.e. Commission empowerment) and plausibly tightening (H5.2).

Opposition is likely to be voiced by governments that expect to be either in a minority position or, as discussed in Chapter 3, noncompliant. The preferences of governments with superior bargaining power, resulting from asymmetric interdependence, eventually shape outcomes. Most influential are those that either (1) place a relatively higher value on the best alternative to an agreement or (2) can form viable alternative coalitions that are costly to the excluded countries. As we established in Chapter 4, the first situation can cast a long shadow on the bargaining dynamics and underlie credible *threats to veto*, the second situation instead lies behind credible *threats to exclude*. Last, *issue linkages* may also play a role, but within issue areas, if interests are asymmetrically distributed, benefits are concentrated and costs are diffused (Moravcsik 1998: 60–67).

Neofunctionalism encompasses more variegated contributions, but a common thread is an emphasis on *endogeneity*, as well as uncertainty, in policy design (e.g. Heipertz and Verdun 2010: 64–67; Schimmelfennig 2014: 326–27). Except for the need for centralized expertise that may justify delegation (H5.3), it suggests new mechanisms, rather than new logics, for policy design (Schimmelfennig 2014: 334). According to its institutionalist variant, past decisions have profound consequences for current bargaining because of endogenous interdependencies, spillovers, and path dependencies (Garrett and Tsebelis 1996; Pan, Hosli, and Lantmeeters 2023; Pierson 1996). Consider an obvious example: for euro area countries, opting for a flexible *national* exchange rate implies leaving the monetary union and re-establishing a national currency. The uncertainty and *exit costs* of this policy option are significantly higher compared to those that a member of the European monetary system would have faced. Then, such a decision would have implied only a shift from an adjustable to a flexible exchange agreement. This option is now effectively precluded. In Chapter 3, we have indeed shown that membership of the euro area shapes governmental attitudes about national discretion and Council involvement in enforcement.

One of the key insights of neofunctionalism is that a more supranational policy process may lead to different outcomes (i.e. a 'cultivated' spillover effect). The procedural models we have analyzed in Chapter 4 are the offshoots of this emphasis on supranational decision-making. Accordingly, the position of the agenda setter, institutional hurdles, such as lower voting thresholds, and inter-institutional conflicts may all shape the final design. For instance, demands for tightening and delegation are more likely to be met under qualified majority voting since recalcitrant governments, preferring ample national discretion and narrowly defined Commission's competences, can be overruled. In light of the findings reported in Chapter 4, this outcome may tilt further in this direction under the ordinary legislative procedure if the position of the European Parliament is closer to that of the supranational executive than to that of the Council (Franchino 2007: 64–65, 285–86).

There is however reason to believe that these traditional rationales may not be at play. According to Genschel and Jachtenfuchs (2018: 181–82), fiscal policy is a core state power where bargaining is zero-sum. Compliance falls predominantly on governmental rather than societal actors; it faces tighter capacity constraints and may require the building up of capacity at the EU level. Negotiations are therefore highly politicized. Moreover, the bargaining context has changed. In a study of six European countries, Kriesi and Grande (2016: 253) report that the latest economic governance reform has been 'the integration debate with the highest public visibility' in the mass media since the early 1970s. Its politicization, including the involvement and polarization of actors, was on par with the debate on the ratification of the Maastricht Treaty. In Chapter 3, we show that governments facing conflicting pressures appear to take clues from the support of their public for the EU on issues concerning the empowerment of the Commission.

In sum, economic governance is more politicized than other policies and its politicization has increased over time. Accordingly, Schimmelfenning (2014: 322) argues that the recent euro crisis contains the conditions for Hooghe and Marks's (2009) postfunctionalism to offer better guidance. For these scholars, in an age of politicization and public dissensus on European integration, outcomes may not reflect functional pressures any longer and identity-based contestation may make all the difference. If European issues are politicized on identity lines, we should see a 'downward pressure on the level and scope of integration' and a narrowing of the 'substantive ground of possible agreement' (Hooghe and Marks 2009: 21–22). For our purposes, this could be interpreted as *loosening, less pooling, and delegation*, but Hooghe and Marks (2009: 21, 22) are more ambivalent. They tentatively conclude that politicization may lead to both less integration (*loosening*) *and* more delegation – the latter is presumably a means to depoliticize an issue.

This indeterminacy is resolved in the recent wave of new intergovernmentalist theorizing that shares postfunctionalist premises such as the relevance assigned to the post-Maastricht rise in public dissensus and politicization (Bickerton, Hodson, and Puetter 2015: 709–11; Fabbrini and Puetter 2016: 486). According to this variant, the post-Maastricht period is marked by 'integration without supranationalism' (Bickerton, Hodson, and Puetter 2015: 703). Initiatives are characterized by *greater reliance on the European Council and the Council for policy execution and implementation* (Fabbrini and Puetter 2016: 481). Delegation of powers 'to traditional supranational institutions such as the Commission [is] increasingly discredited among member state governments' (Puetter 2016: 604), *de novo* institutions are preferred, and unanimous decision-making within intergovernmental institutions acquires greater prominence (Fabbrini 2016: 593; Fabbrini and Puetter 2016: 488). This reluctance to pool and delegate is particularly relevant in highly salient or core state powers such as fiscal policy. These scholars do not seem to associate 'integration' with tighter national obligations but rather with loose coordination measures that marginally encroach upon national policy autonomy. This is plausible in light of how politicization operates. Once an issue becomes politicized, public dissensus restricts governments' room to manoeuvre, making them less inclined to relinquish sovereignty and even temped to reining in lost control (Hooghe and

Marks 2009: 18–22; Puetter 2012: 168). Postfunctionalist scholars do not differentiate the impact of politicization by country or government, but it could be argued for instance that politicization may have led Germany to demand more delegation and tightening in the last reform and Greece to push for the opposite. But this proposition is indistinguishable from liberal intergovernmentalist predictions as it is based on a government's expectation of being compliant, thus making politicization epiphenomenal.

In conclusion, if the euro crisis has been a highly politicized identity conflict (Börzel and Risse 2018) or represents the 'apex of the [new] intergovernmental moment' (Fabbrini 2013: 1010), the functional pressures in policy design identified by liberal intergovernmentalism and neofunctionalism are disrupted and concerns about losing control are heightened. Therefore, *economic governance should rely less on pooling and delegation and* plausibly *more on loosening, especially in politicized contexts* (H5.4).

5.2 Measuring the Design of Economic Governance

The corpus of legal provisions that we consider here includes the chapter on economic policy and the EDP protocol of the Treaty on European Union, seventeen secondary laws on the application of the EDP, the Stability and Growth Pact (SGP), the macroeconomic imbalance procedure (MIB), and the harmonization and monitoring national budgetary procedures, and, last, the fiscal compact treaty.[2] Section 5.1 of the online appendix to this chapter lists the provisions and acts subject to our analysis.

We broadly follow the method of coding provisions developed in the American congressional literature and applied by Franchino (2007) to EU legislation. Each legal act, including treaty provisions and protocols, is subdivided into *major* provisions. Each major provision is coded if it imposes obligations on member states (*tightening*) or gives them leeway in implementing measures (*loosening*). Similarly, each major provision is coded if it pools policy authority within the Council (*pooling*), it delegates authority to the Commission (*delegation*), and it sets *constraints* upon these institutions. A provision can have multiple properties. For instance, it

[2] The MIB and the fiscal compact treaty will be discussed more concisely.

may delegate a policy prerogative, subject to constraints. We also determine whether pooled and delegated authority is related to an enforcement activity, such as establishing noncompliance or monitoring budgets. Provisions have been coded independently first, then disparities have been settled.[3] The inter-coder agreement is 89 per cent greater than would be expected by chance.

This procedure is reliable, easily replicable, and produces data that greatly facilitates comparison across measures, time, and even policies, but it is not devoid of drawbacks. It treats policy prerogatives equally. A provision that confers upon the Commission the power to determine noncompliance has the same weight as one that asks this institution to adopt data collection guidelines. Also, a small change to an existing constraint, such as the shortening of a time limit, has to be either disregarded or double-counted (we opted for the former). The phenomenon we are measuring – the *direction* of reform – should, therefore, be more cautiously interpreted as changes along an ordinal scale rather than an interval one. These shortcomings, however, are not serious enough to distort the broad patterns we observe. Where necessary, we will compensate for this coarseness by distinguishing among types of policy prerogatives. On the other hand, we took two coding decisions to make sure that some important changes were detected. First, we code as a constraint on the Council if this institution has to cooperate or co-decide with the Parliament, while we disregard simple parliamentary consultation. Second, delegation is the granting of substantive policy authority to shape outcomes (Franchino 2007: 84). It excludes the sole examination of documents and the proposal prerogatives of the Commission unless they are enhanced, that is, if less than a qualified majority in the Council is sufficient to adopt proposals. Here, the Commission has a significant chance of affecting outcomes (recall that in Chapter 4 we do not find the standard agenda-setting powers to boost the influence of the Commission, see also Kreppel and Oztas 2017).

Figure 5.1 displays the number of provisions in force after important reforms.[4] Major and tightening provisions have quintupled since the completion of the initial framework in 1997. Initially, no provisions loosened control or conferred some policy leeway to member

[3] Coding rules are listed in Section 5.2 of the online appendix.
[4] See Section 5.3 of the online appendix for more detailed breakdowns.

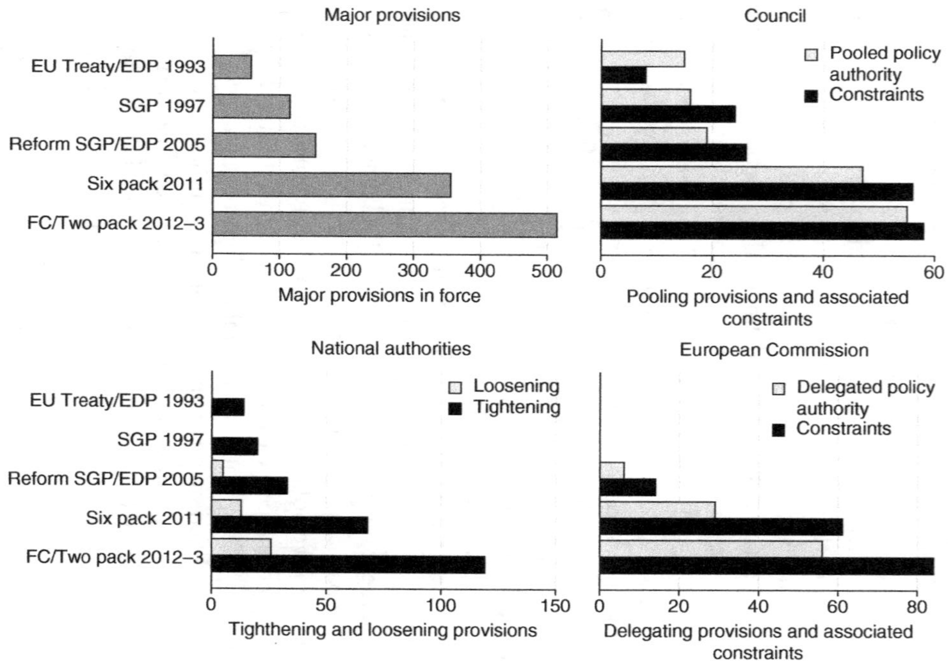

Figure 5.1 Major provisions and design provisions in force
Note: Cumulative figures. EDP: excessive deficit procedure, SGP: Stability and Growth Pact, FC: fiscal compact
Source: Franchino and Mariotto (2020). Reprinted with permission.

states, but since 2005 the number has moderately increased. Pooling provisions remained constant until 2005, and then they almost tripled. The associated constraints tripled both with the initial SGP and with the latest reforms. Instead, apart from standard proposal prerogatives, no provisions delegated powers to the Commission until the 2005 reform of the EDP. The total tally is now almost ten times larger and the associated constraints have sextupled since.

The following analysis of negotiations is also based on information on contested issues and the initial positions of institutional and governmental actors. Recall that the methodology for collecting these data, including a detailed account of the sources and strategies of identification and cross-validation, is described in Section 3.1 of the online appendix to Chapter 3. Aside from the fact that these initial positions are likely to be freer from strategic considerations, they are also particularly useful in this context because they permit evaluating the patterns of concessions in light of the final outcomes.

5.3 The Initial Design: Why So Much Pooling?

5.3.1 Council-centred Enforcement

Figure 5.2 displays the regime after major reforms in terms of shares of design provisions, while Figure 5.3 displays the share of pooling and delegating provisions that are related to an enforcement activity. Only pooling occurred by the time the initial framework was completed in 1997. Apart from proposal competences, no provisions delegated powers to the Commission or granted some leeway to member states. Council constraining provisions and tightening provisions were similarly employed.

The Maastricht Treaty (and the proximate EDP regulation) set some general demands on member states on coordination and reporting of economic policies and public finances, and more specific requirements, such as the well-known obligation to avoid excessive government spending, with the associated reference values of deficit and debt to GDP. We will not discuss this treaty's negotiations here, but the initial design is not fully aligned with liberal intergovernmentalism (H5.1). As expected, prerogatives were pooled where rules on financing, bailout, multilateral surveillance, and the EDP had to be laid down, but pooling occurred also with regard to the publicity

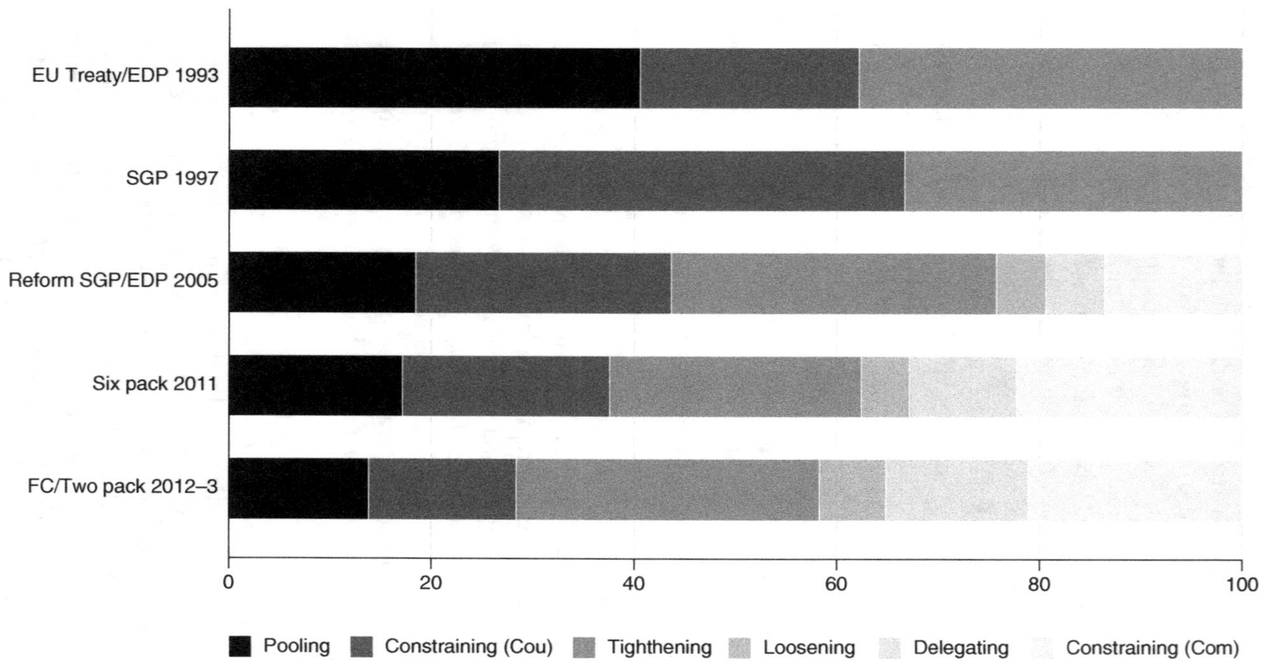

Figure 5.2 Proportion of design provisions in force

Note: Cumulative figures. EDP: excessive deficit procedure, SGP: Stability and Growth Pact, FC: fiscal compact, Cou: Council, Com: Commission

Source: Franchino and Mariotto (2020). Reprinted with permission.

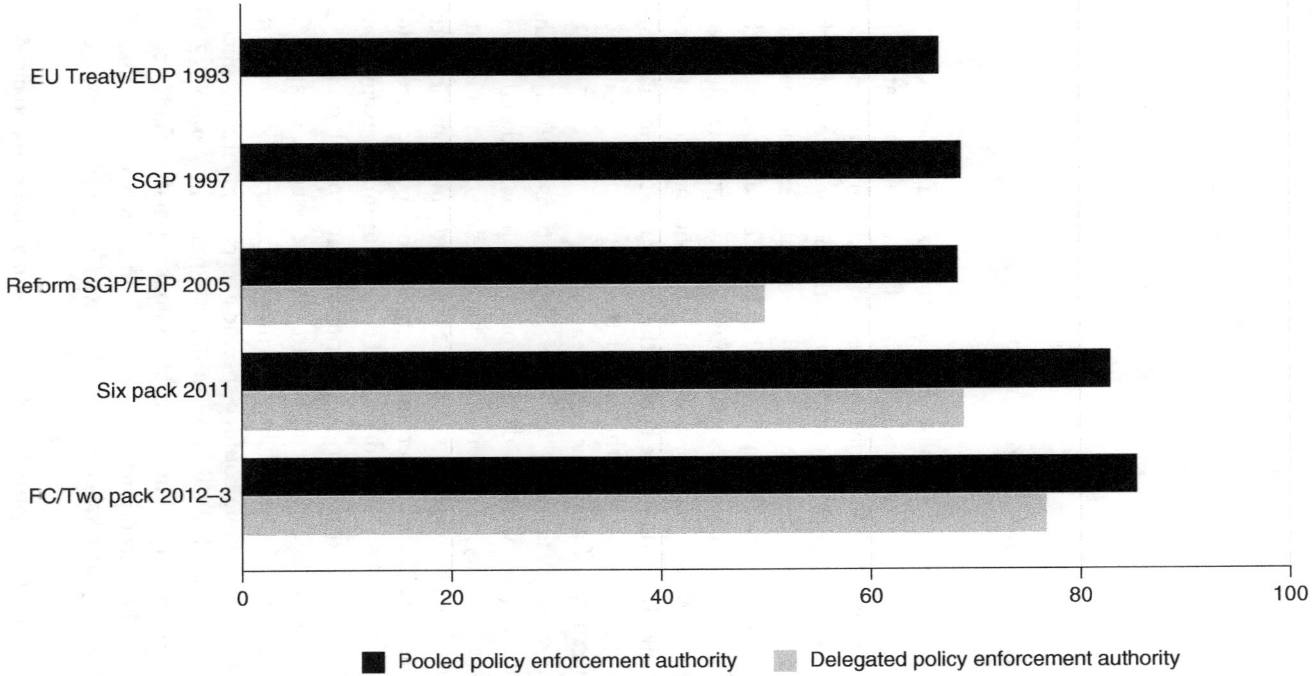

Figure 5.3 Proportion of pooling and delegating provisions related to enforcement
Note: Cumulative figures. EDP: excessive deficit procedure, SGP: Stability and Growth Pact, FC: fiscal compact
Source: Franchino and Mariotto (2020). Reprinted with permission.

of recommendations establishing inconsistency between national measures and broad economic guidelines and the determination and sanctioning of excessive deficits. Two-thirds of pooling provisions concerned enforcement (see Figure 5.3). The absence of delegation betrays a lack of concern about compliance, and it is a likely indication of the unique salience of the policy, as postfunctionalist scholars emphasize (H5.4).

5.3.2 Noncompliance, Threat of Exclusion, and Contested Issues

Noncompliance as well did not have all the consequences expected by liberal intergovernmentalism (H5.2). Figure 5.4 illustrates the periods under which governments have not been compliant with key provisions of the regime.[5] Consider only the deficit criteria for the time being. By 1996, the Council established that every member state had an excessive deficit, except for Ireland and Luxembourg. As the deadline for selecting countries that would have adopted the euro was approaching and as it became clear that those with a history of fiscal profligacy, like Italy, may have been in the first wave, the German government pressed for a strengthening of the regime under an implicit but credible threat of a smaller euro area.

Yet, delegation was barely an issue. Negotiations centred on the circumstances under which a deficit would not be considered excessive, the automaticity of the procedure, and the size of the sanctions. The first two issues were about the Council's room of manoeuvre. The German and Dutch governments argued for specific thresholds (Agence Europe 1996: 5) and proposed that automatic exemptions should apply only to countries experiencing an annual decline in real GDP of at least 2 per cent. As already discussed in Chapter 3, the Belgian, French, and Italian governments preferred keeping the Council free to determine country-specific exceptional circumstances. The 2 per cent threshold was eventually included in Article 2.2 of the SGP corrective arm, but the third comma stipulated that circumstances could be exceptional also for a contraction of less than 2 per cent, '*in light of further evidence*'. It was a modest amendment.

[5] We employ a looser benchmark for debt; for more information, see Section 5.4 of this chapter's online appendix; Chapters 7 and 8 cover compliance.

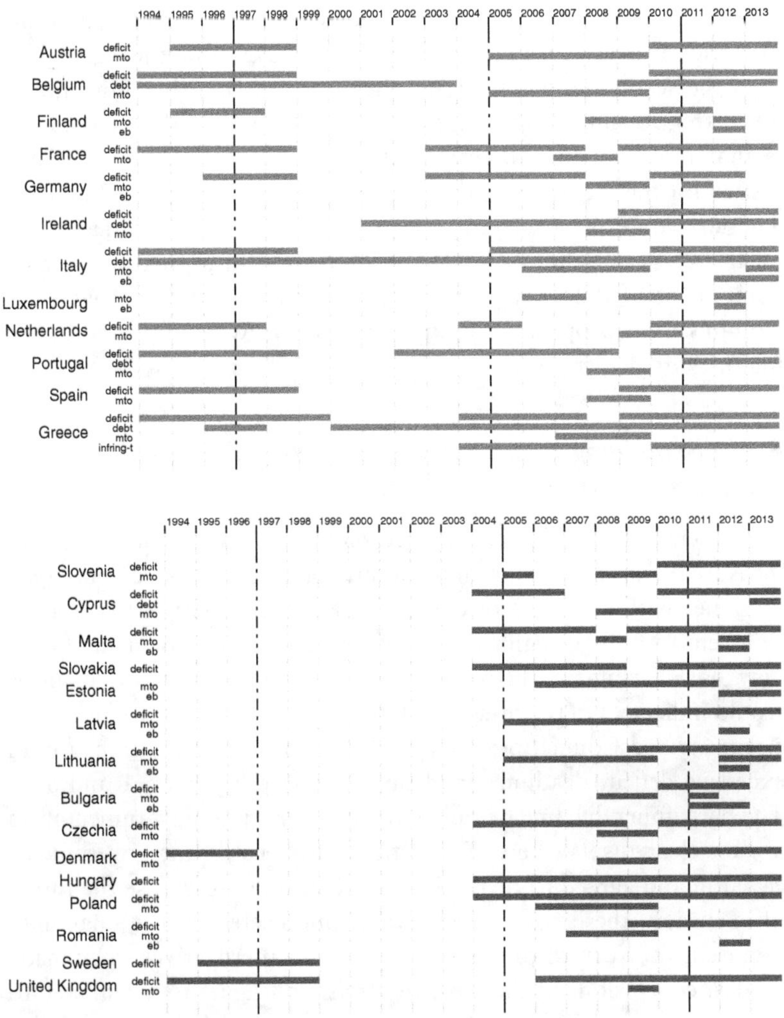

Figure 5.4 Periods of noncompliance with fiscal provisions
Note: Excessive deficit, debt greater than GDP, medium-term objective (mto), expenditure benchmark (eb), infringements. Darker bars for years with euro. Vertical lines separate reforms. See the online appendix for more details.
Source: Franchino and Mariotto (2020). Reprinted with permission.

A resolution of the Amsterdam European Council summit of June 1997 further narrowed the Council's faculty to exempt noncompliant countries in cases when the reduction was more than 0.75 per cent, the so-called 'box model'. In sum, the most recalcitrant countries accepted to limit the Council's powers only in case of mild recessions, and this exception was not even included as a legal provision in the SGP.

In the second contested issue, the German, Danish, Finnish, and Swedish governments proposed to insert the words 'the expectation is that the Council will respect the Commission's decision'. They settled for the inclusion of the words 'as a rule' in Articles 2 and 11. The last contested topic concerned the deposit to be made in case of an excessive deficit. The German government argued for a fixed component of 0.25 per cent of GDP, but it had to settle with the Commission's proposal of 0.2 per cent, which was supported by the majority of governments.

5.3.3 Explaining Pooling in the SGP: Veto Power, Ideational Pressures, and Informational Pressures

Some demands for tightening were met in the SGP. The preventive measure required states to submit annual stability or convergence programmes with an MTO of close to balance or in surplus. The need to assemble only a qualified majority in the Council for its adoption may have facilitated this outcome, as neofunctionalist mechanisms would indicate. On the other hand, the corrective regulation primarily circumscribed Council prerogatives by establishing conditions for an excessive deficit, deadlines, and sanctions (see Figures 5.1 and 5.2). The bargaining dynamics emphasized by liberal intergovernmentalism are on clear display here. While the most recalcitrant governments caved in and agreed to revise the regime in order to defuse the threat of exclusion, these governments were empowered by the unanimity requirement. Keen to preserve the Council's prerogatives, they made modest concessions to the most reformist colleagues to signal a commitment to fiscal stability, but they stalled any delegation of policy competences. However, the SGP remained overall a modest reform in terms of policy design, with pooling still dominant in enforcement despite noncompliance. Two-thirds of pooled prerogatives were related to this activity (see Figure 5.3).

From a postfunctionalist perspective (H5.4), limited tightening and no delegation are the results of the unique salience of the policy. But one ingredient is missing. There is hardly any evidence that the conflicts characterizing these negotiations turned into mass public debates, despite raising politicization in the 1990s (Hutter, Grande, and Kriesi 2016). In our view, other important factors militating against delegation were the *uncertainties* surrounding these rules. As reiterated a few times already, this policy's primary objectives are to prevent moral hazard in public spending in a monetary union and to limit negative externalities associated with the possible combination of expansionary fiscal policies and a contractionary monetary policy (the former resulting from governments' attempts to use fiscal policy to boost output and employment in the short term at the expense of inflation, the latter from an inflation-averse common central bank). These rules should ensure sustainable public debts, allowing enough flexibility for countercyclical policies (e.g. Claeys, Darvas, and Leandro 2016).

At the time of drafting the SGP however, these externalities were hypothetical consequences derived from the application of macroeconomic models to a monetary union. They represented ideational pressures. Some scholars downplayed the magnitude and questioned the direction of externalities. Buiter et al. (1993) explicitly argued for the reference values to be disregarded. They were excessively tight and inflexible, leading to a contractionary bias and impeding the operation of automatic stabilizers. No bailout rules were deemed sufficient to deal with the risk of default and with financial contagion: governments would avoid excessive spending anyway *if* the central bank is credibly inflation-averse and *if* financial markets demand higher risk premia from profligate governments.[6] Fiscal and monetized bailouts of profligate governments would be prevented (see also Buiter, 2006; Eichengreen and Wyplosz, 1998, but cf. Bean's and Gerlach's comments on this work, doubting the small size of the externalities). However, apart from market vagaries, the commitments to no bailout and to stable prices were obviously untested,[7]

[6] And, these scholars added, even if markets turn out to be poor at assessing sovereign risk, a default is primarily a distributional issue that does not need supranational intervention or rules monitoring public deficits on a yearly basis.

[7] After analyzing the bank's appointment and voting procedures, Alesina and Grilli (1994) concluded that its board might not display a conservative bias, despite its mandate and formal independence. In cases of uncertainty about a central bank's commitment to price stability, Chari and Kehoe (2007) show how uncontrolled fiscal authorities may not internalize the union-wide costs of increased inflation, leading to higher debt and inflation. They state that 'the larger the debt the monetary authority inherits, the higher it wants to set the inflation rate and, without some mechanism to prevent that, the higher it sets

while the prospects of countries with histories of fiscal improvidence joining the monetary union were becoming concrete.

Another concern was that these reference values could induce pernicious pro-cyclical policies since governments may have to cut spending or raise taxes during a recession (thus, undermining the credibility of financial sanctions), while they could increase spending or cut taxes during a recovery (Buiter et al. 1993). Surely, numerical values are transparent and easier to monitor and enforce, but, efficacy aside, several different combinations of debt and deficit values are fiscally sustainable, so any given set of parameters is necessarily arbitrary and it risks being excessively constraining. Each set of values has non-trivial distributive consequences because it implies country-specific adjustments between current and future public expenditures, and between public and private debt (Pasinetti 1998).

To illustrate the informational pressures policymakers face, Figure 5.5 plots the forecasting error and bias of the government balance to GDP ratio.[8] The error is the mean absolute deviation, that is, the sum of the absolute differences between the actual ratio in year t and the forecast for year t in the spring of year t–1, divided by the number of member states in year t. The spring of year t–1 is usually when government departments begin drafting the budget for year t and the country-specific recommendations are issued.[9]

Despite the improvement in forecasting and the implementation of a European system of accounts, the mean absolute deviation hovered well above 1 per cent of GDP between 1993 and 1996. This is a substantial degree of uncertainty, considering that the deficit reference value is 3 per cent. The dashed line in Figure 5.5 plots the forecasting

the inflation rate. Thus, without monetary policy commitment, when one of the fiscal authorities issues more debt, the others are made worse off' (Chari and Kehoe 2007: 2400).

8 We employ the forecasts of the European Commission (European Economy) and, for the years 1993 and 1994, the OECD (Economic Outlook). These institutions have fewer incentives to bias the forecasts even though they still depend on data from official government agencies. Over the years, reforms have increased the independence in these agencies with a view of limiting political interference (Frankel and Schreger 2013; Jonung et al. 2006).

9 If we employ the forecast for year t in the autumn of year t – 1, the mean absolute deviation is only 0.22 percentage points lower and the standard deviation of the bias is only 0.27 percentage points lower. We exclude interest payments from the actual deficit ratio, otherwise forecasts would be even more inaccurate.

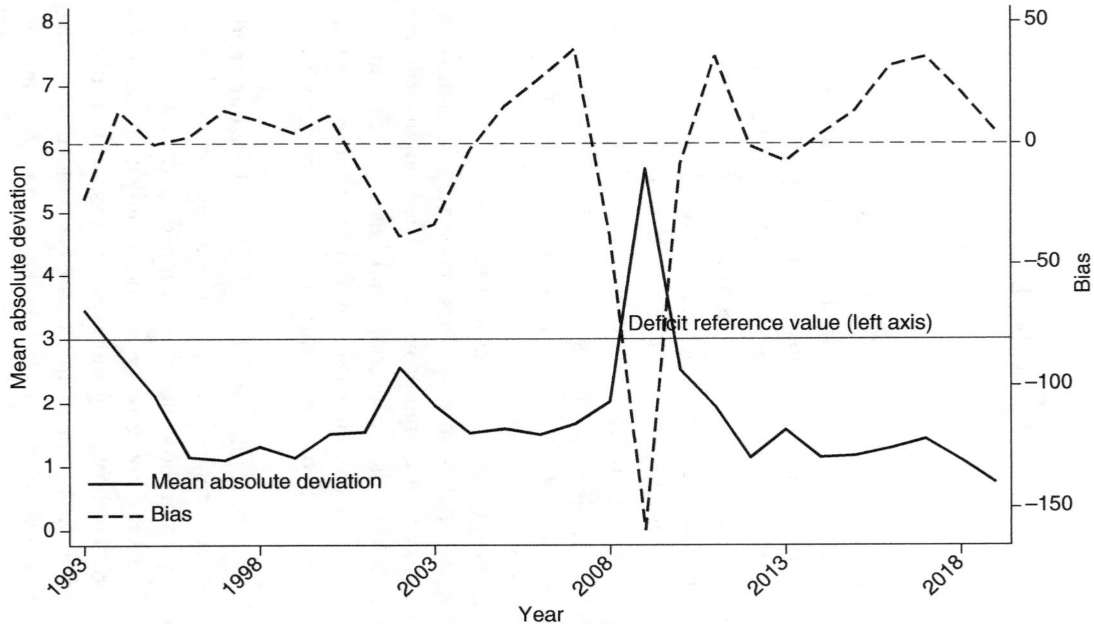

Figure 5.5 Forecasting error and bias of government balance, as a percentage of GDP

Note: The mean absolute deviation is the absolute difference between the actual government balance–GDP ratio in year t and the forecast for year t in the spring of year t–1, divided by the number of member states in year t. Bias is the sum of the difference between the actual ratio in year t and the forecast for the year t in the spring of the year t–1.

bias, which is the sum of the differences between the actual ratio in year *t* and the forecast for year *t* in the spring of year *t*–1. The initial negative values illustrate the significant underestimation of the budget deficit ratios following the early 1990s recession.

5.4 The 2005 Reform: Why Loosening Despite Noncompliance?

5.4.1 Loosening and Modest Delegation

This reform introduces two small but significant changes. First, four provisions (6 per cent of design provisions in force) grant member states greater flexibility. Most were inserted in the preventive SGP regulation. Article 2a replaces a common MTO (recall, the structural budget objective) with a *revisable country-specific* one, which *may* now diverge by no more than 1 per cent of GDP from a balance or surplus position. On the other hand, the EDP regulation adds new obligations regarding the provision of statistical data, professionalism of statistics officials, and assistance to the Commission's inspections. Hence, about a third of the policy design still consists of tightening provisions.

The second significant change concerns six provisions in the EDP regulation conferring policy prerogatives upon the Commission (amounting to 6 per cent of design provisions). The Commission sets statistical formats, adopts data collection guidelines, and determines the implementation of accounting rules. Importantly, the supranational executive can object to the quality of the reported data and amend them.

The role of the Council is unaltered, on balance. On the one hand, the definition of severe economic downturn – a key contested issue in 1997 – is relaxed. The box model is dropped, and now even a protracted period of very low *growth* can be a mitigating factor to avoid the procedure. Decisions can be revised in case of unexpected adverse events and the assessment time frame is extended.[10] On the other hand, the preventive regulation clarifies the criteria for examining

[10] Except perhaps for pension reforms, it is unclear whether the criteria for evaluating budgets listed in the corrective regulation allow for greater discretion.

structural budgets in light of the MTOs; while the corrective regulation specifies that the Council must request minimum annual improvements of the structural budget of 0.5 per cent of GDP from noncomplying states. Deadline extensions cannot exceed one year.

5.4.2 Consequences of EDP Regulation Noncompliance: Tightening and Delegation

As Figure 5.4 illustrates, after a respite of a few years, noncompliance reappeared. In 2004, Eurostat revised upwards the Greek deficit by between 2 and 3 percentage points of GDP for the years 2000 to 2003 and the 2003 debt–GDP ratio by more than 7 percentage points. In December 2004, the Commission initiated an infringement procedure against Greece for failing to comply with the EDP regulation. The new design corroborates liberal intergovernmentalism (H5.2). National obligations were tightened and the Commission's competences expanded. Half of the delegating provisions relate to enforcement, and the remaining half to implementation (see Figure 5.3). Qualified majority voting may have helped address these demands, following, therefore, a neofunctionalist logic. The most contentious issue indeed concerned the Commission's prerogatives (governmental positions have been discussed in Chapter 3). The opposition by the four largest countries to regular methodological inspections and a first in-depth monitoring visit, as proposed by the Luxembourgish presidency, led to adopting Article 8d, which narrowly defines the objectives of these visits and specifies that they should take place only in case of serious problems.

This reform runs counter to postfunctionalist expectations (H5.4), but some of their scope conditions were absent. The conflict remained primarily circumscribed to the elite level in these negotiations. Recent works actually indicate that debates on European issues in the early 2000s were less politicized than in the previous decade (Hutter, Grande, and Kriesi 2016: 281).

5.4.3 Consequences of SGP Noncompliance: Loosening, Reversion Point, and Economic Uncertainty

Governments also failed to comply with the fiscal rules. Between 2000 and 2004, four euro area countries, including France and Germany, had an excessive deficit, while high indebtedness persisted in some other countries. In 2004, for the first time, the Council issued Greece a notice for failing to act – the last step before imposing sanctions (Heipertz and Verdun 2010: 163). Yet, in shifting the focus from correction to prevention, the SGP loosened some national obligations and relaxed some Council constraints, while the Commission obtained no new substantive powers. Moreover, the corrective regulation pools two additional enforcement-related prerogatives concerning the revision of decisions.

This outcome is not easy to reconcile with postfunctionalism (H5.4), given limited politicization, nor with liberal intergovernmentalism (H5.3), given noncompliance. A qualified majority might have been easier to assemble in the preventive arm. Indeed, the 1 per cent floor to the divergence from the MTO was inserted by the Council. But this reform of the corrective arm, which requires unanimity, is unexpected at first sight. By far the most controversial issue concerned the numerousness and specificity of mitigating factors for establishing an excessive deficit. The conflict replicated the 1997 divide, but with the German position reversed. This time chancellor Gerhard Schröder argued for more leniency and proposed a long list of factors that was viewed favourably by France and Italy.

In March 2005, Luxembourgish Jean-Claude Juncker, presiding over the Council, proposed a shorter list, which was criticized by both governments that wanted to add specific spending categories (the three above plus the United Kingdom) and those that considered it too long and insisted on the centrality of the reference values. This list was eventually abandoned in favour of a somewhat fuzzy but still long enumeration of factors in Article 2.3 and an invitation to a 'balanced overall assessment'. As an 'overarching principle', mitigation would be considered only if the deficit remained close to the reference value and its excess was temporary. Nevertheless, considering also the laxer criteria of protracted low growth as a mitigating factor, these changes undeniably expanded Council discretion and diluted control over national authorities.

Why did recalcitrant and mostly compliant governments not veto these developments and push for delegation? Liberal intergovernmentalism proves its usefulness by directing our attention to the outcome in case of failure to agree: The reversion point of these negotiations was the suspension of the EDP – clearly an unpleasant outcome for these fiscally responsible governments.

Let's go back to 2003. In January of that year, the Council established that Germany had an excessive deficit, six months later, it was the turn of France. These events triggered a convergence between these two governments on the appropriate implementation of the policy. French accommodating interpretation of the rules was no news, but Hans Eichel, the German social democratic finance minister, joined the ranks by repeatedly emphasizing the inappropriateness of fiscal consolidation during a recession (Mody 2018: 150). In November 2003, facing recommendations that would have established the insufficiency of their measures and demanded further action under the threat of sanctions, they managed to assemble a minority to block decisions. Only the governments of Denmark, Spain, Belgium, Sweden, Austria, the Netherlands, Finland, and Greece supported the Commission's proposals (Heipertz and Verdun 2010: 142–54). The Council also declared that the procedure was held in abeyance. Although this latter decision was successfully challenged by the Commission before the European Court of Justice in July 2004, the Court upheld the Council's right to block decisions. It was therefore clear that there was a minority blocking *any* new Commission's recommendation – a de facto abeyance. The least reformist countries had therefore to accept looser criteria for establishing an excessive deficit and more emphasis on preventive surveillance in exchange for resuming the procedure and stricter constraints once an excess was determined. The unpalatable consequences of no agreement defused the threats of veto and engendered a willingness to compromise.

Given several governments pushing for loosening and more Council leeway, we should hardly expect delegation. This is in line with postfunctionalism (H5.4), were it not for the limited politicization. But in our view, the prevailing reluctance to delegate may have also been motivated by the renewed emphasis on the structural budget: an unobservable quantity subject to significant estimation errors, which depends on estimates of the output gap – also an unobservable quantity that in turn depends on estimates of, for instance, total factor productivity and (non-accelerating wage) rate of unemployment. Multi-annual forecasting errors of output growth and inflation add further uncertainty. Indeed, Claeys, Darvas, and Leandro (2016: 6) later note that 'the typical yearly revision both in the level and in the change in the structural balance is larger than 0.5 per cent of GDP, that is, larger than the required baseline annual adjustment'.[11]

Moreover, the risk of pro-cyclicality to achieve balance is not averted. Since a structural deficit is positively related to the non-accelerating wage rate of unemployment, episodes of high long-term unemployment could raise this rate, turning a cyclical deficit into a structural one and prompting corrective measures that could further increase unemployment.[12] This hysteretic risk may be asymmetrically distributed. Recessionary episodes (i.e. negative output gaps) of greater than 3.6 per cent have occurred every twenty-second year in the ten core EU member states but every sixth year in the five periphery countries[13] (Claeys, Darvas, and Leandro 2016: 4).

Accuracy did not improve even for the easier-to-estimate government balance-GDP ratio. Its forecasting error not only remained above 1 per cent of GDP, but it also worsened between 1997 and 2004 (see the mean absolute deviation in Figure 5.5). In 2002, the budget deficit ratios for Greece, Sweden, Ireland, and the Netherlands were underestimated by more than 3 per cent. In sum, governments agreed to a preventive surveillance based on an imprecise indicator over which they had limited control, and they faced still large, if not worsening, uncertainty when issuing corrective recommendations. No wonder they were not inclined to delegate.

5.5 The Euro Crisis: Policy Failure and Enforcement Reform

5.5.1 Delegation and Tightening

This overhaul of economic governance was adopted in the midst of the sovereign debt crisis. In Figures 5.1 and 5.2, we distinguish between the six-pack on the one side and the two-pack and fiscal compact on the other. These measures are part of the same reform, even though they span over three years. As Figure 5.1 shows, the number

[11] Given its opaqueness, the objective of a structurally balanced budget may not provide 'a focal point that enables investors to coordinate on when to punish governments for running excessive deficits' (Kelemen and Teo 2014: 366).

[12] The European Commission indeed routinely revises the methodology to calculate the output gap in order to address this issue.

[13] Spain, Portugal, Greece, Ireland, and Italy. The core includes the remaining ten EU countries prior to the 2004 enlargement.

of major provisions more than tripled and, in line with the scholarly consensus (e.g. Bauer and Becker 2014; Seikel 2016; Vanheuverzwijn 2017), the main beneficiary is undoubtedly the Commission. Figure 5.2 reports that the share of delegating provisions has moved from 6 to 14 per cent and the share of pooling provisions has correspondingly decreased from 18 to 14 per cent. Provisions giving national authorities some leeway, mostly exemptions, have marginally increased from 5 to 7 per cent. With more powers, provisions constraining the Commission have correspondently increased from 14 to 21 per cent, while the Council share has decreased from 25 to 15 per cent. The proportion of tightening provisions has barely altered. Almost half of the new ones are included in the two-pack, less than a quarter in the budgetary frameworks directive, and a tenth in the fiscal compact.

The reform establishes more precise assessment benchmarks: an annual real net expenditure growth to assess progress towards the MTO in the preventive regulation and an annual rate of improvement of the debt–GDP ratio for countries exceeding the reference value in the corrective regulation. The fiscal compact narrows to 0.5 per cent of GDP, the acceptable MTO divergence for countries exceeding the debt reference value.

The strengthening of the Commission's power is both procedural and substantive and occurs primarily in four measures (adopted with the ordinary legislative procedure): the SGP preventive regulation, the new SGP enforcement regulation, and the two-pack regulations.[14] Notably, 77 per cent of them are enforcement-related (see Figure 5.3). On the other side, accountability to the Parliament has been strengthened through its involvement in the economic dialogue and its oversight of Commission-delegated acts.

Although the shift in policy design from pooling to delegation is clear, the triplicated pooling provisions are still predominantly enforcement-related (85 per cent, see Figure 5.3). In the SGP enforcement regulation, sanctioning remains centred on the Council. In the two-pack surveillance regulation, this institution approves adjustment programmes, establishes noncompliance, and sets conditionality requirements. A third of the new pooling provisions comes from the MIB, and the enforcement of this measure relies more on the Council than on the Commission, compared to the SGP.

[14] The online appendix summarizes noteworthy delegating provisions.

In sum, there is both continuity and change. This reform may not have constituted a critical juncture – a radical shift in the allocation of policy competences – as Pan, Hosli, and Lantmeeters (2023) contend, but it has been the most extensive in our period of analysis.

5.5.2 Explaining the Overhaul: Noncompliance, Exit Cost, and Issue Linkage

As Figure 5.4 illustrates, the patterns of noncompliance leading up to this reform amounted to a policy failure. The significant revisions of the Greek government deficit in late 2009 raised serious concerns about data quality and led to the opening of an infringement procedure.[15] This was the proximate cause of the sovereign debt crisis, but the preceding financial crisis had already put public finances under serious strain. The structural balance of every single euro area country, except Slovakia, intermittently diverged from the MTOs. Public indebtedness worsened. Then, in 2010, every country, except for Luxembourg, ran an excessive deficit, while Greece, Ireland, and Portugal had to secure bailout loans. Negotiations were also highly mass politicized (Genschel and Jachtenfuchs 2018; Kriesi and Grande 2016), making this reform a sort of critical test of these theories.

Overall, liberal intergovernmentalism and neofunctionalism are more convincingly corroborated (H5.2 and, arguably, H5.3). As Schimmelfennig (2015: 184) aptly puts it, the ensuing bargaining dynamics took the form of a game of chicken between fiscally sound governments and those under pressure to finance their outlays. The significant risks of a dissolution of the euro area – an exit option of vast consequences – compelled them to solve the crisis but each preferred to shift the burden of adaptation onto the counterpart. The former sought commitment to fiscal discipline, the latter to a bailout.[16] For instance, this *linkage* explains why

[15] The repeated reservations by Eurostat on the quality of Greek public accounts materialized in the alarming revisions of the 2009 deficit, initially up to 7 per cent of GDP, ultimately to almost 16 per cent. They triggered a downgrade to junk status of Greece's credit rating, a pan-European capital flight to safety, and bailout measures.

[16] For positions on capacity-building measures, see Lehner and Wasserfallen (2019). As corroborating evidence, we find Germany, Finland, and the Netherlands opposing Article 13.4 of the SGP enforcement regulation that demands the Commission to draft a report on Eurobonds.

the Italian and Greek governments, despite their power to veto the corrective regulation, accepted the new benchmark of a debt–GDP ratio improvement for highly indebted countries (but successfully opposed demands to narrow the mitigating factors for determining an excessive deficit).

In the other measures, the shift in policy design towards tightening and delegation (especially for noncompliance and sanctioning decisions, with the consequence of narrowing Council influence) has also been facilitated by qualified majority voting in the Council (and parliamentary involvement). For instance, in the preventive regulation, the discussion centred on (1) a different MTO adjustment path for highly indebted countries and (2) the consequences of budgetary deviations. The Italian government argued against a differentiated assessment and, together with the Greek government, against sanctions for deviations. The new Article 5.1 instead demands the Council and the Commission to examine whether annual budgetary improvements reach at least 0.5 per cent of GDP for these countries (the Finnish, Dutch, and Luxembourgish governments pressed for a more explicit requirement, which was eventually inserted in the fiscal compact). Moreover, Article 5.1 not only operationalizes the adjustment path through an expenditure benchmark but the new Article 6.2 also demands the Council to act within a month of a warning; and sanctions are envisioned.

Politicization did not engender a convergence of positions over policy design. Benelux governments even proposed to extend the enhanced proposal prerogatives of the Commission to more SGP and MIB provisions. The Parliament was instead instrumental in including sanctions for manipulating statistics in the SGP enforcement regulation and for keeping Council qualified majority voting for approving adjustment programmes in the two-pack, over the opposition of several ministers (recall from Chapter 4 that proximity to the parliamentary position determines bargaining success in the ordinary legislative procedure).

In sum, noncompliance and the pressure of securing commitment to both fiscal soundness and bailout produced a reform in the direction predicted by liberal intergovernmentalism (H5.2). Additionally, prohibitive exit costs limited available options and lower procedural hurdles facilitated tightening and delegation according to a neofunctionalist dynamic. These changes are not unexpected (cf. Bauer and Becker 2014; Dehousse 2016). Delegation may have been also perceived as less risky since the Commission has been building up non-trivial policy capabilities over time (Savage and Verdun 2016) and the new expenditure rule is a step towards more certain and controllable performance indicators (Claeys, Darvas, and Leandro 2016) (H5.3).

Yet, economic uncertainty persevered and the Council's unwillingness to lose further control over policy enforcement should not come as a surprise. As Figure 5.5 documents, the forecasting error of the balance-to-GDP ratio actually increased to around 1.5 per cent of GDP, even before the global financial crisis. Between 2005 and 2007, errors predominantly originated from *over*estimations of the deficit ratio, as the bias line in Figure 5.5 indicates (Greece and Hungary were notable exceptions). Needless to say, the financial crisis and the subsequent European sovereign debt crisis were completely missed by economic forecasters.

Last, as an indication of how the topic is highly contested, the renewed emphasis of this reform on the debt reference value has rekindled the debate on the impact of public debt on growth and on the political sustainability of debt consolidation (e.g. Alesina, Favero, and Giavazzi 2019; Eichengreen and Panizza 2014; International Monetary Fund 2012; Moschella 2017). In the 2019 Presidential Address to the *American Economic Association*, Blanchard (2019) warned how an overestimation of the fiscal and welfare costs of debt may lead to public underinvestment,[17] although acknowledging that 'an aggressive contingent fiscal rule' (i.e. a primary surplus) may be a solution when highly indebted countries are trapped in high-risk premiums – low growth equilibria (Blanchard 2019: 33–34).

5.6 Conclusion

To understand economic governance design, we should not rely on a single theoretical perspective. Contrary to liberal intergovernmentalist expectations (H5.1, H5.2), enforcement has been heavily

[17] Public investment has been reserved special treatment since 2005 and the expenditure benchmark allows public investment to be averaged over a four-year period. For some countries, debt rollovers may well be sufficient to comply with the adjustment benchmark if the growth rate exceeds the safe interest rate.

Council-centred until 2011, despite significant noncompliance, and it remains so in the recent two-pack surveillance regulation and MIB. As postfunctionalist theories (H5.4) suggest (pooling aside), the salience of this policy has quite likely underlain the reluctance to tighten and delegate. But these latter approaches fall short in highly politicized contexts, exactly where they should do most of the explaining. Policymakers do not seem to react to mass politicization by loosening obligations and avoiding pooling and delegation. They do not cave in and ensure that the policy remains or returns under national control. The 'new intergovernmental moment' saw a move from Council- to Commission-centred enforcement, without relying on new institutions. Tightening, pooling, and delegation occurred *despite* the highly politicized negotiations of the recent reform. Perhaps mass domestic politicization was epiphenomenal exactly because it was *triggered by* noncompliance and elite conflict.

On the other hand, the mechanisms emphasized by liberal intergovernmentalism and neofunctionalism, for the expectations H5.1 to H5.3, remain valuable for explaining the overall *direction* of these reforms towards tightening, restricting Council authority and delegation – precipitated by noncompliance and characterized by commitment problems, threats of exclusion and veto, issue linkages, path dependencies, and more supranational decision-making. Attention to these supranational bargaining dynamics helps illuminate outcomes, even when loosening follows noncompliance, while functional pressures, such as the need to secure credible commitments, appear unaltered. To understand why liberal intergovernmentalism comes short requires us to consider the unavoidable arbitrariness and uncertainties of these rules, which must have cautioned against relying on a supranational executive with limited resources, even after recurrent compliance problems. This uncertainty derives from an incomplete and partial understanding of how an economy operates.

The legal provisions we have analyzed in this part of the book matter only to the extent they are complied with by the member states and are effective. Therefore, Part II investigates the implementation of the policy, complementing the bargaining models with theories of compliance and political economy theories of reform and public spending. We begin by analyzing the negotiations that take place between the Commission and the Council in setting the country-specific recommendations that constitute the preventive surveillance of economic governance. We then study the determinants of compliance with both these recommendations and with the fiscal reference values that are at the basis of the EDP and the corrective arm of the SGP. As we will see, the implementation of this policy also consists of navigating economic, national, and supranational pressures.

PART III

Implementing Economic Governance

6 *Supranational Bargaining, Credibility, and Preventive Surveillance*

In the European Union, no good policy goes unamended – only improved through the art of compromise, or what we like to call bureaucratic efficiency.

ChatGPT (after reading this chapter's abstract)

Governing today means giving acceptable signs of credibility.

Jean Baudrillard

If ignored, legal provisions are simply words on a piece of paper, even if printed in publications with imposing titles, such as the *Official Journal of the European Union*. The second part of this book is, therefore, entirely dedicated to the implementation of the economic governance regime. As we explained in Chapter 1, the policy rests on the two pillars of preventive surveillance and correction of excessive deficits. The excessive deficit procedure is the fulcrum of the second pillar. The causes and consequences of this oversight will be thoroughly assessed in Chapter 9. Recall that the first pillar – preventive surveillance – consists of two stages as laid out by the Stability and Growth Pact (SGP). First, every year by the end of April, the governments of euro area countries submit Stability Programmes to the Commission, while the other governments submit Convergence Programmes. The Commission examines these documents, writes an in-depth report on each of them, and proposes *country-specific recommendations* (CSRs) to the Council of the EU. The Council may amend these recommendations if it wishes to, it then adopts them by qualified majority voting.[1]

[1] This procedure has involved every member state since 1997, except for the periods a country has received financial assistance from a so-called Economic Adjustment Programme, namely, Cyprus (2014 and 2015), Greece (2011–2015), Ireland (2011–2013), Latvia (2011), and Portugal (2011–2013). Since 2011, it has been part of the new coordination system of the European Semester, see the overview in Chapter 1.

In this chapter, we investigate (1) what shapes the Council's propensity to modify these proposals and (2) what affects their strengthening or weakening.[2] In Chapter 7, we examine the determinants of national compliance with these recommendations.

These recommendations are the linchpins of preventive surveillance and they are becoming important policy instruments. For instance, to access the 2021 Recovery and Resilience Facility, adopted to mitigate the impact of the coronavirus pandemic, governments had to prepare plans that addressed the challenges identified in such recommendations. At the core of these documents are key priority issues that require immediate attention by the member states. These deal not only with fiscal policy, as established by the SGP, but also with the policies covered by the six-pack measures and aimed at redressing macroeconomic imbalances or pursuing other major economic objectives. They may include growth-enhancing structural reforms or measures that address employment and social issues or financial market stability. Governments are expected to follow these recommendations when they draft their national budget for the following year, and a failure to implement them might eventually result in sanctions under the SGP and the macroeconomic imbalances procedure.

The negotiations over the content of these documents are, therefore, central features of the implementation of economic governance. They are where 'politics', intended as the power and influence of the different EU actors, affects 'policy', intended as the design and calibration of policy instruments (Howlett 2000). As such, they shape the relations among governments and between the Council and the Commission.

As discussed in the first part of the book, scholarly works have predominately studied the factors shaping the design of the policy, but, since the establishment of the European Semester, researchers have begun to investigate the motivations of the Commission in proposing these recommendations (Cova 2022; Guidi and Guardiancich 2018; van der Veer and Haverland 2018), the content of these documents (Copeland and Daly 2018; Haas et al. 2020; Zeitlin and Vanhercke 2018) and how they differ across countries (D'Erman et al. 2019). However, the bargaining process between

[2] As this chapter substantially extends the work of Mariotto (2019), we will emphasize the differences in the methods employed and the results produced.

the Commission and the Council that precedes their adoption has received less attention. Some scholars have noted the more inclusive and accommodating stance that the Commission adopted towards the governments at the end of the presidency of José Manuel Barroso and into that of Jean-Claude Juncker (Schmidt 2020: 198–202; Vanheuverzwijn 2017: 25–27). In a more systematic study that covers the recommendations that have been addressed to fifteen member states between 1999 and 2013, Baerg and Hallerberg (2016) find that the Commission's proposals have been mostly weakened by the Council, especially if the addressees were larger countries or had a more Eurosceptic national public opinion. The text of the recommendations for larger countries has also been more extensively edited. In an extension to the 2011–2018 period, the same scholars find that the recommendations to large euro area countries experiencing economic headwinds are more extensively modified by the Council (Baerg and Hallerberg 2022).

In this chapter, we rely on both bargaining and compliance theories to set out ten expectations about the factors leading the Council to amend the Commission's assessments of national macroeconomic programmes. We consider both the extent of the Council's modifications to the Commission's proposals and the nature of the changes. We confirm some of the results of Baerg and Hallerberg (2016; 2022) and Mariotto (2019), take issue with some other results, and suggest additional explanatory factors.

Our analysis indicates that the Council is particularly active in modifying the Commission's assessments, and, contrary to Baerg and Hallerberg's findings, it strengthens four-fifths of the recommending provisions that it decides to modify. Economic and supranational pressures dominate this process. We find that the divisiveness within the Council, the extremeness of the position of the Commission, the noncompliance record of the target country and the economic context are associated with the extent to which the Council modifies the CSRs proposed by the Commission. Similarly, the noncompliance record and the position of the government which is pivotal for adopting the CSRs shape the direction of these changes. Like Baerg and Hallerberg (2016) and Mariotto (2019), recommendations addressed to countries that may exert greater influence within the Council (i.e. net contributing countries or those with higher voting power) are more likely to be watered down, but these effects are weak.

Overall, controlling for the specific economic contexts under which they operate, governments balance the pressures originating from the bargaining dynamic within the Council with the need to preserve the credibility of the policy in the face of noncompliance.

6.1 Bargaining over the Country-specific Recommendations

6.1.1 Gridlock and Failure to Agree

We begin with the supranational factors that may shape these recommendations. The negotiations over the CSRs between the Commission and the Council and among governments within the Council resemble a situation of (super)majority-rule bargaining under open rule (Baron and Ferejohn 1989), with an agenda-setter that has no gatekeeping or voting power. The influence of the Commission resides in its prerogative to propose the initial document, but the final text is likely to be shaped by the Council's open rule. On the other hand, the proposal power of each minister is mitigated by the supermajority voting since any amendment requires a qualified majority for approval.

This procedure is essentially equivalent to the qualified majority voting variant of the consultation procedure that we discussed in Chapter 4, although without parliamentary consultation. Since a qualified majority in the Council suffices for the adoption of the Commission's proposal, the minimum winning coalition comprises the Commission and the governments that make up such a majority (Crombez 1996: 209; Steunenberg 1994). The pivotal Council member(s) is the government that is closest to the status quo (or the best alternative to a negotiated agreement) and can form a blocking minority.

The target member state has plausibly an interest in weakening any recommendation proposed by the Commission. Had a recommended measure been considered beneficial by the incumbent government, it would have been already implemented and it would have dropped from the Commission's agenda. But the likelihood of modifying a proposed recommendation depends on the size of the gridlock interval, which represents the set of policies that cannot be changed under a given decision-making rule.[3] If we look back

[3] For applications of the gridlock interval to the EU, see Citi and Justesen (2016), Crombez and Hix (2015), and Junge, König, and Luig (2015).

at Figure 4.1 in Chapter 4, this interval is $G - [x_3, x_5]$, if a qualified majority requires five out of seven votes. Any proposed recommendation that lays to the left of x_3 or to the right of x_5 can be modified, any proposal belonging to G cannot. A Commission's proposed recommendation that is located inside the gridlock interval is less likely to be amended by the Council, and, therefore, *the larger the gridlock interval, the less extensively a proposed recommendation is changed* (H6.1).

A changed recommendation implies that either the Commission has failed to anticipate the positions of Council ministers or the supranational executive sees some benefit from taking a different position.[4] This benefit is likely to be higher when the Commission's stance differs significantly from that of ministers. Accounting for both factors, we should, therefore, expect *a proposed recommendation to be more extensively changed if the Commission is more uncertain about the position of the Council ministers* (H6.2) or *if the Commission's position is located outside the gridlock interval* (H6.3).

The procedural model of Chapter 4 can also be used to produce expectations about the *direction* of change when it occurs. Assume that the dimension in Figure 4.1 represents the tightness of a specific recommendation to a given state, from weak at the left end of the spectrum to strong at the right end. A failure to agree produces no recommendation and this outcome is the status quo *sq* at the left end because no recommendation is clearly the weakest 'recommendation' as it would leave governments with complete autonomy on how to conduct their policies. The Commission's position *COM* is at the strongest endpoint of the dimension. In this context, government 3 is the 'acceptance pivot', that is, it is the government whose support is necessary for the adoption of the recommendation. This implies that *the more the acceptance pivot supports weakening, the more likely a proposed recommendation is weakened* (H6.4). Recall, however, as we discussed in Chapters 4 and 5, that the failure to adopt a recommendation could be very costly as it could signal an unwillingness to

4 For example, Guidi and Guardiancich (2018) find that, when the Commission drafts CSRs on pensions, it follows a 'technochratic' approach based on objective data, rather than a 'discretionary' approach based on the member state's ideal preference.

reform to both fellow governments and the markets. If that were the case, the acceptance set of the pivot would not constrain the set of adoptable measures and we would not find support for H6.4.

6.1.2 Council Bargaining and Vote Trading

In this context, Council bargaining is about trading votes across proposed recommendations. If a government has an interest in weakening the recommendations it receives from the Commission, it needs to assemble a minimum winning coalition within the Council. To successfully do so, it can offer in exchange support for weakening the recommendations addressed to fellow governments. *If* we assume that governments attach more importance to the recommendations they receive than to those addressed to fellow governments, exchange models become particularly useful (Arregui, Stokman, and Thomson 2006; König and Proksch 2006). The adoption of CSRs turns into orthogonal multidimensional bargaining – a setup that encourages logrolling (Aksoy 2012). Accordingly, governments with greater bargaining resources should be in a better position to finalize the exchange. Following these and other similar works (e.g. Bailer 2004; Thomson 2011: 220–24) as well as our discussion in Chapter 4, voting and economic power are common proxies for bargaining resources. We, therefore, expect that *a proposed recommendation addressed to a member state with greater voting or economic power to be more extensively changed* (H6.5a) *and more likely weakened* (H6.5b).

These large country governments may also be in greater *need* of carrying out this exchange because the proposed recommendations are first discussed *within* a College of commissioners that guarantees equal representation to member states[5] and votes by a simple majority (see Chapter 3). Proposals may, therefore, be characterized by a small-country bias. Indeed, Baerg and Hallerberg (2016; 2022) find that more powerful states are more likely to water down or edit the Commission's recommendations because of the influence they exert on the Council. There is some more evidence that this power may matter, but it is not overwhelming. For instance, the compromise model is indeed very robust in explaining bargaining outcomes (see Chapter 4), and it includes a measure of the power of actors.

[5] Before the 2004 Barroso Commission, larger countries had two commissioners.

This factor, however, does not seem to affect bargaining success. Moreover, models that account for vote trading are not necessarily more accurate. König and Proksch's (2006) procedural exchange model is an improvement only over standard procedural models that normally perform poorly. Arregui, Stokman, and Thomson's (2006) position exchange model instead does not seem to be more accurate than the compromise model upon which it is built.

Last, a country's position in relation to the EU financial transfers may also represent an important resource or liability in these bargaining exchanges. Several works have found evidence that some coalitions in the Council are formed around net contributors and net beneficiaries of the EU budget on structural and agricultural funds (Bailer, Mattila, and Schneider 2015; Carrubba 1997; Zimmer, Schneider, and Dobbins 2005). This divide intensified during the sovereign debt crisis as new financial mechanisms were established to support countries that were experiencing financial difficulties (Târlea et al. 2019).[6] We expect net-contributing countries to be more successful in their attempts at loosening their recommendations since net-beneficiaries and countries receiving financial assistance (i.e. Greece, Hungary, Ireland, Latvia, Portugal, Romania, and Spain) may be more willing to accommodate their requests in exchange for their financial support. In other words, we expect that *a proposed recommendation addressed to a net contributor to be more likely weakened* (H6.6).

6.1.3 Noncompliance, More Logrolling, and Reputation

Noncompliance is likely to alter the dynamics of trading votes. How exactly this may occur is not straightforward, though. The Commission, as the guardian of the treaties, is likely to demand tougher policy actions from governments of countries already in more perilous fiscal circumstances, that is, with high debts or excessive deficits. After all, the purpose of surveillance is to prevent unsustainable fiscal positions and corrective actions in case of excessive deficits.

6 For euro area countries, these efforts culminated with the establishment in December 2010 of a permanent intergovernmental organization called the European Stability Mechanism, which replaced two earlier temporary funding programmes. Non-euro countries rely on a balance-of-payment assistance facility.

But tougher proposals may offer even more opportunities for vote trading. Similar to the small-country bias effect, tougher proposals may raise the target government's willingness to trade votes since such government would attach a higher value to a weakened recommendation. In return, fellow governments, especially those at future risk of noncompliance, may be more willing to entertain the trade and to weaken the Commission's recommendation, also because they would gain from such an exchange in case they run into the same situation. We may, therefore, expect that *a proposed recommendation addressed to a noncompliant member state to be more extensively changed* (H6.7a) *and more likely weakened* (H6.7b).

On the other hand, noncompliance may affect the relative importance governments assign to their and their fellow governments' recommendations. Expected negative externalities and reputational losses could engender an opposite dynamic. As discussed in Chapter 2, this regime is designed to prevent negative externalities arising from fiscal profligacy. Fellow governments may be unwilling to trade votes for weaker recommendations if they anticipate negative externalities from the actions of noncompliant countries. More plausibly, they may try to tighten up such recommendations. Moreover, governments that support the weakening of recommendations addressed to noncompliant countries may face significant reputational losses as this behaviour could be interpreted as an attempt at undermining the Commission's assessments and, ultimately, the credibility of the whole policy. Indeed, governments that breached the deficit reference value in the early years of application of the SGP and pushed for a loosening of the rules appear to have faced a significant reputational loss. Instead, toughening things up may preserve such a reputation before fellow compliant governments. As a result, we may, therefore, expect that *a proposed recommendation addressed to a noncompliant member state to be more likely strengthened* (H6.8) or, as a minimum, to remain unaltered.

6.1.4 Economic Distress

Consider now economic pressures. The sensitivity to negative externalities may be heightened during periods of economic distress. Sure, the Commission could already incorporate the need to address externalities by proposing more demanding recommendations, but the minds of economic and finance ministers of the Council are likely to be tilted, if anything, towards tougher preventive surveillance. Editing appears, indeed, to be associated with the economic conditions a country is experiencing (Baerg and Hallerberg 2022). In other words, we expect *a proposed recommendation addressed to a member state under economic distress to be more extensively changed* (H6.9a) *and more likely strengthened* (H6.9b).

6.1.5 *Public Support*

Last, we consider the possibility that national factors shape these recommendations. As Van der Veer and Haverland (2018) have found, the Commission may be responsive to national political pressures when drafting the CSRs. These scholars show how the supranational executive addresses more demanding reforms to governments facing a more polarized public opinion on the EU, probably in order to protect its reputation and signal resolve to its audience. From the Council side, however, we have already seen in Chapter 3 that governments facing a more Eurosceptic public opinion are less supportive of the expansion of the Commission's enforcement prerogatives. As we said, this finding resonates with the results of Hagemann, Hobolt, and Wratil (2017) about governments opposing the extension of EU policy authority in these circumstances. In other words, more diffuse EU support should plausibly make re-election-seeking ministers warier of trying to weaken the Commission's recommendations – let not such easing be publicly criticized by opposition parties, while more public Euroscepticism should embolden governments in their attempts at weakening them. Fellow ministers, who understand electoral pressures, may well accommodate these demands. Indeed, Baerg and Hallerberg (2016) find that, between 1999 and 2013, governments of countries with lower EU public support have been more successful at weakening the Commission's proposed measures. We, therefore, expect *a proposed recommendation addressed to a member state with a more Eurosceptic public opinion to be more extensively changed* (H6.10a) *and more likely weakened* (H6.10b). Note however that a secondary finding in Chapter 3 indicates that these governments appear also to be slightly more in favour of *tighter* national oversight, at least as far as the overall design of the policy is concerned.

6.2 Modifications of the Country-specific Recommendations and Their Explanans

6.2.1 Extent and Direction of the Modifications of the Major Recommending Provisions

Between 1999 and 2019, the Council adopted 487 CSRs.[7] As in Mariotto (2019), we broadly follow the text-analysis methodology employed by Baerg and Hallerberg (2016), based on hand-coding, to measure the changes of the Council to the CSRs proposed by the Commission. Unlike these scholars, however, we focus solely on the major *recommending provisions* of the Commission's proposal, rather than the entire document, because these provisions are the cornerstones of preventive surveillance. This approach makes the process of aggregating the changes to individual recommending provisions into a measure of change of an entire document (i.e. the CSR) more transparent. Our original coding procedure consists of two steps.[8] First, the Commission's recommendation and the Council's opinion on the stability or convergence programmes (i.e. the CSR) are subdivided into major provisions. Second, a major provision is labelled 'recommending provision' if it lists clearly the policies or reforms to be implemented. Our first dependent variable, *Council change*, is the sum of the major recommending provisions in a given CSR that have been modified by the Council. For the second dependent variable, each Council's modification to a major recommending provision is coded as either 'strengthening' or 'weakening'.[9] *Council severity* is an ordinal variable that measures the direction of change as follows:

$$Council\ severity_{it} = \begin{cases} -1 & if\, S - W < 0 \\ 0 & if\, S - W = 0 \\ 1 & if\, S - W > 0 \end{cases} \tag{1}$$

[7] Recommendations issued before 2002 have been requested from the Commission Directorate General for Economic and Financial Affairs. Since 2002, they have been downloaded from the Directorate General's website. Countries that are subject to an Economic Adjustment Programme are excluded because they are exempt from this procedure.

[8] For a detailed description, see the online appendix to this chapter.

[9] We use the Compare feature of the Review tab in Microsoft Word 2016 for this comparison.

If more recommending provisions of a proposed CSR to a member state *i* in year *t* have been weakened (*W*) than strengthened (*S*), *Council severity* takes the value of –1. If more provisions have been strengthened than weakened, it takes the value of 1. If no provisions have been changed or the CSR contains the same number of strengthened and weakened provisions, *Council severity* takes the value of 0.[10] In the online appendix, we assess the validity of these estimates by comparing them with those produced by Baerg and Hallerberg (2016) and we run robustness checks with alternative dependent variables.

Considering the long period of investigation and the subsequent reforms to the governance regime, these major recommending provisions display some systematic differences. Before the establishment of the European Semester for economic policy coordination, they were more general, and they were concerned with fiscal policy only, in line with the provisions laid out in the SGP. With the introduction of the six-pack, two-pack, and the fiscal compact, the provisions became more specific and covered more objectives, such as addressing macroeconomic imbalances or other major economic policy goals such as growth, employment creation, social cohesion, and financial market stability. Moreover, while the 1999–2010 provisions were rather unsystematic and unstructured, after the 2011–2013 overhaul, the new coordination mechanism has systematized the requests towards the member states. For these reasons, unlike Mariotto (2019), we run two separate analyses in the empirical section. One focuses on the period between 1999 and 2010, while the second concentrates on the period when the European Semester is operating. This strategy allows us to compare and contrast the two phases more accurately.

6.2.2 *Explanatory Factors*

The measurement of some explanatory, both national and supranational, factors requires that we identify the more plausible dimension that underlies the adoption of these recommendations. In our view, the left–right cleavage is the best fit. In the literature, there is a broad

[10] Only thirty-three CSRs have the same number of strengthened and weakened recommending provisions, 73 per cent of which contain only one strengthened and one weakened provision.

consensus that left-leaning parties tend to prefer a larger public sector and a more interventionist fiscal policy than right-leaning parties because their constituencies benefit from generous social programs and prefer lower unemployment even if it produces higher inflation (e.g. Alesina, Roubini, and Cohen 1997; but cf. Clark 2003). Left-leaning governments indeed tend to be associated with more public expenditure (Bawn and Rosenbluth 2006; Fortunato and Loftis 2018; Martin and Vanberg 2013), although not necessarily with more fiscal profligacy.[11] We have therefore calculated the left–right ideology of each government as the parliamentary seat-weighted mean of the left–right scores of cabinet parties from the Chapel Hill expert surveys.[12] Following, among others, Crombez and Hix (2015), we have associated each government's ideological score with its country's voting weight and calculated the *Gridlock interval* as the absolute difference between the ideological positions of the two so-called pivotal governments whose support is necessary, under qualified majority voting, for a rightward and a leftward policy shift. Also following Crombez and Hix (2015), we have assigned a left–right ideological score to each commissioner according to her party affiliation and determined the position of the median commissioner under simple majority voting. *Commission outlier* takes the value of one if this position is located outside the gridlock interval, and zero otherwise. Last, the *Acceptance pivot* is the ideological score of the government whose support is necessary for a rightward policy shift. We expect a weakening of the CSR as the position of this pivot takes lower values, that is, as it moves to the left.

To measure the Commission's *Preference uncertainty* in estimating governmental positions, we follow Boranbay-Akan, König, and Osnabrügge (2017) and count the number of elections that occurred in the year before the proposed recommendations. As far as the

[11] Some scholars have found an association between government ideology and public deficit or debt (e.g. Balassone and Giordano 2001; Fabrizio and Mody 2006; Mink and De Haan 2006), but others have not (e.g. Fortunato and Loftis 2018; Franzese 2002; Harrinvirta and Mattila 2001; Perotti and Kontopoulos 2002; Volkerink and De Haan 2001; Wehner 2010a). We discuss this literature in Chapter 8.

[12] The scale ranges from zero to ten. Data come from the CHES dataset at www.chesdata.eu/. We use McElroy and Benoit's (2012) dataset for the positions of Cypriot, Luxembourgish, and Maltese parties.

factors that should facilitate vote trading within the Council are concerned, *Voting power* (already used in Chapter 3) is measured by the Penrose–Banzhaf index in the Council's qualified majority voting rule at the time of negotiation of the proposed recommendation. *Economic size*, that is, the logarithm of the addressee country's GDP in the year of negotiation, measures power in the economic area, while *Budget contribution* is the difference, in billion euros, between the EU budget total revenues and expenditures for each country-year.[13] For noncompliance, we employ the one-year lagged reference values, that is, the ratios of the general government's gross *Debt* and *Deficit* to the country's GDP. Economic distress is captured by two business cycle variables: *GDP growth rate* and *Inflation rate*,[14] and a dichotomous variable, *Economic crisis*, that takes the value of 1 if the CSR is adopted during the sovereign debt crisis, that is, between the first Greek bailout in 2010 and 2015. For public opinion, a type of political pressure, we employ the same Eurobarometer survey item used in Chapter 3. *Public support* is the post-stratification weighted share of respondents answering that membership is good, net of the share of respondents answering that membership is bad in the survey preceding the adoption of CSRs. Last, as control variables, we also include the *Left–right position* and *Anti–pro EU position* of the governments, which are used in Chapter 3.[15]

6.3 How the Council Shapes the Country-specific Recommendations

The Council has modified almost two-thirds of the CSRs, although most major recommending provisions are unaltered. Figure 6.1 displays the yearly number of major recommending provisions as well as the proportion of provisions that have been strengthened and weakened in the CSRs. The number of provisions more than doubled after

[13] Budget data prior to 2000 is available from the 2008 Financial Report (European Commission 2009), while data between 2000 and 2020 can be found at the Commission's website dedicated to EU spending and revenues.

[14] We use the Eurostat dataset for countries' GDP, debt, deficit, GDP growth, and inflation rate.

[15] We have excluded the euro area variable, also used in other chapters, because it is highly correlated with debt. Descriptive statistics are reported in Table A6.1 of the online appendix to this chapter.

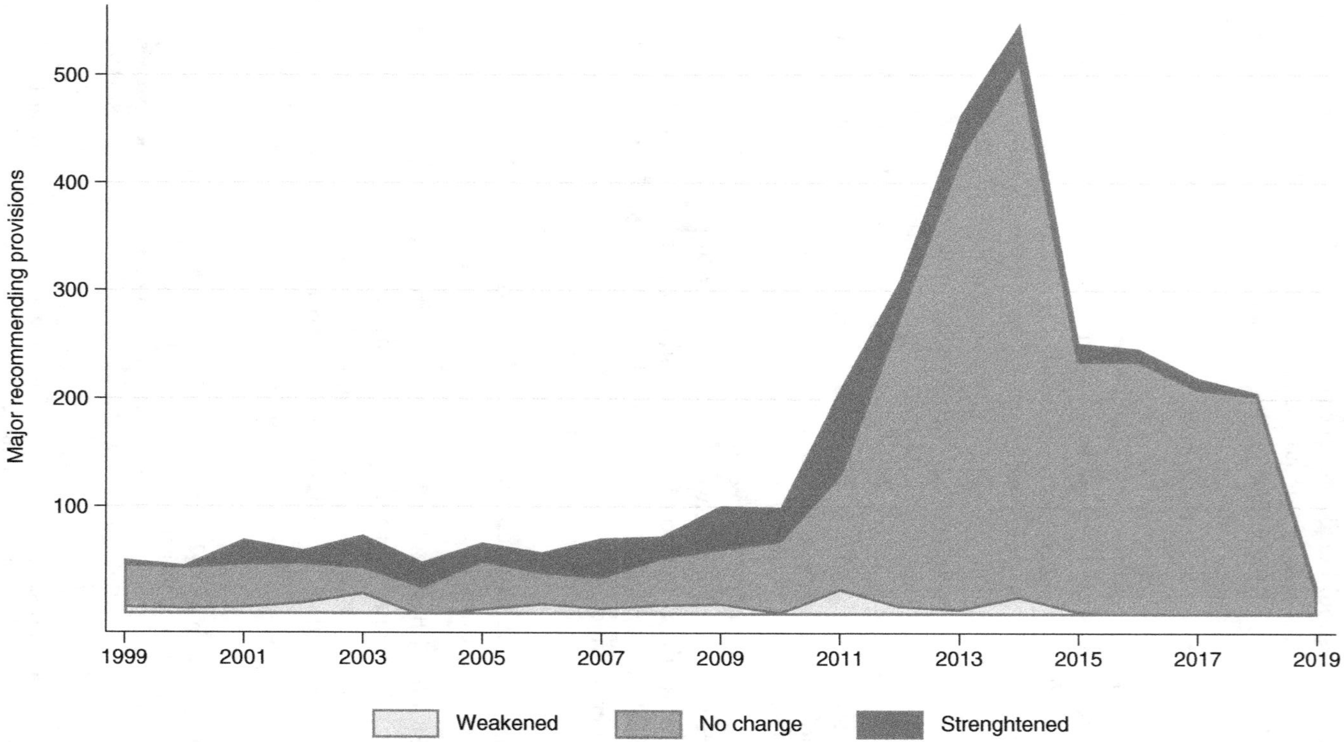

Figure 6.1 Major recommending provisions and Council modifications

the introduction of the European Semester in 2011, peaking at 549 in 2014. Although unchanged provisions represent the lion's share, more provisions have been strengthened than weakened throughout the entire period, and increasingly so: more than twice as many between 1999 and 2010 and more than three times as many in the European Semester period.

Recall that a CSR has been coded as strengthened if the number of strengthened major recommending provisions within such CSR exceeds the number of weakened ones. Unlike Baerg and Hallerberg (2016), we find that the Council has strengthened more than 40 per cent of the CSRs (213 out of 487) and weakened only 10 per cent. Forty-six per cent of the CSRs are, however, left unchanged.

Figure 6.2 shows the number of CSRs by addressee country and type of change, before and after the introduction of the European Semester. Except for three years at the onset of the policy (1999, 2000, and 2002), the Council has tended to be stricter than the Commission both in the period before and after the 2011 overhaul. The most demanding modifications of the Council occurred in 2010 when 81 per cent of the proposed Commission's CSRs were strengthened. Over the recent years, during the Jucker presidency of the Commission, the Council has left unaltered about two-thirds of the CSRs, while it has strengthened the remaining one-third, perhaps because the two institutions were facing a less uncertain negotiating environment or because of the greater effort by the Commission at taking governmental positions into account, as some scholars argue (Schmidt 2020: 198–202; Vanheuverzwijn 2017: 25–27).

These patterns are broadly confirmed across member states, but there are also non-trivial differences. Most strengthened CSRs are addressed to Greece (10 out of 13 documents), Cyprus (9 out of 13), followed by Slovenia (11 out of 16) and Hungary (10 out of 16). Except for Slovenia, these countries received financial assistance in the meantime.

Only four of the ten founding member states of the euro area (Luxembourg, Finland, Austria, and Ireland) have faced strengthened demands by the Council in less than half of the CSRs. This should not be surprising as surveillance is primarily designed to prevent negative externalities from spreading across euro area countries. The Mediterranean and less fiscally virtuous countries, such as Italy, France, and Spain, are the addressees of the highest number of major recommending provisions.

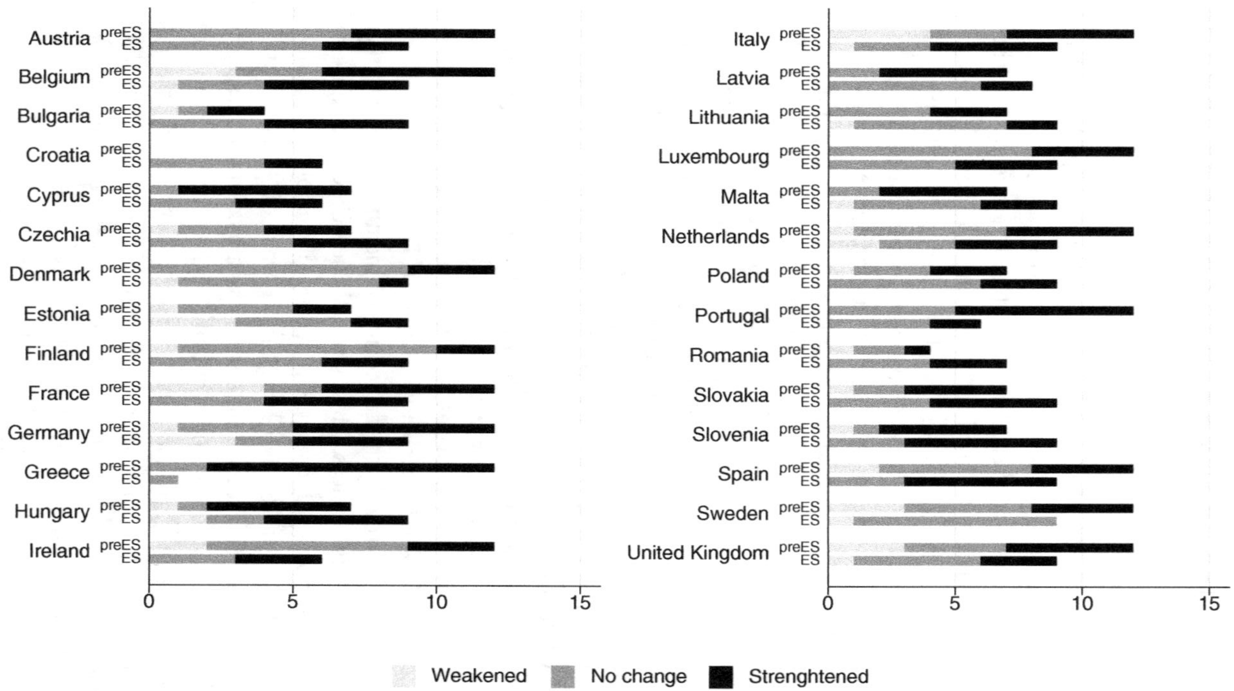

Figure 6.2 Changes to CSRs by addressed member state and period

Note: Before (preES) and after (ES) the introduction of the European Semester. A CSR is strengthened if more major recommending provisions have been strengthened than weakened, and the opposite for a weakened CSR.

We first examine what prompts the Council to modify the Commission's proposal. Because *Council change* (the sum of modified major recommending provisions in a CSR) is an overdispersed count variable, we use a negative binomial regression with country and year fixed effects. Next, we investigate the determinants of the direction of these changes (*Council severity*), employing an ordinal logistic regression with country and year fixed effects (Long and Freese 2014). In light of the above considerations, Table 6.1 reports the results of these two models, testing separately for the period before and after the introduction of the European Semester.

Supranational bargaining and credibility: Starting from the supranational pressure politicians face, greater divisiveness within the Council (i.e. a larger gridlock interval) is associated with *more* extensive changes to the proposed CSR. As the gridlock interval widens by a standard deviation (i.e. the difference between the 2019 and 2014 interval), the number of amended recommendations in a CSR increases by between 15.1 (in the 1999–2010 period) and 42.9 percentage points (in the 2011–2019 period). This is opposite to the expectation H6.1. A possible reason for this surprising result could be that the documents that are adopted in these negotiations are addressee-specific rather than binding for *all* member states, as the models we introduced in Chapter 4 assume. The larger the ideological distance between pivotal governments, the more likely some governments will demand changes to the proposed CSR and, perhaps, succeed in modifying it through vote-trading *across* CSRs.

Uncertainty does not seem to affect the extent of the modifications to the proposed CSRs (expectation H6.2), but, as expectation H6.3 suggests, we find that the Council modifies the proposals more extensively if the median commissioner is located outside the gridlock interval, at least before the introduction of the European Semester.[16] The number of amended recommendations increases

[16] We can test this hypothesis only for the period 1999–2010. After the introduction of the European Semester, the position of the median commissioner is always located within the gridlock interval. We cannot, therefore, test directly the argument about the Commission's more conciliatory position as the Barroso's second term at the helm of the supranational executive was drawing to a close and during Juncker's presidency (Schmidt 2020: 198–202; Vanheuverzwijn 2017: 25–27). This test would have required pooling the data from the two periods, which we do not deem advisable. The result is nevertheless coherent with this argument and it is stronger than in Mariotto (2019) where the relevant coefficient does not reach the nominal level of statistical significance.

Table 6.1 ***Determinants of the extent and direction of Council revisions of proposed CSRs***

	Council change		Council severity	
	1999–2010	2011–2019	1999–2010	2011–2019
Supranational factors				
Gridlock interval	0.2727†	0.7588**		
	(0.1527)	(0.2009)		
Commission outlier	0.6665**			
	(0.1981)			
Preference uncertainty	-0.1030	0.0112		
	(0.1407)	(0.1398)		
Acceptance pivot			0.4025*	1.9456**
			(0.1623)	(0.6361)
Voting power	0.0922	0.0989†	-0.1779†	0.1097
	(0.0713)	(0.0557)	(0.0972)	(0.1050)
Economic size	-0.0286	-0.1301	-0.0077	-0.1881
	(0.1200)	(0.0949)	(0.1687)	(0.1925)
Budget contribution	0.0109	-0.0047	0.0758	-0.0554†
	(0.0269)	(0.0142)	(0.0685)	(0.0313)
Debt	0.0041	0.0120**	0.0145*	0.0100*
	(0.0032)	(0.0026)	(0.0074)	(0.0048)
Deficit	-0.0507*	-0.0172	-0.0707	-0.0807
	(0.0230)	(0.0283)	(0.0474)	(0.0798)
Economic factors				
GDP growth rate	-0.0341*	-0.0054	-0.0292	-0.0590
	(0.0159)	(0.0289)	(0.0428)	(0.0665)
Inflation rate	0.0530†	0.1365**	0.0697	0.0035
	(0.0312)	(0.0530)	(0.0889)	(0.1378)
Economic crisis	-0.0940	1.5030**	1.0551*	0.3380
	(0.2573)	(0.1887)	(0.5265)	(0.5468)
National factors				
Left–right position	-0.0144*	-0.0026	0.0028	-0.0162†
	(0.0060)	(0.0053)	(0.0125)	(0.0086)
Anti–pro EU position	-0.0039	0.0003	-0.0204†	0.0166
	(0.0087)	(0.0173)	(0.0114)	(0.0293)
Public support	0.0011	-0.0009	0.0033	0.0049
	(0.0040)	(0.0043)	(0.0073)	(0.0072)
Constant	2.3782	-1.3156		
	(5.0084)	(1.1644)		

Table 6.1 (*cont.*)

	Council change		Council severity	
	1999–2010	2011–2019	1999–2010	2011–2019
Constant (cut 1)			0.6784	11.1334*
			(1.2105)	(4.4742)
Constant (cut 2)			3.0849*	14.4620**
			(1.2372)	(4.3675)
Observations	258	229	258	229
Number of countries	27	28	27	28
Log-pseudolikelihood	−366.9	−282.2	−227.9	−183.8

Note: Negative binomial regressions for *Council change*, ordinal logistic regressions for *Council severity*. Robust standard errors are in parentheses. $^{**}p < 0.01$, $^{*}p < 0.05$, $^{\dagger}p < 0.1$. Public finance data are considered supranational factors because they are measures of compliance with the reference values.

by 66.6 percentage points when the Commissioner is an outlier. In other words, suspicions of bias of the Commission engender changes to its proposals.

The position of the government that is pivotal for accepting a proposal (i.e. the acceptance pivot) appears to play an important role in shaping the nature of the changes in both periods, as expectation H6.4 indicates. A proposed CSR is between 6.3 (in the period before the semester) and 11.2 percentage points (under the semester) less likely to be strengthened if the position of this government shifts leftward by a standard deviation, implying a preference for weaker recommendations.

Bargaining resources facilitate vote trading (H6.5), somewhat. The effects are weak (p-values <0.10) and vary across periods. CSRs that are addressed to countries with higher voting power are more extensively modified (during the European Semester period) and are more likely to be weakened (prior to the European Semester period). For instance, an increase in voting power by a standard deviation (i.e. the difference between Poland and the United Kingdom in 2017) leads to an average increase in the expected number of changed recommendations by 23.3 percentage points. This resonates with Baerg and Hallerberg's (2022) findings. And in line with the results of Baerg and Hallerberg (2016) and Mariotto (2019), recommendations addressed to larger countries are more likely to be weakened by the Council, at least in the pre-European Semester period. If the target country is Germany, which has a voting power index of 8 per cent, the likelihood of weakening the proposed CSR is 8.8 percentage points higher than that of Sweden, which has a voting power index of 3 per cent. Net beneficiaries to the EU budget also saw the strengthening of their CSRs during the European Semester period, but this effect is weakly significant (p-value <0.10). For example, the probability that the Council strengthens a CSR increases by 6.5 percentage points if net contributions diminish by a standard deviation (4.7 billion euros, the mean difference between Italy and Cyprus). Raw economic power, however, does not seem to matter.

Results are more robust when it comes to the impact of non-compliance, at least as far as the debt-to-GDP ratio is concerned. In line with H6.7a, a standard deviation increase in this proportion – for instance, the difference between Germany and Belgium in 2015 – is associated with an increase in the expected number of amended recommendations of 38.1 percentage points, under the European Semester (this variable fails to reach significance in Baerg and Hallerberg 2022). In terms of the direction of changes, the reputational logic (H6.8) convincingly trumps the logrolling logic (H6.7b). In other words, governments toughen up recommendations addressed to noncompliant (i.e. highly indebted) states in order to preserve their reputation and the credibility of the policy. As also found by Mariotto (2019), governments do not use more demanding Commission proposals as bargaining chips to soften the CSRs. Take a state that has experienced an increase in the debt-GDP ratio from the reference value of 60 per cent to above 100 per cent. The probability that the Council strengthens a CSR addressed to such a country increases by between 14.2 (in the 1999–2010 period) and 8.9 (under the European Semester) percentage points. Given that before 2011, the debt criterion had been largely ignored in the determination of whether a country was running an excessive deficit, in this period, the governments in the Council may have been even more inclined to strengthen the preventive recommendations when assessing highly indebted countries.[17]

[17] A higher deficit is associated with fewer changes but only before 2010, while it is unrelated to the direction of the modifications.

Economic conditions: Economic pressures prompt more mixed results. In the pre-European Semester period, lower growth is weakly associated with fewer modifications: a standard deviation decrease in the growth rate – for instance, the difference between Luxembourg and Spain in 1999 – is associated with a decrease of 13.4 percentage points in the expected number of changed recommendations. But after the launch of the European Semester, the intergovernmental institution has revised extensively the recommendations to countries with higher inflation as well as during the crisis years. A standard deviation higher inflation rate is associated with an increase of 18 percentage points in the expected number of modified recommendations. Changes increased by a notable 150.3 percentage points during the crisis years of the 2011–2019 period. The Council has been more active during the crisis most likely because of concerns about contagion, but greater activism does not imply strengthening, at least in this period. Only prior to the European Semester, the crisis years (2007–2010) are associated with a 25.3 percentage point increase in the probability that the Council strengthens the CSRs. Most economic conditions are not associated with the direction of the modifications of the proposed CSRs.

National pressures: Finally, as far as national pressures are concerned, the Council appears to be more lenient towards countries with higher levels of Euroscepticism. This is in line with Baerg and Hallerberg's (2016) findings, but the effects fail to reach the nominal level of statistical significance. Before 2010, more left-leaning governments saw their recommendations more extensively modified by the Council. The expected number of changed recommendations increases by 15.7 percentage points for governments whose position moves a standard deviation to the left (approximately a shift equivalent to when D66 replaced the Pim Fortuyn List in the Balkenende government in the Netherlands in October 2002). Eurosceptic governments and left-leaning governments also appear to induce the Council to strengthen the recommendations, before and after the European Semester, respectively. But these effects are marginally significant and substantively weak.

6.4 Conclusion

When the Commission's proposals for CSRs reach the desks of the ministers in one of the conference rooms of the Justus Lipsius or Europa buildings in Brussels, the haggling begins. These negotiations may appear disorderly, but this is only on the surface. On an aggregate level, our innovative text analysis indicates that the Council has amended almost two-thirds of the Commission's proposals. And, perhaps counterintuitively, it has strengthened rather than weakened the proposed CSRs.

These patterns vary significantly across time and countries, though, and they can be explained primarily by the economic and supranational pressures surrounding policymakers. First, ministers intervene more extensively in the proposed recommendations when the economic conditions of the target country or across Europe worsen. Lower growth, higher inflation, and economic crisis are associated with greater ministerial activism, without however taking a specific direction of change. Second, the supranational bargaining dynamic matters a great deal. The configuration of preferences within the Council and vis-à-vis the Commission shapes both the extent and nature of Council amendments. A more divided Council and a more extreme Commission are associated with greater changes. If the position of government which is pivotal for adopting these proposals shifts to the left, the Council weakens the CSRs. And recommendations addressed to countries that exert greater influence within the Council, via voting or budget contributions, are more likely to be watered down (the effects of these latter factors remain statistically weak, however, as we also found in Chapter 4). Third, these political pressures are powerfully counterbalanced by the risks of incurring reputational losses and undermining the credibility of the whole preventive surveillance system. Ministers, therefore, intervene more actively and strengthen the Commission's proposals when the addressee country has a track record of fiscal profligacy, exemplified primarily by high debt-to-GDP ratios. Such strengthening was more likely in the pre-European Semester period, probably to balance the limited prominence assigned to the debt criterion in the determination of excessive deficits and the opening of the related corrective procedure in this period. We will analyse these aspects in Chapter 8.

Around July of each year, the Council gives its final endorsement to the CSRs. In Chapter 7, we investigate the determinants of national compliance with these recommendations.

7 *Navigating the Pressures of Preventive Compliance*

… the necessity to limit our deficit and public debt, [so that Italy will] be seen by Europe not as the suspicious source of infection, but as, again, a point of strength

Mario Monti, Prime Minister of Italy (2011–2013)

We are here to find solutions through dialogue and that is the spirit in which the letter is intended.

Pierre Moscovici, Commissioner for Economic Affairs (2014–2019)

As soon as his government was sworn in on 16 November 2011, in the midst of the euro area crisis, Italian Prime Minister Mario Monti pledged his commitment to implement the specific recommendations that have been addressed to his country and to do what he called his 'homework' on budget discipline and structural reforms. Such measures were required by the Commission and the Council for a long time and they could not be postponed for much longer (Sacchi 2015). In a few months, between December 2011 and July 2012, the Monti cabinet reformed the pension system and the labour market and proposed a package of liberalization that Italian governments have ignored for years. Moreover, it ensured fiscal consolidation and the achievement of the medium-term objective of structural budget balance by 2013.

This performance is the exception rather than the rule, not only for Italy but also for the other EU countries. Almost half of the recommendations in the period between 2002 and 2019 have been either disregarded or scarcely considered and even the introduction of the European Semester – a more structured system of policy coordination between the EU and national governments – has not ameliorated the implementation record.

In this chapter, we explain what drives the national implementation of these country-specific recommendations (CSRs) and we assess whether there are differences between the periods preceding and following the introduction of the European Semester.[1] Although it is an increasingly popular topic of scholarly investigation, most studies cover either specific countries or policies, or they are limited to the post-European Semester period (e.g. Al-Kadi and Clauwaert 2019; Bokhorst 2022; Darvas and Leandro 2015; D'Erman et al. 2022; Di Mascio et al. 2019; Eihmanis 2018; Guardiancich and Guidi 2020; Mariotto and Franchino 2020). Several works point to the limited effectiveness of the European Semester in light of the poor implementation record (Al-Kadi and Clauwaert 2019; Darvas and Leandro 2015; Efstathiou and Wolff 2019; Hennis 2022), and some emphasize how economic conditions and financial pressure stimulate the implementation of recommended reforms. For instance, Guardiancich and Guidi (2020), Di Mascio et al. (2019), and Darvas and Leandro (2015) find that governments tend to implement more recommendations when they are experiencing pressures from the market. Other studies, instead, analyze how political factors, such as the positions of the governments along the economic left–right and anti–pro integration divides, have driven implementation in some countries, such as Latvia (Eihmanis 2018) and Italy (Mariotto and Franchino 2020). Efstathiou and Wolff (2019), so far the most systematic research even though limited to the 2013–2018 period, find that the rate of implementation improves with the worsening of the economic conditions and the tightening of market pressures, but such a rate is also associated with the quality of national governance and the fragmentation of government coalitions.

Country-specific recommendations have been introduced with the adoption of the Stability and Growth Pact (SGP) in 1997, with the first set being issued in 2002. Yet, extant works ignore these early recommendations perhaps because they were not issued within the more structured process of policy coordination, represented by the European Semester, and they tended to focus more on budgetary measures that addressed excessive deficits. On the other hand, as already discussed in Chapter 6, the recommendations issued under the European Semester system deal with a wider variety of policies and rely upon additional sanctioning mechanisms, such as the excessive (macroeconomic) imbalance procedure and, perhaps,

[1] This chapter extends the study of Mariotto (2022).

stronger peer pressure or persuasive argumentation. Yet, the recommendations of the two periods share also important commonalities as they are both intended to enhance surveillance and coordination of economic policies.

We cover the full set of recommendations released between 2002 and 2019, thus we offer a unique opportunity to compare and contrast expectations of how economic conditions, enforcement costs, and electoral pressures shape national implementation, both before and after the entry into force of the European Semester. To measure compliance, we extend to the pre-European Semester the approach employed by the Commission to evaluate the implementation of the recommendations adopted during the European Semester period. We show that proximity to electoral contests is associated with lower rates of implementation, even though this effect weakens after the establishment of the European Semester. In 2002–2010, inflationary pressures acted as drivers of compliance with recommendations in euro area countries and as obstacles to compliance in non-euro area countries. After the introduction of the European Semester, it was the euro area crisis that triggered a fuller implementation of the recommended measures. Moreover, governments adopted especially those actions that were associated with a more established system for sanctioning noncompliance.

Raw country power has had different implications. Countries with higher voting power were initially less compliant. Later on, economically larger countries complied more.

7.1 Why Do Member States Implement Recommendations?

7.1.1 Economic Conditions and Euro Area Membership

Scholars offer two contending mechanisms for the impact of economic factors on reforms. A well-established research tradition sees reforms as the silver lining of economic crises (Drazen and Grilli 1993). When countries face difficult economic conditions, such as recessions, high inflation, and fiscal imbalances, they have more incentives to remove obstacles to policy change and undertake reforms. Although there are several reasons developed in the literature (Drazen and Easterly 2001), the variant that is relevant to our inquiry argues that only when the economic situation has sufficiently deteriorated do policymakers perceive that the solution requires a major policy change rather than transitory measures. Empirical evidence on this so-called 'benefit of the crises' argument suggests that the nature of the crisis significantly affects the likelihood of reforms (see, for example, Agnello et al., 2015). For Drazen and Grilli (1993), the severe costs of high inflation and the related emergency provide the incentives for the resolution of social conflicts and, thus, facilitate the introduction of economic measures. However, crises originating from current account deficits, budget deficits, or negative per capita growth rates do not appear to operate in the same way. Perhaps these differences can be explained by the difficulty of dealing with different types of crises.

Other empirical studies have found evidence that other macroeconomic factors stimulate the implementation of reforms. In particular, recessions, high unemployment rates, and low potential economic growth play an important role in promoting the necessary consensus for financial, capital, banking, and trade reforms (Agnello et al. 2015; Dias da Silva, Givone, and Sondermann 2018). In sum, we expect that *the worse the economic conditions of a country, the more likely its government will implement the European recommendations* (H7.1a).

What if this country is a member of the euro area? As extensively discussed in Chapter 5, countries that share a common currency may be more exposed to the negative externalities arising from the fiscal indiscipline of fellow member states. If the central bank has a strong mandate of keeping inflation under control, these externalities may take the form of higher interest rates, currency appreciation, current account imbalances, financial contagion, default, and lower capital accumulation. But, because of the irrevocably fixed nominal exchange rates, deteriorating economic conditions may diffuse more rapidly across members of a monetary union, leading, in turn, to lower purchasing power, higher unemployment, fiscal imbalances, and, in the long run, capital outflows. Sure, there are glaring economic differences among euro area countries (Copelovitch, Frieden, and Walter 2016; Walter, Ray, and Redeker 2020), but, in the aftermath of the launch of the European Monetary Union, inflation rates and government bonds' yields converged, affecting extensively the workings of the financial markets. These trends however reversed with the sovereign debt crisis, and reducing yield differentials and the vulnerable exposure to the vagaries of financial markets, especially in the euro area, became a top priority to mitigate the knock-on effects on borrowing costs. In other words, when the economic conditions are difficult, euro area governments are more likely to feel pressure from supranational institutions, fellow governments, and the financial markets to implement the European recommendations. In other words, *the worse the economic conditions of a Euro area country, the more likely its government will implement the European recommendations* (H7.1b).

Other scholars argue instead that worsening economic conditions hinder structural and fiscal reforms because governments have a smaller room for manoeuvre to compensate the social groups that are negatively affected. For instance, Lodge and Rodriguez-Vives (2013) contend that fiscal and macroeconomic conditions appear to influence governments' success in sustaining lengthy fiscal consolidation. This argument finds support in the literature on the implementation of the SGP. The several episodes of recession and economic downturn experienced by member states since its entry into force appear to be associated with the lack of compliance with the deficit and the debt rules, corroborating the view that crises impede the implementation of policy reforms (De Haan, Berger, and Jansen 2004; Heipertz and Verdun 2010). Hansen (2015), for instance, finds that the rates of unemployment and GDP growth are the two major factors behind the violation of the debt and deficit criteria.[2] This line of reasoning can therefore be extended to the preventive side of the EU economic governance, leading to the contending expectation that *the worse the economic conditions of a country, the less likely its government will implement the European recommendations* (H7.1c).

7.1.2 Costs of Noncompliance

Consider now another important source of supranational pressure: the rules for sanctioning noncompliance. After the introduction of the European Semester, recommendations fall under four categories.

[2] These recommendations are annually released country-specific soft laws that leave extensive national discretion for implementation, hence comparisons with the broader literature on EU compliance, especially concerning directives, should be taken with due caution. Neverthless, it is worth pointing out that Pircher and Loxbo (2020) show that, between 1997 and 2007, higher economic growth is associated with greater compliance in transposing EU single market directives. On the other hand, Toshkov (2007) finds that unemployment does not affect the transposition of social policy directives in Central and Eastern Europe.

The first group includes recommendations that are based on the preventive regulation of the SGP. This type of multilateral surveillance is centred around budgetary positions. Noncompliance could eventually lead the Council to open an excessive deficit procedure and demand corrective measures (this procedure will be extensively investigated in Chapter 8). All the recommendations for the 2002–2010 period fall under this category. The second group of recommendations is designed to prevent macroeconomic imbalances as determined by a scoreboard of indicators. Similarly, noncompliance may lead the Council to open an excessive imbalance procedure as detailed in the six-pack Regulation 1176/2011. The third group is hybrid. Its recommendations have implications for both budgetary positions and macroeconomic imbalances. Finally, the last group of recommendations falls under the general rubric of integrated guidelines. These are more general, spanning social, education, infrastructure, and energy policies. No corrective procedure is associated with noncompliance with some specific benchmarks.

Noncompliance with recommendations designed to address budgetary positions is considered a more serious violation of the premises upon which the euro area is built than noncompliance with the other types of recommendations. Aside from the economics of negative externalities arising from fiscal profligacy, which we extensively discussed in Chapter 5, European politicians have clearly assigned primacy to sanction noncompliance with fiscal rules. The correction of excessive deficits was set out in Article 126 of the Treaty on the Functioning of the European Union and its Protocol on the excessive deficit procedure. The related regulation was adopted in 1993, well before the adoption of the SGP, and the preventive and corrective procedures have been extensively revised as we have discussed in Chapter 4. Regardless of whether the oversight of national finances is effective (this will be discussed in Chapter 8), the reputational losses associated with noncompliance with recommendations related to budgetary positions are likely to be larger than those associated with the other types of recommendations.

Consider the following example. In 2018, the Italian government introduced a new early retirement scheme, which would have caused 'a risk of significant deviation from the preventive arm requirement', according to the Commission (2019). The supranational executive threatened to propose the opening of an excessive deficit procedure.

After intense negotiations between Giovanni Tria, the Italian Minister of Finance, Pierre Moscovici, and Valdis Dombrovskis, the Commissioners respectively for Economic and Financial Affairs and for Financial Services, the Italian government agreed to a deficit reduction from 2.4 to 2.04 per cent of GDP by cutting pension spending and delaying the introduction of the new scheme, as required by the CSRs (Guardiancich and Guidi 2020). In other words, the government ended up partially complying with the recommendations, under the threat of the excessive deficit procedure. It is less likely that we would observe a similar outcome in the case of integrated guideline recommendations since legislators have not even bothered to adopt a corrective procedure.

An alternative explanation emphasizes policy complexity to explain differences in implementation. According to this interpretation, measures that are related to budgetary positions or macroeconomic imbalances are less problematic to implement because they are less complex than the measures on employment and economic policies, which are primarily listed in the integrated guidelines. This premise is untenable, however. As the earlier example illustrates, SGP-based recommendations do not refer only to issues concerning budgetary positions, but they may also refer to feverishly complex topics such as pension reforms and other measures designed to pursue the long-term sustainability of public finances. These measures are far from being simple to implement.

Hence, we expect that *the higher the costs of noncompliance with a given European recommendation, the more likely the government will implement it* (H7.2). The different corrective procedures associated with recommendations related to budgetary positions, macroeconomic imbalances, and other issues reflect these costs of noncompliance. In formal models of the general EU Treaty-based infringement procedure, they would be equivalent to sanctioning costs (König and Mäder 2014) or litigating costs (Fjelstul and Carrubba 2018), which are associated with greater compliance.

7.1.3 Electoral Pressures

Last, national electoral pressures may, as well, affect the implementation of European recommendations – a factor that is mostly ignored in the literature on the implementation of the SGP. Any reform is associated with costs and benefits and re-election-seeking national politicians are keenly aware of the need to ensure that their supporters either benefit or are compensated for the costs arising from such reforms. Electoral pressures build upon retrospective voting behaviour (Key 1966) and anticipatory representation (Mansbridge 2003). In concise terms, voters tend to reward or punish government parties in the upcoming elections in light of their performance in the more recent past. Anticipating this, governments are more likely to take those actions that they believe voters will reward in the next election. And these actions may include the delivery of precisely those electoral pledges that put those parties in office. The more the government parties' actions deviate from these pledges, the more they are likely to be sanctioned by their voters.

We can plausibly assume that we are likely to observe European recommendations in precisely those areas where government parties are more reluctant to act, possibly because of the costs that these reforms may impose on their constituencies. Measures that are coherent with the objectives of preventive surveillance and deliver benefits to government supporters would be adopted and, therefore, we would not see them in the list of European recommendations. Said differently, European recommendations are likely to advise measures that deviate from the political agenda of government parties. Because of retrospective voting behaviour and anticipatory representation, we should, therefore, expect that *the closer the elections, the less likely a government will implement the European recommendations* (H7.3). Indeed, Efstathiou and Wolff (2019) find that the implementation rate of recommendations lowers in the proximity of elections.[3]

7.2 Measuring Compliance and Its Determinants

7.2.1 Rate of Progress in Implementing the Recommendations

We have constructed a measure of the implementation of a recommendation in two steps. First, as we explained in Chapter 6, we have identified the *major recommending provisions* in all the CSRs

[3] Between 1994 and 2004, elections appear to have had a delaying (accelerating) effect on the transposition of EU transport directives if they occur at the beginning (end) of the transposition period (Kaeding 2008). Even the use of the infringement procedure is delayed by the Commission in the proximity of elections (Cheruvu 2022).

issued between 2002 and 2019.[4] These provisions differ and, surely, a request to comply with the fiscal reference values is more demanding than one asking to adopt data collection guidelines. However, despite these differences, we have decided to avoid (arbitrarily) weighting recommendations. Second, since 2011, the Commission has published country reports on the implementation of CSRs – eight months after they are adopted. The *Progress rate* of each recommendation is evaluated on a three-level ordinal scale[5]: one (no progress) if a member state has not implemented the recommendation, two (some progress) if some implementation has occurred, and three (full progress) if the recommendation has been fully adopted. We extended this evaluation to the CSRs released between 2002 and 2010.[6]

Although there might be some reliability issues, scholars who have used these assessments, such as Efstathiou and Wolff (2019) and Al-Kadi and Clauwaert (2019), consider them free from strategic considerations, given the information-rich environment surrounding economic coordination (European Court of Auditors 2018).[7] This assumption is particularly warranted for the CSRs since the evaluations are supported by in-depth reports and publicly available statistics. Admittedly, an annual evaluation might underestimate the rate of implementation, especially if some measures require more time to be put into effect. Indeed, since 2018 the Commission has provided multiannual assessments, but they are still in their embryonic form

[4] The Commission began yearly assessment of the convergence or stability programmes on the basis of the CSRs in 2002. For more details, see the online appendix to this chapter.

[5] Since 2014 the Commission has been using a five-point scale: 'no progress', 'limited progress', 'some progress', 'substantial progress', and 'full progress'. Despite the loss of some information, we adopt a three-point scale to facilitate comparison across the two periods. Following the European Parliament's colour code, 'limited progress' is assigned to 'no progress', while 'substantial progress' to 'full progress' (European Parliament 2013). We run an analysis with a five-level progress rate as a robustness test (see Table A6.6 in the online appendix).

[6] The online appendix to this chapter explains the coding rules to measure the *Progress rate* from the official documents and it reports descriptive statistics about the implementation record across countries and years. Inter-coder agreement in measuring implementation of the recommendations released before the introduction of the European Semester is 78 per cent greater than would be expected by chance.

[7] Al-Kadi and Clauwaert (2019) discuss how the Commission's evaluations reflect actual implementation.

and cannot be used for our purposes (European Court of Auditors 2020). For the time being, tracking the annual progress of implementation is a more reliable measure of actual operationalization. Since the recommendations prior to the introduction of the European Semester focus solely on budgetary positions, we run two separate analyses for the periods preceding and following this enhanced process of coordination. This allows us to bring into better light our contribution given that most of the extant analyses focus on the European Semester.

We have collected information on the rate of progress of 1,481 major recommending provisions, of which 488 were adopted before the introduction of the European Semester and 993 after.[8] Figure 7.1 displays the *Progress rate* by country and period. Overall, it is poor. Only 12 per cent of the recommendations are fully implemented, while 46 per cent of the time progress is limited. However, the progress rate varies significantly across countries and periods. Scandinavian and Baltic countries are the best implementers (aside from being fiscally sound for most of this period). After the introduction of the European Semester, progress has worsened for most countries, except for Germany and Ireland. This however could be due to both the broader nature and, perhaps, greater ambition of the recommendations, as well as the strengthened monitoring functions of the Commission, which may lead to stricter assessments of the rate of progress.

7.2.2 *Determinants of Compliance*

For the competing expectations on economic conditions and reforms, we consider several measures (most of them already used in Chapter 6): *Inflation rate*, *Unemployment rate*, and *GDP growth rate*, as well as the period indicator for the *Economic crisis*. The rate of inflation was at the core of the traditional 'benefit of the crises' argument, according to which high rates of inflation trigger economic reforms (Drazen and Grilli 1993; Drazen and Easterly 2001). The other proxies have been used by Hansen (2015),

[8] CSRs are not issued when a country has signed an adjustment programme. For instance, no CSRs have been issued for Portugal between 2011 and 2013. During the European Semester period, Greece has received only two recommendations in 2019.

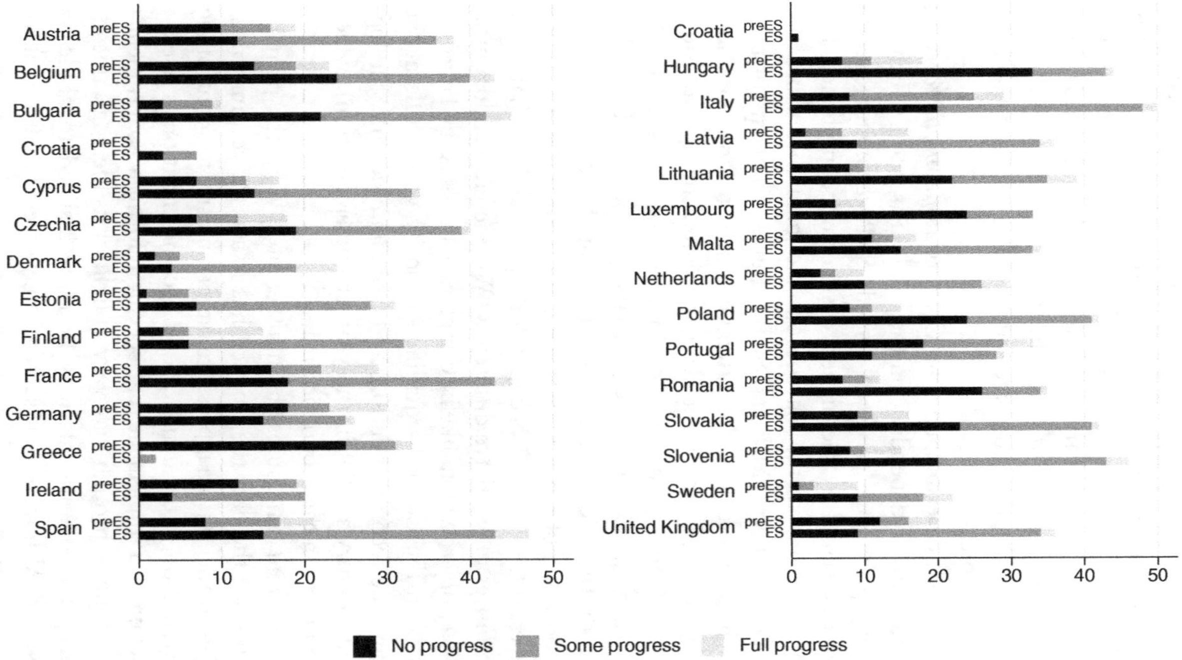

Figure 7.1 Progress rate by member state and period

Note: preES = 2002–2010 period; ES = 2011–2019 period. No CSRs are issued for countries under an adjustment programme.

Source: Mariotto (2022). Reprinted with permission.

Efstathiou and Wolff (2019), and Lodge and Rodriguez-Vives (2013). Unemployment rates, for instance, vary significantly across EU countries, from 1.9 to 26 per cent, indicating that economic distress along this dimension is far from trivial. As in Chapter 6, *Economic crisis* captures the exceptional economic conditions triggered by the euro area crisis from the first Greek bailout in 2010 to 2015. The variable *Euro area* takes the value of one if the country uses the single currency when a recommending provision has been issued, and zero otherwise.

As supranational determinants, the *Costs of noncompliance* vary across four categories, depending on the legal basis upon which the recommending provision has been issued. SGP recommendations should be characterized by the highest costs of noncompliance, followed by those related to the macroeconomic imbalance procedure (MIP) and those blending MIP and SGP features. The costs of noncomplying with the so-called integrated guidelines recommendations should be the lowest. Data on the type of recommending provisions come from the Country-Specific Recommendation database of the European Parliament's Economic Governance Support Unit.

Following the broader literature on EU compliance (e.g. Börzel et al. 2010; Börzel, Hofmann, and Panke 2012; Fjelstul and Carrubba 2018; Mbaye 2001), we also account for the possibility that more powerful countries may behave differently. We, therefore, add a measure of *Voting power*, which, like in Chapters 3 and 6, is the Penrose–Banzhaf index in the Council's qualified majority voting rule at the time of issuing the recommendation, and *Economic size* (i.e. the logarithm of the country's GDP in the year of implementation), which accounts for power in the economic area.

Electoral proximity measures the number of days to the planned next election since the date the Council has issued the recommendation.[9] We add further national pressure factors, mostly for controlling purposes. Even though the issuance of a recommendation is itself a sign of reluctance to implement that specific reform, a government's propensity to follow through may vary in light of its ideological leaning. Pro-European governments may be more inclined to abide by these suggestions. Although some scholars may object (see Chapter 8), right-leaning executives may be keener implementers given the general

[9] Data come from Döring and Manow (2019).

emphasis of surveillance on fiscal sustainability and prudence.[10] We control for these potential confounders by including a government's *Left–right position* and *Anti–pro EU position.*[11] Finally, following several broader analyses (e.g. Fjelstul and Carrubba 2018; Mbaye 2001; Spendzharova and Versluis 2013; Williams 2018), we account for the national pressures arising from public opinion by including the variable *Public support* that we derived from the Eurobarometer surveys and used in Chapter 6.[12]

7.3 Explaining Compliance with Recommendations

Each recommending provision is nested within a country and a year, and the dependent variable has three ordered categories. Although the number of second-level units (year) is not large on average,[13] we

[10] The broader EU compliance literature suggests that the presence and direction of these ideological effects are highly policy-dependent (e.g. Falkner et al. 2005; Jensen 2007; Spendzharova and Versluis 2013; Toshkov 2007, 2008; Williams 2018).

[11] In this chapter, we rely on the comparative manifesto dataset (Volkens et al. 2020) to construct the EU (the difference between categories per108 and per110) and left–right (the *rile* scale) positions. More pro-EU and right-wing positions have higher values. For the few missing data, we used the scores from either the previous elections, the originating party (in the case of fission), or, after being re-scaled, from Döring and Manow (2021). For the cabinets of Monti in Italy in 2012 and of Cioloș in Romania in 2016, we used the positions of the parties in the parliamentary support coalition. We use time-weighted and, like in Chapter 3, legislative seat-weighted means.

[12] The online appendix to this chapter provides a summary of the variables and descriptive statistics.

[13] The literature suggests various thresholds, often in the range of 15–30 observations per group, as necessary to accurately estimate standard errors (Hox, Moerbeek, and van de Schoot 2017). But Monte-Carlo simulations conducted by Clarke (2008) indicate that even when there are as few as two observations per group on average, researchers may run the risk of producing downward biased standard errors when using single-level models. Underestimation is more problematic for non-linear models than for linear models. However, as Clarke notes, 'the multilevel approach still generates valid fixed parameter estimates and standard error with two or more observations per group' (2008, 757). To our knowledge, there are no simulations with ordinal dependent variables. Our dataset has on average 2.5 (in the 2002–2010 period) and 4.7 (in the 2011–2019 period) observations per second-level grouping, which are considered to be robust for unbalanced data and discrete outcomes. We have therefore opted for a country- and year-nested model.

use a multilevel ordinal logistic regression analysis with a random intercept at the country and year level. In the online appendix, we investigate whether the results are robust under alternative model specifications.

Table 7.1 reports the results of the analysis on the determinants of the implementation of the recommendations released in the 2002–2010 period and under the European Semester. We first consider electoral pressures (H7.3). We then move on to the noncompliance costs (H7.2), while we leave the impact of economic conditions (H7.1) last as it requires a more detailed discussion.

Electoral pressures and other national factors: As far as the period 2002–2010 is concerned, the closer the election, the poorer the implementation record. Electoral proximity has a small but robust impact on the progress rate. The probability of full implementation decreases by 5.2 percentage points when elections are scheduled four months rather than two years after the Council's issuance of the recommendation. This result is in line with anticipatory representation and retrospective voting. Assuming that a European recommendation represents measures where government parties are reluctant to act, politicians will procrastinate to avoid electoral sanctions in the proximity of elections. Note however that the effect has weakened since the introduction of the European Semester, which was a response to the global financial crisis and the euro area crisis.

As for the other national factors, we find a significant association between public Euroscepticism and compliance after 2010. The relation is not substantively large. A standard deviation decrease in public support (approximately the difference between Romanian support in 2017 and 2013) is associated with an increase of 1.7 percentage points in the probability of fully implementing a recommendation. This relation is also found in studies on the use of the treaty-based infringement procedure (Fjelstul and Carrubba 2018; Mbaye 2001; Sczepanski and Börzel 2023) but, as we will see, in our circumstances it simply reflects the fact that several measures have been implemented in the midst of the euro area crisis when public support was at historically low levels. Instead, governmental positions along the left–right and the anti–pro EU dimensions do not appear to be associated with the progress in implementing these recommendations.

Costs of noncompliance: The costs associated with noncompliance, resulting from the sanctioning mechanism, have a significant effect on

Table 7.1 ***Determinants of compliance with recommendations***

	Period	
	2002–2010	2011–2019
Economic and supranational factors		
GDP growth rate	-0.00209	0.0279
	(0.0293)	(0.0421)
Inflation rate	-0.146*	0.0633
	(0.0634)	(0.0995)
Unemployment rate	0.0177	0.0441
	(0.0407)	(0.0349)
Economic crisis	0.206	0.694*
	(0.302)	(0.338)
Euro area	-1.520**	0.255
	(0.476)	(0.387)
Inflation rate × Euro area	0.347**	0.195
	(0.134)	(0.138)
Economic crisis × Euro area		-0.209
		(0.391)
Supranational factors		
Costs of noncompliance		
MIP		-0.752**
		(0.264)
SGP/MIP		-1.412**
		(0.392)
Integrated guidelines		-0.677**
		(0.228)
Voting power	-0.152*	-0.152
	(0.0677)	(0.118)
Economic size	0.176	0.297†
	(0.130)	(0.176)
National factors		
Left–right position	0.00795	0.00400
	(0.0123)	(0.00811)
Anti–pro EU position	0.0113	-0.000257
	(0.0246)	(0.0209)
Public support	-0.01000	-0.0171*
	(0.00736)	(0.00718)
Electoral proximity	0.184*	0.116†
	(0.0828)	(0.0677)
Constant (cut 1)	-0.588	0.780
	(0.815)	(0.866)

Table 7.1 (*cont.*)

	Period	
	2002–2010	2011–2019
Constant (cut 2)	0.799	4.306**
	(0.811)	(0.882)
var(Country)	0.202	0.327**
	(0.154)	(0.162)
var(Year)	0.301	0.422**
	(0.269)	(0.162)
Observations	488	994
Number of countries	27	28
Log-pseudolikelihood	–489.5	-800

Note: Standard errors are in parentheses. Reference category for the costs of noncompliance: SGP. $^{**}p < 0.01$, $^{*}p < 0.05$, $^{\dagger}p < 0.1$.

the rate of progress (H7.2, recall that this expectation applies only to the 2011–2019 period). Figure 7.2 displays the predicted probabilities of the degrees of implementation across the different sanctioning regimes, keeping the other covariates at their mean values.

The predicted probability of fully complying with a recommending provision that is based on the SGP is 9.3 per cent, while it is only 4.8 per cent for MIP recommendations, 2.6 per cent for combined ones, and 5.8 per cent for the integrated guidelines. It is also highly likely that we see some progress towards implementing SGP recommendations: The predicted probability of partial compliance exceeds 60 per cent. Notable instead is the poor performance of MIP-based recommendations. The short history of this regime and the complex use of scoreboard indicators to evaluate progress may obfuscate the rationality for action and undermine the credibility of sanctioning. Or the complex nature of these issues may lead the Commission to particularly pessimistic assessments about progress. The two mechanisms are not necessarily mutually exclusive and may be related.

Last, results are contradictory as far as raw country power is concerned. Prior to the European Semester, countries with greater voting power were more likely to disregard the recommendations. This relation is commonly found in studies on standard infringements

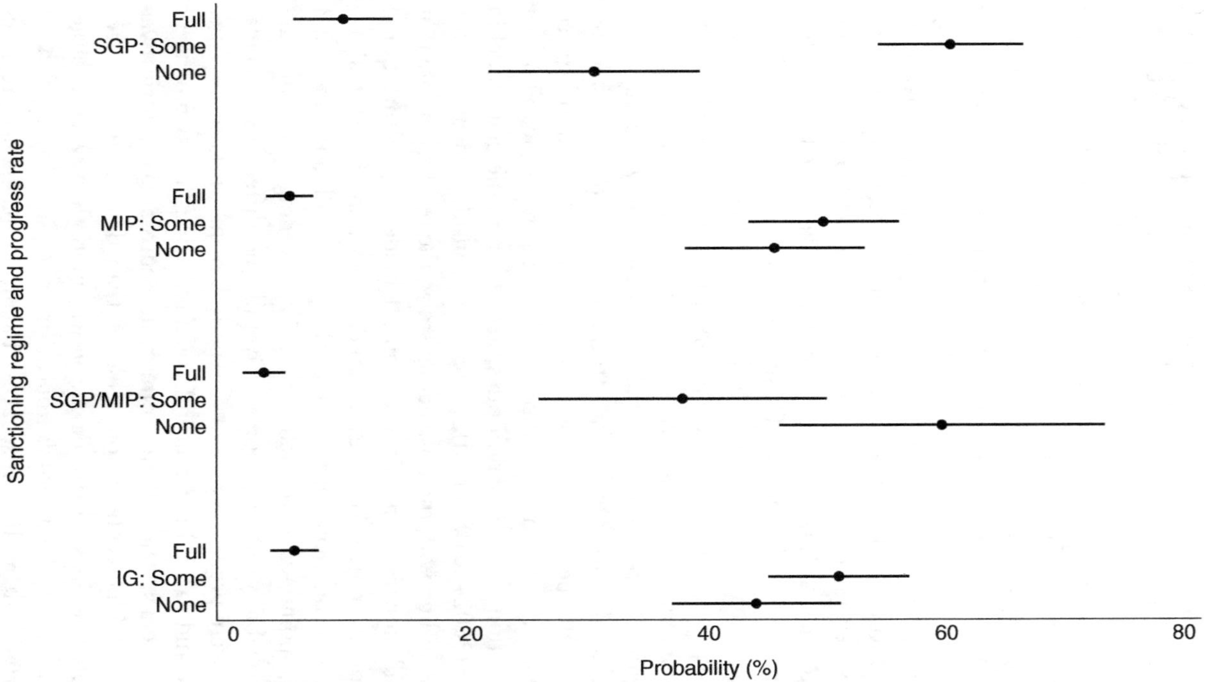

Figure 7.2 Predicted probabilities of compliance across sanctioning regimes
Note: SGP = Stability and Growth Pact; MIP = macroeconomic imbalance procedure; SGP/MIP = combination of SGP and MIP; IG = integrated guidelines. 2011–2019 period only.

(Börzel et al. 2010; Börzel, Hofmann, and Panke 2012; Fjelstul and Carrubba 2018; Jensen 2007; Mbaye 2001; Sczepanski and Börzel 2023). Going back to the comparison between Germany and Sweden we made in Chapter 6, the likelihood of no implementation increases by 16.9 percentage points when the addressed country has the voting power of the former, compared to that of the latter. Perhaps more powerful countries faced a less credible threat of sanctions as they would have been capable of assembling a blocking minority. Recall that we discussed in Chapter 5 how a coalition built around France and Germany managed to stall the progress of the excessive deficit procedure in November 2003. Such a coalition would be harder to assemble during the European Semester period because of the introduction of reverse qualified majority voting in the Council. Indeed, larger countries, at least in terms of economic size, have been slightly more compliant in this period. Comparing the size of the economies of, again, Germany and Sweden, the likelihood of no implementation now *decreases* by 10.8 percentage points when the addressed country has the economic size of the former, compared to that of the latter.

Economic conditions and euro area: Consider now the impact of economic conditions. On balance, the evidence appears to support the 'benefit of the crises' theory (H7.1a) more than the obstructing story (H7.1c). Figure 7.3 displays the predicted probabilities of implementation across inflation rates, derived from the first model in Table 7.1 (2002–2010 period), for countries inside and outside the euro area. In line with the obstructing story, the results indicate that a more inflationary economic environment hindered implementation among non-euro area countries: a standard deviation increase above the country-recommendation mean of the rate of inflation (about 2.3 percentage points) is associated with a 7.2 percentage point increase in the probability of no progress. Overall, the differences in inflation rates were pretty notable in this period, from a negative 1.7 per cent in Ireland to 15.3 per cent in Latvia, reflecting the asymmetry of economic shocks. The inflation rate in non-euro area countries was on average 1.5 percentage points higher than the rate in euro area countries, while the standard deviation was more than twice as large. Several Central and Eastern European member states were also hit particularly hard by the crisis, facing balance-of-payments pressures and experiencing inflation rates that were on average more than two and a half times larger than the rates in euro area countries.

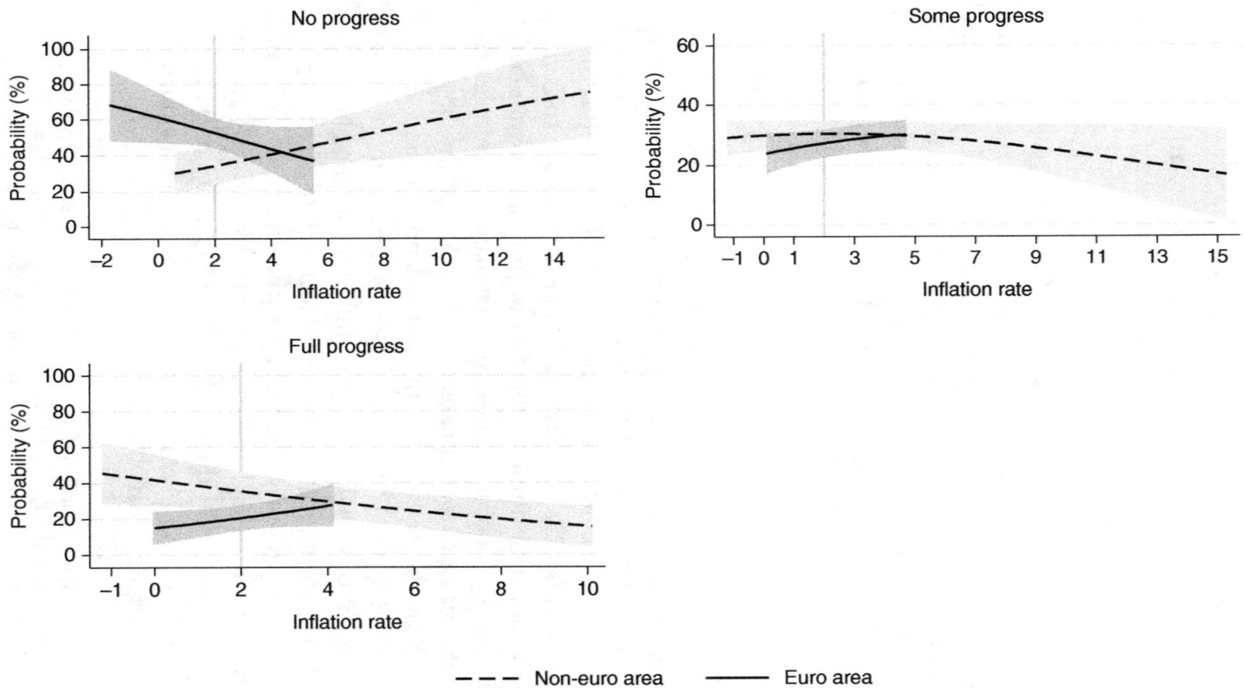

Figure 7.3 Predicted probabilities of compliance across euro area membership and inflation rates

Note: The curves extend over the observed rates of inflation only. The grey vertical line is at the 2 per cent medium-term inflation rate target set by the European Central Bank. 2002–2010 period.

However, higher inflation boosted compliance in euro area countries, in line with the 'benefit of the crises' theory (H7.1b). Keeping all other covariates at their means, the results indicate that if in a euro area country like Belgium, the rate of inflation exceeds the country-recommendation mean by one standard deviation, the probability that its government would fully implement the recommendations increases by 8.2 percentage points. On the other hand, if a non-euro area country such as Lithuania in this period were in the same situation, this probability would drop by 6.3 percentage points. Last, deflation or near-zero inflation, which are also signs of economic malaise, deterred compliance among euro area countries: a shift from 2 per cent inflation (the medium-term target set by the European Central Bank) to 0 per cent is associated with an 8.9 percentage point increase in the probability of no progress. Admittedly, deflation is rare, but it has been almost three times more frequent among euro area countries than non-euro area ones in this period.

To conclude, deflation aside, euro area countries experiencing relatively higher inflation face stronger pressures to address the possible loss of competitiveness and to implement politically contentious measures since they cannot avail themselves of currency depreciation. These governments may also face more intense pressure to comply from supranational institutions and fellow euro area governments, given their greater exposure to negative externalities. Countries outside the euro area can procrastinate.

Consider now the period after the introduction of the European Semester. In line with H7.1a, countries experiencing more difficult economic conditions, such as higher inflation or unemployment, are more likely to implement the recommendations, regardless of whether they have adopted the euro. But the economic crisis indicator is even more strongly associated with compliance. Keeping all the other covariates at their means, the probability of no implementation decreased by 11.9 percentage points during the turbulent years of the euro area crisis.[14]

[14] As robustness tests, we added to the models another measure of economic strain (the expected inability to pay and service the debt) and a measure of states' administrative capacity (the inflation-adjusted total government expenditure per capita). These variables do not reach statistical significance and the main results hold, see the online appendix.

7.4 Conclusion

What happens once the Council adopts the CSRs? Are they mostly ignored or are governments going to follow through? What explains differences in implementation? We have addressed these questions by analyzing an original dataset that includes the entire history of European recommendations, from 2002 to 2019. Assessed eight months after adoption, the overall record of implementation is underwhelming. Less than 60 per cent have been partially or fully implemented, and things have worsened after the introduction of the European Semester.

A combination of economic and electoral pressures, as well as the costs of noncompliance, are associated with these patterns. In general, worsening economic conditions tend to speed up implementation, supporting the thesis that economic reforms are the silver lining of crises. Exceptions have been the countries outside the euro area before the introduction of the European Semester. These mostly Central and Eastern European states were poor implementers despite the inflationary pressures. Exchange rate flexibility may have plausibly given them the luxury to procrastinate reforms, but, after 2010, they too fell into line. Before 2010, deflation had also been an obstacle to compliance in the euro area.

The proximity to elections poses obstacles to adopting recommended measures that are, by their very nature, costly to the governing parties. But these pressures appeared to have receded somewhat after 2010 – a period characterized by severe economic crises – notwithstanding the increased politicization that characterized the economic governance reforms that we analyzed in Chapter 5. In this period instead, the progress in implementing recommendations is associated with the noncompliance costs that the underlying sanctioning regime engenders: better for the recommendations based on the SGP (i.e. budgetary positions) than on the integrated guidelines. Budget-related recommendations are of much greater importance and are underpinned by an established set of rules to address noncompliance that, predating the SGP, were enshrined into the Treaty of Maastricht: the excessive deficit procedure. It is this important corrective mechanism that we turn our attention to in Chapter 8 of this part of the book.

8 *Causes and Consequences of Overseeing Fiscal Deficits*

In a society in which there are no class privileges, in which every man is legally equal to every other man, the concept of *pax publica* cannot fail to be recognized as preeminent and prevail over that of mere social peace.

Luigi Einaudi (2004 [1949])

The Pact helps a government to tie itself to the mast and resist the sirens who are trying to lure us to destruction with seductive songs of more state spending and bigger bureaucracies.

José Manuel Barroso, Portuguese Prime Minister (2002–2004) and President of the European Commission (2004–2014) (cited in Heipertz and Verdun 2010: 137)

While in exile in Switzerland between October 1943 and December 1944, Luigi Einaudi, perhaps one of the most renowned Italian liberal economists, who would later become president of the fledgling Italian Republic, was invited to give a series of lectures on social policy at the University of Geneva and the School of Engineering of Lausanne. Prompted by the recent publication of the Beveridge Report in November 1942, Einaudi, by no means a Keynesian or a fiscal dove, recognized the central role of the state in the provision of social insurance and emphasized how Bismarckian welfare systems will have to move beyond the instrumental objective of accommodating the demands of socialist movements that threaten social peace. The legitimacy of the regimes emerging from the tragedy of the war will have to depend on a *pax publica*, that is, an expanded affirmation of the democratic commitment to social insurance.

Such a commitment came in abundance. The average fiscal activity – the consolidated central government revenue and expenditure – of fourteen European countries, which would eventually be members of the European Union, increased from 41.8 per cent in 1950 to 76.7 per cent of GDP in 1991 when the twelve members of the then European Economic Community began negotiating the

Treaty of Maastricht. Public transfer payments, such as welfare and pension benefits, increased from 7.3 to 18.8 per cent of GDP. To finance such a massive increase in the public provision of social insurance, the consolidated general government gross debt increased from 38.3 to 68 per cent of GDP.[1]

Until the 1960s, high growth and low real interest rates facilitated the financing of these commitments and, concomitantly, engendered a reduction of public debt. But the adverse economic shocks of the 1970s and the anti-inflationary policies of the 1980s rendered debt management particularly arduous. High real interest rates, persistent slow growth, and high unemployment severely strained public finances (Franzese 2002: 166). Importantly, some governments struggled significantly more than others. By the time countries were negotiating the Treaty of Maastricht, the debt–GDP ratios in Belgium, Italy, Ireland, and Greece hovered at around or above 100 per cent, twice as much as those in France, Germany, Spain, and the UK. As shown by Franzese (2002: 166), political factors had a lot to do with these differences. This scholar unveils the political and economic determinants of the public debt dynamics in twenty OECD countries from the late 1950s to 1990. Starting from a benchmark model that accounts only for temporal and spatial effects, he proposes an encompassing political-economic model that improves by 39 per cent the share of explained variance in debt–GDP ratios. Assuming, rather heroically, that economic factors are fully exogenous to political decisions, between one-fourth and one-half of this improvement is due to political factors. One should therefore not be surprised that the second pillar of European economic governance in the Treaty of Maastricht was a procedure to correct excessive deficits, designed as a policy flanking the planned monetary union.

To briefly recap, starting in 1994, states had to report to the Commission twice a year their planned and actual (or estimated) levels of government deficit and debt for the current year and the preceding four years. If the Commission considers that an excessive deficit exists in a member state, it recommends that the Council of the EU (specifically, the Economic and Financial Affairs configuration) adopt a decision to that effect. An excessive deficit procedure is then opened and the Council issues recommendations to the member state concerned with a view to reducing the deficit within a given period.

[1] The data comes from Franzese (2002).

Failure to act leads to a ratcheting up of the pressure with further decisions up to the imposition of fines. The procedure is terminated once the Council abrogates its initial decision.

In this chapter, we address two key questions about implementation: What explains the opening and continuation of an excessive deficit procedure? What are the consequences of this supranational oversight for national public finances? Public spending has been the object of investigation of a rich array of political economy theories – each with its own measure of (national) political and economic pressures. To account for this vast scholarship, we expand significantly the set of measures that operationalize these factors. In this way, if we find that some supranational predictors exert influence, we will be more confident in our results.

8.1 Why Corrective Surveillance?

There are several scholarly narratives on the opening of the excessive deficit procedure and the decisions that have (or have not) been adopted after the onset of oversight. A few of these studies focus on the early period (Beetsma and Giuliodori 2010; De Haan, Berger, and Jansen 2004; Heipertz and Verdun 2010; van der Veer 2022), most concentrate on the euro area crisis and the succeeding years (Mérand 2022; Miró 2021; Pan, Hosli, and Lantmeeters 2023: 20–21; Sacher 2021; Schmidt 2016b: 1043–48; 2020: 138, 176–207; van der Veer 2022; Vanheuverzwijn 2017: 25–27). However, as far as we are aware, no scholarly work has tried to explain systematically the opening and continuation of the procedure since its establishment.

These are important questions because, to repeat, the actual numerical breach of the 3 per cent deficit-to-GDP ratio is neither a necessary nor a sufficient condition for determining the existence of an excessive deficit. It is not a necessary condition because the Commission can recommend to the Council to make such a determination also if the *planned* ratio exceeds the reference value, as is stated in both Article 126 of the TFUE and the Protocol on the excessive deficit procedure. In other words, the *risk* of an excessive deficit embedded in a governmental fiscal plan can trigger the opening of the procedure. In theory, one could see the Council establishing the existence of an excessive deficit even if the relevant country's public finances are compliant with the reference value at the time of such determination. The actual numerical breach is also not sufficient since there may be extenuating circumstances that would advise against determining the existence of an excess. Indeed, as we have extensively discussed in Chapters 3–5, several divisive issues that have characterized the negotiations over policy design have been centred on the exact nature of such extenuating circumstances.

In light of the complexities and uncertainties surrounding this procedure, one could sympathize with Jones's (2013: 157) assertion that 'deciding whether a government is actually running an excessive deficit is essentially a political choice'. And even if one sees this statement as taking a step too far, these complexities and uncertainties strongly suggest that the decisions to open and close a procedure are far from being purely technical and automatic affairs.

8.1.1 Compliance, Euro Area, and Economic Conditions

What is therefore likely to explain the opening and continuation of an oversight procedure? First, consider temporal and spatial effects, both country-specific and EU-wide, that are related to compliance. High *lagged and expected deficit-GDP ratios* should be positively associated with an open procedure and, if ministers are concerned about debt sustainability as well, high *lagged debt–GDP ratios* may also be positively associated with it. These are, in a nutshell, the criteria set out in Article 126 of the TFUE. Although uncodified, spatial concerns about the level of deficit *across* the whole EU may induce ministers to exercise greater vigilance. For similar reasons, *larger and euro area economies* may be subject to greater scrutiny because the EU-wide negative externalities associated with fiscal indiscipline in larger economies are greater, and euro area countries cannot take advantage of currency fluctuations to soften the transmission of these effects.

Moreover, as we have extensively discussed in Part II of the book, the provisions of this procedure allow for economic conditions to provide extenuating circumstances for the determination of an excess. Recall, for instance, that the 1997 corrective regulation of the SGP established that a deficit excess was deemed exceptional when resulting from an annual fall of real GDP of at least 2 per cent. We, therefore, account for *lagged and expected spending, revenues, and open-economy shocks*, which are derived from the basic economic tax-smoothing theory of the deficit dynamics (Franzese 2002: 128–35, 151), to affect the likelihood of opening a procedure.

That factors related to compliance and economic conditions affect oversight is not a given. References to discretionary, if not almost arbitrary, interpretation of the rules abound in the literature (e.g. Mérand 2022; Sacher 2021; Schmidt 2016b; Vanheuverzwijn 2017: 17).

8.1.2 National Pressures and Supranational Bargaining

Next, we account for national political pressures. Considering the general pro-European orientation of governments, commissioners and ministers may display a degree of reticence in determining the existence of an excessive deficit in cases of *public or governmental scepticism about the EU* in the addressee country. Alternatively, governments in these circumstances may feel less compelled to comply with these fiscal rules for either ideological reasons or electoral rewards. Indeed, public attitudes towards the EU and the political orientation of the concerned governments play no secondary role in the narratives on the implementation of fiscal surveillance (Mérand 2022; Miró 2021; Schmidt 2020: 138; van der Veer 2022). The procedure could also be used strategically. Governments may *choose* to be subject to supranational monitoring. A *right-leaning executive* facing the prospect of losing office may loosen its fiscal stance to purposely face oversight. It may then implement the tighter policy it actually prefers and shift the blame on the EU (admittedly, this behaviour should also be captured by lagged and expected deficits).

Last, opening and closing a procedure result from a process of supranational bargaining. Article 126 of the TFUE specifies that a qualified majority in the Council, excluding the vote of the government that is the addressee of the decision, is necessary for opening and closing an excessive deficit procedure. This procedure is equivalent to the qualified majority voting variant of the consultation procedure discussed in Chapters 4 and 6, without parliamentary involvement, where the minimum winning coalition includes the Commission and the governments that make up such a qualified majority. When deciding on the existence of an excessive deficit and opening a procedure, the pivotal Council member is the government that can form a blocking minority and is the least inclined to support the oversight. When deciding on the termination of the procedure, the pivotal Council member is the government that can form a blocking minority and is the least inclined to conclude the oversight. The coalitional dynamic within the Council is seldom the main focus of extant studies. The Commission, on the other hand, frequently takes centre stage. For instance, there is almost unanimous consensus that the turnover in 2014 from the centrist liberal Olli Rehn to the socialist Pierre Moscovici as the commissioner in charge of the procedure played no small role in shaping its more accommodating implementation (Mérand 2022; Miró 2021; Sacher 2021; Schmidt 2016b; 2020: 176–207; Vanheuverzwijn 2017).

8.1.3 Data and Measurement

We investigate both the probability and the exposure to oversight. In the models on the probability of oversight, the dependent variable (*Excessive deficit procedure – EDP)* takes the value of one for any year a country has been under surveillance and the value of zero otherwise. In the models on the exposure to oversight, the variable measures the proportion of a given year a country has been under surveillance. Between 1994 and 2019, the Council established the existence of an excessive deficit fifty-two times. The government deficit of every country, except for Estonia and Luxembourg, has been deemed excessive at least once, and in some cases twice or thrice. A procedure has lasted on average four years, from a minimum of about ten months (Germany in 1994–1995) to a maximum of ten years (Spain in 2009–2019).

For the lagged *Deficit* ratios, we use the measure employed in the excessive deficit procedure: the difference between the total expenditure and the total revenue of the general government, as defined in the European system of national and regional accounts, as a percentage of the GDP at current prices. Similarly, the measure of lagged gross public *Debt* as a percentage of GDP is the one employed for the procedure.[2] For the *Expected deficit*, we use the OECD and the European Commission forecast in the autumn of year $t-1$ for year t.[3] Spatial effects (*Average deficit* and *Expected average deficit*) are measured by the means of other EU countries' lagged or expected deficit ratios. Like in Chapters 6 and 7, *Economic size* is gauged by the logarithm of

[2] Data come from the AMECO database and the OECD for the 1993–1994 missing information. AMECO is linked to Eurostat, which is the source for the similar variables used in Chapters 3 and 6.

[3] The autumn (or, if missing, the spring) forecasts are used for all the variables based on economic expectations.

the GDP, while for euro area membership we use the binary indicator *Euro area* that takes the value of one if a country uses the euro in a given year, including the year preceding adoption, which is when the European Council approves the applications of membership.

To account for revenue, spending, and open-economy shocks to public finances, we use the lagged and expected *Real GDP growth rate*, *Unemployment rate*, and the interaction between *Trade openness* (exports plus imports of goods and services as a share of GDP) and the *Terms of trade* (the ratio of export prices to import prices).[4] To account for market concerns about a country's ability to pay and service the debt, we include the *Expected real interest rate*, that is, the difference between the annual average of the long-term government bond yields and the forecast of the GDP deflator in the autumn of year $t-1$ for year t.[5]

For the *Anti–pro EU position* and the *Left–right position* of a government, we use the same measures we employed in Chapter 7. Likewise for the variable *Public support*, however, we use the earliest Eurobarometer survey of each year. We interact the *Left–right position* with the *Replacement risk* of a government, which is the expected probability of losing office in a year (the inverse of the actual government duration) times the standard deviation of the government's left–right ideology across nine years, centred on the present year. This risk measures the probability of being replaced by ideologically different governments.[6] We interact government ideology also

[4] Data come from Eurostat and the World Bank and the forecasts from the OECD and the European Commission, except for *Expected trade openness* and missing values of *Expected terms of trade*, which are forecast by regressing the current value on two lags with country fixed effects.

[5] An optimizing government borrows wisely when the expected real growth rate exceeds the expected real interest rate because the ability to repay (the increased tax base associated with higher growth) is expected to exceed the total debt burden associated with the real interest rate. And it saves wisely if the opposite conditions hold. Franzese (2002: 150) uses the difference between the expected real interest and real growth rates to measure the expected ability to pay and service the debt. We disaggregate the two items since the latter is explicitly provided for in the legal provisions on economic governance. Forecasts are available from the OECD and the European Commission, while bond yields come from the OECD and the European Central Bank.

[6] This operationalization follows Franzese (2002: 148–49). In the case of more than one government a year, the hazard rate is weighted by the part of the year a government has been in office (caretaker cabinets and post-election government formation periods are disregarded). For presidential and

with the *Expected government duration*, which measures the risk of parliamentary dissolution. Here, we broadly follow the procedure employed by Fortunato and Loftis (2018). We first re-estimate Chiba, Martin, and Stevenson's (2015) competing risks model of government survival using an expanded dataset of 673 governments. We then employ a non-parametric bootstrap to produce a duration mean from a distribution of 1,000 predicted survival times for each cabinet. Next, we subtract from these values the number of days the cabinet has been in office at the time the budget for a given year has been submitted to parliament. If this value exceeds the constitutionally mandated deadline for legislative elections, it is trimmed back to such maximum duration.[7]

We use the economic left–right dimension of the comparative manifestos project to determine the positions of the pivotal governments for opening and terminating a procedure. According to the standard partisan theory of fiscal discipline, left-leaning governments are expected to run and, therefore, to be more tolerant of larger deficits than their right-leaning counterparts because their core supporters favour a larger government. Opening a procedure is then equivalent to a rightward policy shift, while terminating is a leftward shift. Starting from the yearly distribution of these left–right positions (i.e. the *Left–right position* variable introduced earlier), we have identified the positions of the governments that are pivotal for starting and terminating a procedure (i.e. a rightward and a leftward policy shift) with regard to each specific country. These positions are mostly country-specific because the government that is the potential addressee of a measure cannot vote.[8]

semipresidential systems, the hazard rate is the mean of the hazard rates of the president and the cabinet. Data on actual government duration comes from Döring and Manow (2021).

[7] More details are provided in the online appendix.

[8] Until the Treaty of Lisbon, the Council decided on the opening of a procedure by a qualified majority (Article 104.6 EC Treaty) and on its closing by a majority of two-thirds of the weighted votes of its members, excluding the concerned state (Article 104.13 EC Treaty). Since then, a qualified majority comprising at least 55 per cent of the Council members, representing at least 65 per cent of the combined population but excluding the concerned state, is necessary for both opening and closing the procedure (Articles 126.13 and 238.3a TFEU). Article 7 of the Fiscal Compact, an international treaty, establishes that a qualified majority of euro area countries is needed to reject a Commission's proposal concerning euro area

However, a government faces a different pivotal actor depending on its oversight status. Those that are not under oversight face this prospect as a function of the position of the government that is pivotal for a rightward policy shift. Those that are under oversight may see the termination of the procedure as a function of the position of the government that is pivotal for a leftward policy shift. In both cases, higher values – more rightward positions – should be associated with more oversight. We have therefore assigned to each observation the left–right position of the relevant pivot depending on the oversight status of the country at the beginning of each year (*Council pivot position*). For the positions of the two sets of pivotal actors to be comparable, we have rearranged their values by anchoring their minimum at zero. Moreover, we have added the difference between the pivotal positions at the beginning and the end of the year (*Change in Council pivot position*). Higher values should also be positively associated with oversight. Last, several studies attribute considerable relevance to the positions of the Commission on whose recommendations the Council decides (e.g. Mérand 2022; Sacher 2021; van der Veer 2022), we, therefore, include the left–right position of the party or the appointing government of the Economic affairs commissioner.[9]

countries. Some scholars argue that this rule covers all the stages of the procedure (Bauer and Becker 2014: 221; Seikel 2016: 1405). This is not the Commission's interpretation (see https://economy-finance.ec.europa.eu/economic-and-fiscal-governance/stability-and-growth-pact/corrective-arm-excessive-deficit-procedure/legal-basis-and-related-stages_en). But even if that were the case, this article lacks a credible enforcement procedure in our view. If a proposed decision is rejected by a blocking minority, in violation of the Fiscal Compact, and an interested party brings an action before the European Court of Justice for failure to act, it is unlikely to succeed because the (lack of) decision respects the procedural requirements of the TFEU (which the Fiscal Compact affirms to fully respect, according to Article 2 and the same Article 7). The only tools at the disposal of the interested party are the standard retaliatory measures available in international law, which do not appear particularly credible in this context. We thank Emanuela Pistoia for sharing her legal expertise on this issue.

[9] We have excluded two variables that were used in the earlier chapters. A time indicator for the economic crisis is correlated with economic conditions and fiscal performance, while a voting power measure should not be included because ministers cannot vote on the oversight of their own country (and voting power is correlated with economic size). If included, results change only marginally, and these variables are never significant.

8.1.4 *Analysis of Results*

Table 8.1 reports the results from autoregressive distributed lag models that include the lagged dependent variable, the expected and lagged deficit ratios, and the lagged debt ratios. For spatial effects, we add the expected and lagged average deficit ratios, the concurrent economic size, and the euro area membership status. The economic tax-smoothing variables that operationalize the extenuating circumstances enter the regression with their lagged and concurrent realizations while only the concurrent values of the political variables are included. The following analysis is based on models 2 and 4 of Table 8.1 unless specified otherwise. Note that models 3 and 4 account for the autoregressive properties of oversight. They indicate that, if a country has been under surveillance throughout the entire year $t-1$, it will likely be under surveillance for more than a third of the following year t. This means that the effects of the other covariates are *additional* to these temporal effects, and, therefore, their sizes are going to be necessarily small, even if statistically significant. In models 1 and 2 instead, the effect sizes are substantially larger since they ignore these autoregressive features.[10]

Supranational pressures: Public finance data are considered supranational pressure factors because they are measures of compliance with the fiscal reference values. As far as these parameters are concerned, country-specific lagged values of the deficit ratio matter greatly for the opening and duration of a procedure, while the forecasts for year t appear to influence the duration despite the uncertainty we discussed in Chapter 5. A standard deviation increase in the concerned country's deficit ratio in year $t-1$, approximately 3.7 per cent of GDP, is associated with an increase of 24 percentage points in the probability of oversight,[11] and an extension of oversight of 19 days in any given year. A standard deviation increase in the expected deficit ratio for year t (2.8 per cent of GDP) is associated with a prolongation of oversight of 21 days per year.

Interestingly, forecasts about the EU-wide fiscal outlook appear to matter (weakly), despite the lack of legal provisions specifically

[10] They would not converge if they accounted for them. Some political variables are dropped from model 1 for the same reason.

[11] A similar rise of the two-year lagged deficit ratios is associated with an increase of about 23 percentage points in the probability of oversight.

Table 8.1 ***Determinants of the excessive deficit procedure***

	Probability of oversight		Exposure to oversight	
	(1)	(2)	(3)	(4)
Supranational factors				
Excessive deficit procedure $_{t-1}$			0.3057**	0.3643**
			(0.0330)	(0.0288)
Expected deficit	0.5568	0.6319	0.0191†	0.0209*
	(0.3512)	(0.4871)	(0.0110)	(0.0096)
Deficit $_{t-1}$	1.3189*	0.6815*	0.0135†	0.0140*
	(0.6101)	(0.2881)	(0.0068)	(0.0062)
Deficit $_{t-2}$	-0.0639	0.5949*	0.0031	0.0029
	(0.4097)	(0.2325)	(0.0037)	(0.0034)
Expected average deficit	3.6480*	1.1949	0.0357	0.0413†
	(1.6317)	(0.8937)	(0.0261)	(0.0237)
Average deficit $_{t-1}$	-1.5119	-0.5642	-0.0153	-0.0168
	(1.1116)	(0.7759)	(0.0219)	(0.0189)
Debt $_{t-1}$	0.3379†	0.0736	0.0032	0.0030
	(0.1941)	(0.0941)	(0.0031)	(0.0031)
Debt $_{t-2}$	-0.2443	-0.0771	-0.0026	-0.0028
	(0.1702)	(0.0949)	(0.0030)	(0.0028)
Euro area	-3.3901	-0.7960	-0.0739†	-0.0425
	(3.4286)	(0.9895)	(0.0406)	(0.0272)
Council pivot position	0.3465†	0.3240*	0.0064**	0.0045*
	(0.1791)	(0.1359)	(0.0021)	(0.0019)
Change in Council pivot position	1.2257**	0.8141**	0.0265**	0.0261**
	(0.4159)	(0.1148)	(0.0026)	(0.0025)
Commissioner left–right ideology	0.2019†	0.0773*	0.0044**	0.0034**
	(0.1152)	(0.0376)	(0.0013)	(0.0011)
Economic factors				
Economic size	13.7966**	0.9040*	0.0993	0.0063
	(5.2940)	(0.4493)	(0.0614)	(0.0078)
Expected unemployment rate	-0.3594	-0.2096	0.0031	0.0026
	(0.9251)	(0.4311)	(0.0160)	(0.0116)
Unemployment rate $_{t-1}$	0.6586	0.2815	0.0060	0.0039
	(0.9702)	(0.4219)	(0.0147)	(0.0113)
Expected real GDP growth rate	-1.1089	-0.7055*	-0.0006	-0.0031
	(0.8849)	(0.3543)	(0.0095)	(0.0085)
Real GDP growth rate $_{t-1}$	1.1620*	0.2302	-0.0029	-0.0012
	(0.5437)	(0.2114)	(0.0048)	(0.0052)

Table 8.1 (*cont.*)

	Probability of oversight		Exposure to oversight	
	(1)	(2)	(3)	(4)
Expected trade openness	1.6769	0.3180	0.0261	0.0145
	(2.4735)	(0.4585)	(0.0200)	(0.0190)
Expected terms of	-4.4077	33.3899	2.1992	1.1910
trade (ToT)	(157.7945)	(44.1165)	(2.8101)	(2.6120)
Ex. trade openness ×	0.4021	-0.0564	-0.0190	-0.0138
Ex. ToT	(1.6856)	(0.4453)	(0.0185)	(0.0193)
Trade openness $_{t-1}$	-2.4274	-0.3726	-0.0115	0.0010
	(2.5914)	(0.5282)	(0.0183)	(0.0195)
Terms of trade (ToT) $_{t-1}$	-158.5082	-24.8345	0.3051	1.2338
	(176.0364)	(53.4374)	(2.7891)	(2.6480)
Trade openness $_{t-1}$ ×	0.4316	0.1312	0.0035	-0.0019
ToT $_{t-1}$	(1.6140)	(0.5106)	(0.0205)	(0.0195)
Expected real	0.5618	0.1035	-0.0134†	-0.0122†
interest rate	(0.5712)	(0.1805)	(0.0078)	(0.0066)
National factors				
Left–right position	[a]	0.0367	-0.0031	-0.0028
		(0.0651)	(0.0020)	(0.0017)
Anti–pro EU position	[a]	-0.0046	-0.0085**	-0.0058**
		(0.0539)	(0.0020)	(0.0018)
Public support	0.0065	-0.0094	-0.0018†	-0.0010*
	(0.0451)	(0.0134)	(0.0010)	(0.0005)
Expected government	[a]	-0.0004	-0.0000	-0.0000
duration		(0.0006)	(0.0000)	(0.0000)
Left–right position ×	[a]	-0.0001	-0.0000	-0.0000
Ex. duration		(0.0000)	(0.0000)	(0.0000)
Replacement risk	[a]	0.6480	0.0092	0.0069
		(0.4745)	(0.0146)	(0.0119)
Left–right position ×	[a]	0.0156	0.0013†	0.0014*
Repl. Risk		(0.0278)	(0.0007)	(0.0006)
Constant		-31.9513	-4.5668**	-2.1754**
		(26.2435)	(1.2257)	(0.6651)
Effects	fixed	random	fixed	random
Observations	538	580	580	580
Number of countries	26	28	28	28
R^2			0.757	0.789
Log-likelihood	-16.77	-53.78		

Table 8.1 (*cont.*)

Notes: Dependent variable: probability of EDP oversight (models 1 and 2), proportion of a year under EDP oversight (models 3 and 4). Robust standard errors in parentheses adjusted for country clusters. $^{**}p < 0.01$, $^{*}p < 0.05$, $^{\dagger}p < 0.1$. Time period: 1994–2019. Public finance data are considered supranational factors because they are measures of compliance with the reference values. Observations from Luxembourg and Estonia are omitted from model 1 because they have never been under oversight. [a]Variable dropped to reach convergence.

referring to them. A standard deviation increase in the expected average deficit across the EU, approximately 1.8 per cent of GDP, is associated with a yearly extension of oversight of about 27 days. Lagged debt and membership of the euro area are instead not significantly correlated with the probability and the yearly proportion of oversight.[12] These results overall indicate that, despite the shenanigans associated with this procedure, especially during the euro area crisis, the pursuit of sound finances remains a guiding principle of its use.

And supranational bargaining matters too. The left–right preferences of the Council ministers and the Economic affairs commissioners have the expected effects. Recall that we have identified the ideological positions of the governments that are pivotal under qualified majority voting, excluding the concerned country, selected the position of the relevant pivot depending on the country's oversight status, and anchored these values at zero. Opening and terminating the procedure is equated to respectively a rightward and leftward policy shift. Results indicate that positions of the Council pivot member at the beginning of a given year that are a standard deviation to the right are associated with a 21 percentage point increase in the probability of oversight and that a standard deviation shift of such positions to the right in a year is associated with a 26 percentage point increase. Similarly, these changes are associated respectively with nine and, notably, fifty days longer oversight. In our view, we should be pleased with this responsiveness, at least from the normative perspective of democratic decision-making. Finally, in line with extant qualitative studies, the Commission as a non-voting agenda setter is also relevant. If the ideological position of the Economic affairs commissioner shifts a standard deviation to the right (approximately the difference between,

[12] As a within-country effect (model 3), euro area governments tend to spend less time under surveillance after they adopt the common currency.

indeed, socialists like Moscovici and centrist liberals like Rehn), the probability of surveillance increases by 14 percentage points and the oversight is extended by 15 days a year.

Economic conditions: We cannot exclude the possibility that any past or expected economic shocks have no consequences for the duration and likelihood of oversight.[13] This is an interesting result. As we have extensively analyzed in Part II, extenuating circumstances have been at the centre of animated debates during the reforms. They led to the adoption of elaborated sets of decision-making rules, which, in turn, have engendered heated discussions during implementation. However, it seems that simple compliance heuristics about expected and past country-specific fiscal performance and, less robustly, EU-wide fiscal outlook guide decision-making. Indeed, detailed analyses of the application of the procedure, such as Sacher (2021) and van der Veer (2022), corroborate the pre-eminence assigned by policymakers to these factors.

Finally, larger economies are also associated with an 18 percentage point increase in the probability of oversight. This result may reflect these countries' greater propensity to either overspend or be monitored, given the potentially larger negative externalities. It also echoes a general pattern: larger economies are more likely to be subjected to the general EU treaty-based infringement procedure (Hofmann 2018; Sczepanski and Börzel 2023).

National pressures: Last, consider national political pressures. They do not seem to affect the probability of oversight. Instead, more pro-EU governments and countries with more pro-EU public support spend proportionally less time under oversight. Although the size of these effects is not large (between seven and eight days for standard deviation shifts), pro-European governments and executives facing a more pro-European public may try to shorten oversight because prolonged exposure is probably electorally costly. We instead find limited evidence that the ideology of the relevant government, its expected duration, and its risk of replacement are associated with the duration or the probability of oversight. If anything,

[13] Except for the forecasts about economic growth, if the rate is expected to increase by a standard deviation (1.8 percentage points), the probability of oversight diminishes by 29 percentage points. An increase in the expected real interest rate is also weakly associated with shorter oversight. Fiscal consolidation may be a more pressing concern under these circumstances.

more right-leaning governments spend less time under surveillance, about 14 days a year, if they face a low risk of replacement and expect to rule for two years.[14]

In sum, if we use a model with only lagged oversight as a benchmark, the improvement in explaining the overall observed variation in the yearly proportion of oversight amounts to about 17 percentage points – the R^2 goes from 0.57 to 0.73 – from including compliance-related factors, that is, expected and past country-specific fiscal performance and EU-wide fiscal sustainability considerations. Other economic conditions hardly make any difference, while the addition of variables related to national politics and supranational bargaining improves the overall explanation by a further 5 percentage points.

8.2 The Consequences of Corrective Surveillance

8.2.1 Supranational Surveillance of Public Deficit

That a group of finance ministers have established that a country has an excessive deficit does not imply that the relevant country will rein in such excess. However, it may.[15] The institutional design of economic governance displays several features that are deemed important to ensure observance of its provisions (Tallberg 2002; e.g. Chayes and Chayes 1995; Downs, Rocke, and Barsoom 1996). As we have extensively discussed in Part II, supranational monitoring is associated with recommendations, notices, and ratcheting sanctions.[16] These have never been imposed and may be counterproductive by aggravating an already perilous budgetary position of a government, but, as our review of economic theory in Chapter 2 indicates, fiscal recklessness may *per se* have dire consequences for a monetary union. To facilitate compliance, the policy also puts emphasis on the comparability and transparency of public accounts, with the Commission operating as the rule interpreter and issuer of guidances. A European system of national and regional accounts was adopted in 1996. The 2005

[14] See Figure A8.1 in the online appendix.

[15] This section builds on Franchino (2024).

[16] As we pointed out in Chapter 5, sanctions were not laid out until the SGP of 1997. Although in the preceding period, and after 1999 for non-euro area countries, the determination of an excessive deficit represented a credible threat of being excluded from the monetary union.

reform we have analyzed in Chapter 5 set significant obligations for member states and, following prominent infringement cases, delegated important powers to the Commission to improve the quality of statistical data. In July 2015, the Council for the first time imposed a fine on Spain for the manipulation of deficit data.[17]

Yet, the impact of supranational oversight on national budgeting is poorly investigated. Some studies ignore it, even though they include EU countries in the post-1993 period in their analysis (Brender and Drazen 2005; Harrinvirta and Mattila 2001; Perotti and Kontopoulos 2002). Other works seem to suggest that this policy made a difference only when there was a credible threat of exclusion from the euro area. Wehner (2010b: 222), for instance, finds that the countries expected to adopt the euro (including Greece) ran lower deficits in the two years prior to 1999 (see also De Haan and Sturm 2000; Volkerink and De Haan 2001).[18] Mink and De Haan (2006) report the presence of political budget cycles in the post-1999 period, suggesting that abiding by the fiscal rules may not pay politically once a country has joined the monetary union. These results have led some scholars to consider the policy 'failed' (De Haan, Berger, and Jansen 2004: 235) or 'irrelevant' (Leblond 2006: 970). And some economic studies have reached similar conclusions (Fatás and Mihov 2010; Ioannou and Stracca 2014). Things may have even gotten worse during the euro area crisis. Several qualitative analyses tend to underscore the selective, if not ineffectual, use of the procedure (Schmidt 2016b: 1046; 2020: 138; van der Veer 2022: 96; Vanheuverzwijn 2017: 18–19). Rules have been reinterpreted 'by stealth' without any public admission (Schmidt 2016b). 'Understandable fudging' has continued even after the crisis (van der Veer 2022: 96).

But a more careful analysis of recent works suggests that the procedure may not be so irrelevant. Fortunato and Loftis (2018) find, in their pooled regression, that the post-Maastricht period has a weak negative impact on deficits. Similarly, De Haan et al. (2013) report

[17] On misreporting and sanctioning, see Alt et al. (2014), Savage and Howarth (2018), and von Hagen and Wolff (2006).

[18] Wehner (2010a) finds no association between a binary indicator for expected euro area membership since 1992 and deficits, perhaps because this variable covers too long a period. However, a pre-Euro area convergence variable in Hallerberg, Strauch, and von Hagen (2009: 91) fails to be significant in their full sample, the same applies to an EU accession indicator for Central and Eastern European countries in Fabrizio and Mody (2006).

that the post-1999 period is associated with greater fiscal discipline.[19] These works use time indicators that do not distinguish between countries in or out of the euro area, let alone those under an excessive deficit procedure. They also do not extend beyond 2004, or 2009 for some countries in Fortunato and Loftis (2018).

De Jong and Gilbert (2020: 18) provide the strongest indication that the regime may matter. Considering EU countries from 1999 to 2016, these scholars find that a recommendation for a 1 per cent fiscal adjustment is associated with a 0.51 per cent improvement in the structural budget balance if a country is not receiving financial assistance. However, aside from the focus on the structural balance, the only political variable included in this work is a planned election-year indicator.

The oversight of the excessive deficit procedure may engender a reduction of budget deficits for two related reasons. First, a decision by a collective body of finance ministers that establishes the presence of an excessive deficit and the subsequent scrutiny may lead to charges of fiscal irresponsibility by the national mass media and opposition parties. This could engender political costs for parties in governments by tearing off at least somewhat the veil of ignorance of fiscally illuded voters that would have otherwise rewarded them for debt-fuelled economic growth and may now instead punish them for economic mismanagement. Van der Veer (2022: 91, 93, 95) offers several examples of reactions from national parties and the media to (the threat of) the opening of the procedure. Even the British media

[19] Related evidence indicates that: the adoption of the euro has engendered lower debt than it would have otherwise been for some countries and higher debt for others (Koehler and König 2015); fiscal deficits have tended to gravitate around 3 per cent after the adoption of the Maastricht criterion (Caselli and Wingender 2018); and forecasted deficits have fallen faster when they exceeded this threshold (R. Beetsma and Giuliodori 2009; Cimadomo 2012).

Hansen (2015) finds that economic growth helps countries to comply with both reference values. Right-leaning governments are more likely to comply with the debt–GDP criterion, and smaller, non-EU founding states with the deficit–GDP one. However, using actual numerical noncompliance with the reference values as a dependent variable is problematic. First, recall that numerical noncompliance is neither a sufficient nor a necessary condition for determining the existence of an excessive deficit. Second, this operationalization is equivalent to dichotomizing the debt–GDP and deficit–GDP ratios. This not only leads to a considerable loss of information but also obfuscates the fact that these ratios are perhaps one of the most extensively theorized objects of inquiry in political economy.

used it to criticize Gordon Brown, the Chancellor of the Exchequer, for economic incompetence in 2008.

Second, regardless of the credibility of the sanctions, protracted noncompliance could encourage emulation by fellow governments, thus undermining the whole regime with possible serious repercussions. As we discussed in Chapter 2, the primary objective of this policy is to prevent negative externalities arising from fiscal indiscipline. Assuming an inflation-averse central bank, in a monetary union, recall that these externalities range from higher interest rates, (common) currency appreciation, trade imbalances, up to default, financial contagion, and, in the long run, lower capital accumulation and output. Regardless of the appropriateness of precisely these fiscal rules, governments, which share a common monetary policy and cannot take advantage of currency fluctuations to soften the transmission of these effects, can plausibly try to reduce their exposure and set up an efficacious system of oversight of national fiscal policies. Finance ministers are not oblivious to these issues and, if their country's deficit is considered excessive, they are likely to be receptive to the pressure to comply from their colleagues in the Council as they would not wish in the future to be at the receiving end of negative externalities originating from fiscal indiscipline in fellow member countries. Finance ministers are also in charge of one of the most important portfolios of the national cabinet (Warwick and Druckman 2001) and they tend to be more fiscally hawkish than their colleagues. On the back of supranational oversight and the risks of electoral sanctions, they may successfully use these arguments and their elevated stature with colleagues in charge of spending ministries to rein in the excess. These dynamics should operate more cogently in countries that are members of the euro area, but compliance with fiscal rules is also a condition for joining the monetary union. Oversight may therefore display its effects on those governments wishing to adopt the single currency as well.

8.2.2 National Pressures: Political Economy Theories of Public Deficit

As the abundance of political economy theories of public spending on offer indicates, there is a vast array of national political factors that need consideration. These factors are in essence associated with the pressures to win (or remain in) office and to adopt policies.

Multiple constituencies and distributive politics: One of the most established theories sees public spending being confronted by a tragedy of the commons. According to one variant of this perspective, political parties have priorities for spending programs that provide, at least in part, disproportionate benefits to their supporters. Parties are primarily held electorally accountable for spending decisions in these domains of interest of their voters and can successfully shift the blame on coalition partners for fiscal outcomes in other policy areas. As a result, their demand for spending will fail to fully internalize the costs of these programs. Since the benefits are concentrated on their supporters while the costs are shared across the electorate through taxation, the demand will be excessive, and spending will increase and deplete the tax base.

Coalition governments are more severely beset by this common pool resource problem than single-party governments. In the latter circumstance, the party as a whole is held accountable by the electorate for all its spending decisions because voters do not distinguish among party factions. For coalition governments instead, the possibility to discriminate and hold electorally accountable individual parties creates an electoral common pool problem (Persson, Roland, and Tabellini 2007: 157). Moreover, smaller parties internalize these costs even less than large parties because they represent a smaller portion of the electorate. Spending, therefore, increases with the number of parties in government (Bawn and Rosenbluth 2006). Evidence indeed indicates that coalition governments and larger coalitions are associated with more public spending (Bawn and Rosenbluth 2006; Bräuninger 2005; Perotti and Kontopoulos 2002; Persson, Roland, and Tabellini 2007; Volkerink and De Haan 2001). However, a larger public sector does not imply less fiscal discipline. Studies on OECD or Western European countries, which cover up to the mid-1990s, report an association between executive fractionalization and budget deficits (Balassone and Giordano 2001; Perotti and Kontopoulos 2002; Roubini and Sachs 1989; Volkerink and De Haan 2001).[20] But other works, that extend further into the 1990s, fail to unearth this relation (Fortunato and Loftis 2018; Harrinvirta and Mattila 2001).[21]

[20] Fabrizio and Mody (2006) find supporting evidence for ten Central and Eastern European countries in the late 1990s and early 2000s.

[21] De Haan et al. (2013) also report corroborating evidence for EU countries from the mid-1980s to the early 2000s, but their dependent variable is the cyclically adjusted primary budget balance.

One reason for these inconclusive results could be that this problem operates at the level of the legislature or the broader political system, rather than within the executive. Volkerink and de Haan (2001), for instance, find a positive association between the effective number of legislative parties and budget deficits in OECD countries between the 1970s and the early 1990s, but, again, Fortunato and Loftis (2018) fail to corroborate this finding for the following period. Taking a broader perspective of the multiple constituencies involved in a political system, Franzese (2002: 158–59) shows that the effective number of electoral districts has exacerbated, while presidentialism has attenuated, this problem in his study of twenty OECD countries from the late 1950s to 1990.[22] To our knowledge, no work has extended this analysis beyond this period.

Fractionalized and polarized governments and delayed stabilization: A second reason could be that executive fractionalization operationalizes a different causal mechanism that emphasizes a government's weakness or inability to make decisions. According to the theory of veto players, fractionalized and polarized coalitions, composed of different parties who can veto policy, may retard fiscal adjustments *when* facing a high debt burden (and may hinder deficits at low levels of debt). Indeed, unlike earlier works (De Haan and Sturm 1994; 1997), Franzese (2002: 158–59) finds executive fractionalization and (more weakly) polarization to be critical in delaying fiscal stabilization in these conditions. Again, to our knowledge, no work has replicated this analysis beyond 1990.

Fractionalized governments and budgetary rules: A final reason for the inconclusive impact of fractionalization in the more recent period could be in the rules of the budgeting process that operate within each country. Maintaining fiscal discipline may be easier if the budgetary powers are centralized in the hands of actors with incentives to internalize costs, and if constraints to limit the size of the budget are in place. For instance, the minister of finance may explicitly set, at the formulation stage, budgetary limits for the spending ministers, or the possibility to amend the budget during parliamentary approval may

[22] Franzese (2002: 126–95) as well as other works (De Haan and Sturm 1994; 1997; and, in part, Hallerberg, Strauch, and von Hagen 2009) study the *changes* in the ratio of public debt to GDP. This has some important implications that we will address later.

be severely curtailed. Although earlier works on EU countries focus on the direct impact of rules on fiscal outcomes (De Haan and Sturm 1994; Fabrizio and Mody 2006; von Hagen and Harden 1995), their effect is more probably conditioned by the nature of the political environment. Indeed, in a study covering fifty-seven countries over the 1975–1998 period, Wehner (2010b) finds that legislative fragmentation is no longer associated with higher deficits *if* there are limits on parliamentary amendments. Results, however, do not appear to be consistent. In a seminal work on budget rules in Western European EU countries between 1985 and 2004, Hallerberg, Strauch, and von Hagen (2009: 89–93) find that, in some states, a budgetary process with more delegating features improves fiscal discipline, in the case of ideologically homogenous governments.[23] However, covering the same countries and time periods, De Haan, Jong-A-Pin, and Mierau (2013) show that greater delegation attenuates deficit spending only for ideologically *divided* governments if the full set of countries is considered.[24] Here, we extend the study of Hallerberg, Strauch, and von Hagen (2009: 89–93) beyond 2004 and the fifteen EU countries.

Electoral budget cycles: A second important theme in political economy theories of fiscal discipline emphasizes electoral effects. First, the pressure to accrue electoral support should intensify with the prospect of new elections. Since voters tend to reward government parties for good economic performance in the more recent past, the executive may be tempted to stimulate the economy by increasing deficit spending, preferably targeted on its electoral base, in the period closer to the elections. These dynamics engender political business cycles. Evidence from OECD or Western European countries indeed indicates that governments run higher deficits in election years (Franzese 2002: 179–81; Hallerberg, Strauch, and von Hagen 2009: 81–83; Harrinvirta and Mattila 2001; Hübscher and Sattler 2017; Mink and De Haan 2006; von Hagen 2010).[25] Recently, Fortunato and Loftis (2018) have shed

[23] In other countries, the use of budgetary targets by heterogeneous governments appears to attenuate increases in the changes in the debt–GDP ratio.

[24] The result holds also if a different set of rules, which comprise a so-called contracts index, is used. De Haan, Jong-A-Pin, and Mierau (2013) however focus on the cyclically adjusted primary budget balance.

[25] On the other hand, Fabrizio and Mody (2006) fail to find an association between elections and deficits in their study of ten Central and Eastern European countries between 1997 and 2003.

new light on these dynamics. Since legislative election timing is not fixed and known in advance in semipresidential and parliamentary democracies, governments may begin to ramp up spending in the *expectation* of parliamentary dissolution, and if they outlive their expected duration, they would keep up spending until the elections to maintain such support, accumulating deficits as a result. Focusing on Western European countries between the early 1970s and the late 2000s, Fortunato and Loftis (2018) find shorter expected government duration to be associated with higher deficits.

Partisan budget cycles and strategic debt-manipulation: A last important theme addresses partisan effects. According to the standard partisan theory of fiscal discipline, left-leaning governments are expected to run larger deficits than their right-leaning counterparts because their core supporters favour a larger government. However, most of the time, government ideology appears to have no significant impact on deficits (De Haan and Sturm 1994; Fortunato and Loftis 2018; Harrinvirta and Mattila 2001; Perotti and Kontopoulos 2002; Volkerink and De Haan 2001; Wehner 2010a; 2010b). In some cases, it has a modest effect (Fabrizio and Mody 2006; Mink and De Haan 2006), especially if a government faces a high risk of replacement (Franzese 2002: 181–83). An augmented variant of this argument, therefore, asserts that governments facing a high risk of being replaced may attempt to manipulate deficits to constrain the fiscal situation inherited by future governments. They may simply accumulate debt (Alesina and Tabellini 1990) or the manipulation may depend on the ideological inclination of the government (Franzese 2002: 154). For instance, right-wing governments may produce deficits while left-wing governments may reduce deficits as the replacement risk increases (Persson and Svensson 1989). Again, this augmented theory of partisan effects has not been subject to an empirical analysis covering European countries post-1990.[26]

[26] Two secondary theories should be briefly mentioned. First, if public debts serve transfer functions between and across generations that are imperfectly supplied by capital markets, older and poorer countries should run larger deficits. Second, voters failing to incorporate the Ricardian equivalence between current deficits and future taxes tend to reward public spending and punish taxing. Politicians may be more inclined to exploit this fiscal illusion to run deficits and get re-elected when tax structures are more complex. Our expanded models control for both transfer functions and fiscal complexity.

8.2.3 Data and Measurement

Our dependent variable is the measure of *Deficit* that is employed in the excessive deficit procedure as already discussed in Section 8.1.3. Similarly, the key independent variable of interest is *Excessive deficit procedure (EDP)*, that is, the proportion of a given year a country has been under surveillance, which interacts with the binary indicator *Euro area* to account for euro area membership.

Also, as earlier, we include five economic condition variables drawn from the basic economic tax-smoothing theory.[27] The *Unemployment rate* accounts for spending shocks and the *Real GDP growth rate* for revenue shocks. Open-economy shocks are measured by an interaction between *Trade openness* (the ratio of exports and imports over GDP) and the *Terms of trade* (the ratio of export prices to import prices). Market pressure is measured as the *Expected inability to pay* and service the debt: the difference between the expected real interest and real growth rates.[28] To account for the possibility that poorer and older societies may favour more public borrowing – the so-called inter- and intragenerational transfer functions of debt – we employ the *GDP per capita* at constant 2010 US dollars and the *Dependency ratio* of people younger than 15 or older than 64 (dependents) to those of age 15–64 (the working-age population).

We use the number of *Parties in government* and the *Effective number of parties* in the legislature (Laakso and Taagepera 1979) to account for common-pool resource issues. In the case of more than one cabinet per year, we weigh the sum of the number of parties in each cabinet by the share of the year in office, excluding periods of caretaking and post-election government formation. In the case of elections, party fusion, or fission, we compute a similar time-weighted sum for the effective number of parties in the legislature.

We then add three macroinstitutional variables that may further attenuate or aggravate this problem. Given their slowly changing nature, they are promising factors that could explain cross-country

[27] Since our measure excludes interest payments, we disregard the cost of servicing the debt.

[28] Recall that an optimizing government borrows wisely when the expected real growth rate exceeds the expected real interest rate, and it saves wisely if the opposite conditions hold. The expected real interest is the difference between government bond yields and expected inflation (see the online appendix to this chapter).

differences. Powerful presidents may ease this problem since they face a nationwide constituency. Twelve countries are semipresidential during the period of our inquiry (plus Czechia since 2013 with the introduction of a popularly elected president) (Elgie 2011: 29), but presidential powers vary considerably. We, therefore, include an indicator variable for effective *Semipresidentialism*, which takes the value of one for those five countries where presidential powers in legislative and non-legislative matters score six or above in the measure developed by Roper (2002: 260). On the other hand, the resource problem may worsen as the number of electoral districts and effective federal regions increases, since geographically concentrated interests enjoy greater representation. To measure the *Effective number of electoral districts*, we use a variety of sources, including Golder (2005), Birch (2001), the election reports in *Electoral Studies*, and the political data of the *European Journal of Political Research*. If more than one electoral tier is used, the effective number is the seat-weighted sum of the number of districts at each tier. For the *Number of regions* in effectively federal countries, we take into account both the regionalization that occurred across Europe in the 1990s as well as the important differences in effective fiscal decentralization across countries. We count the number of subnational authorities that set the rate of at least one major tax, which is equivalent to having a score of three or above on the regional fiscal autonomy measure produced by Marks, Hooghe, and Schakel (2008).[29] Last, we add a variable measuring the share of legislative seats held by agrarian and ethnic cabinet parties out of the total number of seats of government parties. Franzese (2002) suggests that these parties could exacerbate the resource problem because they tend to concentrate geographically. We use Döring and Manow's (2021) classification of party families to identify these parties as well as Franzese's (2002: 141) operationalization.

Following Fortunato and Loftis (2018), the number of *Parties in government* is interacted with the *Budgetary constraint index* to account for the effect of rules on budgetary outcomes. This is a measure of the formal rules that act as constraints on government spending, employed by Martin and Vanberg (2013). The number of cabinet

[29] Unlike Franzese (2002: 154), we do not add the squared terms of these variables since we do not find evidence of a curvilinear effect. The *p*-levels of Wald χ^2 tests for curvilinear relations are above 0.66.

parties is also the linchpin to the theory that emphasizes the delaying effects of executive fractionalization and polarization on fiscal consolidation. We, therefore, interact the number of *Parties in government* and the *Government range* (the absolute distance between the highest and lowest left–right scores of cabinet parties from the comparative manifestos project – see more details later), with the previous year's debt-to-GDP ratio (Franzese 2002: 144–46).[30]

For electoral and partisan effects, we use the same measures that we introduced earlier: the *Expected duration* and the *left–right position* of the executive, in interaction with its *Replacement risk*. Like Fortunato and Loftis (2018), we include a *Caretaker time* variable that measures the share of a given year that a caretaker government has been in power, including the post-election government formation period. Like Franzese (2002: 135–37), we add fiscal illusory effects measured by the *Total tax share* of government revenues. Higher values indicate simpler tax structures that should discourage opportunistic deficits.[31] We also account for the periods during which countries applied for, or received, financial assistance from the EU and the International Monetary Fund during the global financial crisis and the euro area crisis to address the difficulties they were experiencing in refinancing their debts. Since financial support depends on the implementation of economic adjustment programmes, this conditionality may have engendered fiscal discipline. *Financial assistance* measures the proportion of a given year a country has been negotiating or receiving assistance.[32]

We estimate an autoregressive distributed lag model that includes one-year lags of both the dependent and independent variables, concurrent realizations of the economic and demographic variables, two

[30] A variant of this argument asserts that the failure to rein in deficits may be due to polarized governments that cannot avail themselves of suitable budgetary rules to offset spending demands (De Haan, Jong-A-Pin, and Mierau 2013; Hallerberg, Strauch, and Hagen 2009).

[31] Of the three measures used by Franzese (2002: 135–37), this is the only one with a significant effect in the expected direction, at least in one model. The coefficients of the other two variables (the share of indirect taxes to revenues, and the share of central to general government revenues) are wrongly signed, sometimes even significantly, raising doubts as to whether they accurately measure the complexity of the tax structure.

[32] The online appendix to this chapter provides additional information on data sources, measurement, and descriptive statistics.

further temporal effects (the two-year lagged deficit and debt[33] as a percentage of GDP), and a spatial effect (*Average deficit*$_{\sim i}$, the average of other EU countries' deficit ratios). This specification accounts for the autoregressive and spatial properties of spending patterns and for the fact that the effects of political variables are primarily felt not when budgets are implemented, but when they are drafted and adopted (Bawn and Rosenbluth 2006: 261; Martin and Vanberg 2013: 961). Only the indicator variable *Euro area* enters the model in its concurrent realization since it measures membership or *expected* membership of the euro area in a given year. For instance, the 1998 budget is affected by the realizations of the political variables in 1997 as well as the *expectation* that the European Council would decide on membership in 1998 (hence, *Euro area* = 1).

8.2.4 Analysis of Results

The first model in Table 8.2 includes only Western European countries from 1994, or the year of membership of the EU, up to 2019.[34] The next model extends the analysis to all EU countries since their membership, except for Croatia, Cyprus, and Malta, which are excluded because of missing data.[35]

Supranational oversight: The bottom two rows in Table 8.2 report the average marginal effects, for all countries and conditioned on euro area membership, of the scrutiny of the excessive deficit procedure.

[33] Since the political variables that interact with the debt ratio are included at the time the budget is drafted, we use the two-year lag because it should relate to the year preceding the drafting. The one-year lagged debt ratio performs worse. In Franzese (2002), temporal persistence plays a more prominent role because he studies the *changes* in the ratio of public debt to GDP, which is *not* equivalent to the ratio of public deficit to GDP (the correlation between the two measures is 0.64). In Franzese (2002), time effects operate via both economic growth and the interests accrued on the accumulated debt.

[34] Namely, Austria, Belgium, Denmark, Finland, France, Germany, Ireland, Italy, Luxembourg, the Netherlands, Spain, Sweden, Portugal, and United Kingdom – the same set of countries used by Fortunato and Loftis (2018).

[35] *F*-tests from regressing the residuals from the models in Table 8.2 on country fixed effects are far from reaching statistical significance (p-values > 0.34 and 0.52). Their inclusion obscures substantive explanations based on slowly changing variables and worsens the overall performance in explaining the observed patterns by at least 10 percentage points. However, we reintroduce fixed effects later in models that extend to the pre-Maastricht period in order to compute treatment effects.

Consider all EU countries. A full year of oversight during budget drafting leads a government of a euro area country to reduce the deficit on average by 0.57 per cent of GDP. Considering the 3 per cent deficit ceiling of the Treaty of Maastricht, this is quite a substantial impact. For a country like the Netherlands (GDP of €639 billion in 2010), it means an impressive improvement of the budget balance by €3.67 billion. The unconditioned impact of oversight on deficits is slightly lower (0.56 per cent of GDP on average), but it is still large and significant, indicating that surveillance displays its effects on governments outside the euro area as well. That actual monetary union membership does not matter much seems plausible if we consider that even Danish and Swedish governments tried to adopt the euro, only for their plans to be rebuffed in referendums.

The impact of oversight is also not confounded by that of financial assistance, which is substantial as expected. In the full sample, governments that have been negotiating or benefiting from assistance throughout the full year when the budget is drafted reduced their deficits on average by 1.14 per cent of GDP. Even if we exclude assisted countries because budgetary consolidation may be attached to disbursements, a full year of oversight leads to a deficit reduction of 0.66 per cent of GDP ($p < 0.01$).

One concern is that right-leaning executives, with the prospect of losing office, may decide to loosen their fiscal stance to purposely face oversight, then implement their preferred tighter policies and shift the blame on the EU. If governments self-select into being monitored, this kind of procedural manipulation would cast doubt on the notion that supranational oversight exogenously engenders fiscal discipline. However, as we discussed in the previous section, we find no evidence of governmental left–right ideology, across any level of replacement risk, or expected duration to be significantly related to periods under scrutiny. Given the uncertainty, perhaps it should not be surprising that executives do not engage in such procedural strategizing. On the other hand, we have found the fiscal performance of the relevant country, such as the lagged deficit, to be associated with the likelihood and duration of oversight. This non-random assignment begs the question of what governments would have done had they not been subject to oversight. In our dataset, we do not observe the deficit of non-supervised countries that have, for instance, high lagged deficits,

Table 8.2 *The consequences of surveillance*

	Western Europe	European Union
Lagged variables (t – 1)		
Supranational factors		
Excessive deficit procedure (EDP)	–0.4853	–0.5332
	(0.4067)	(0.3709)
Euro area[a]	0.0241	–0.0842
	(0.4259)	(0.2546)
EDP × Euro area[a]	–0.0039	–0.0411
	(0.4130)	(0.3249)
Financial assistance	–2.8659	–1.1433*
	(1.8986)	(0.5493)
National factors		
Left–right position	–0.0312*	–0.0253†
	(0.0148)	(0.0133)
Expected duration	–0.0006**	–0.0004*
	(0.0002)	(0.0002)
Parties in government	–0.3095	–0.0939
	(0.5119)	(0.2769)
Budgetary constraint index (BCI)	0.0297	–0.0804
	(0.8539)	(0.7956)
Parties in government × BCI	0.3236	0.5260†
	(0.2501)	(0.2866)
Parties in government × Debt $_{t-2}$	0.0047	–0.0004
	(0.0052)	(0.0024)
Government range	–0.0153	0.0001
	(0.0161)	(0.0126)
Government range × Debt $_{t-2}$	–0.0001	–0.0002*
	(0.0001)	(0.0001)
Effective number of parties	–0.3000	–0.1134
	(0.1873)	(0.1107)
Semipresidentialism	–1.2541*	0.0004
	(0.5723)	(0.2794)
Ethnic-agrarian party share	–1.4669	–0.2596
	(1.1692)	(0.5489)
Number of regions	–0.0282	–0.0375**
	(0.0184)	(0.0135)
Eff. num. of electoral districts	0.0030**	0.0009
	(0.0011)	(0.0009)
Replacement risk (RR)	–0.0363	–0.0215
	(0.2022)	(0.1409)

Table 8.2 (*cont.*)

	Western Europe	European Union
Left–right position × RR	0.0145†	0.0088
	(0.0084)	(0.0073)
Total tax share	−13.8186*	2.0414
	(5.4614)	(4.7878)
Caretaker time	1.0815	1.1898*
	(0.7317)	(0.5954)
Temporal effects		
Deficit	0.3940**	0.5056**
	(0.0855)	(0.0548)
Deficit $_{t-1}$	0.0270	0.0662
	(0.0440)	(0.0410)
Debt $_{t-1}$	−0.0044	0.0196**
	(0.0108)	(0.0070)
Economic factors		
Unemployment rate	−0.4169**	−0.4057**
	(0.1108)	(0.1386)
Real GDP growth rate	−0.1003	0.0024
	(0.0646)	(0.0548)
Expected inability to pay	−0.0479	−0.0171
	(0.0395)	(0.0386)
Trade openness	0.1139*	0.1683*
	(0.0513)	(0.0701)
Terms of trade (ToT)	31.6512*	31.1153*
	(14.2352)	(15.0277)
Trade openness × ToT	−0.1307†	−0.1780*
	(0.0721)	(0.0834)
GDP per capita	−0.2162†	0.2421†
	(0.1157)	(0.1396)
Dependency ratio	−1.1604*	−0.2027
	(0.4853)	(0.2785)
Concurrent variables		
Spatial effects		
Average deficit$_{-i}$	0.3535**	0.3147**
	(0.0634)	(0.0579)
Economic factors		
Unemployment rate	0.4956**	0.4651**
	(0.1275)	(0.1628)
Real GDP growth rate	−0.2344**	−0.0153
	(0.0873)	(0.0731)

Table 8.2 (*cont.*)

	Western Europe	European Union
Expected inability to pay	−0.0081	−0.0321
	(0.1230)	(0.0728)
Trade openness	−0.2071	−0.1629
	(0.1279)	(0.1103)
Terms of trade (ToT)	−49.2517†	−31.1924
	(26.2749)	(21.6820)
Trade openness × ToT	0.2412	0.1676
	(0.1668)	(0.1301)
GDP per capita	0.1293	−0.2518†
	(0.0992)	(0.1372)
Dependency ratio	1.1239*	0.0973
	(0.5043)	(0.2773)
Constant	35.6926**	3.9934
	(11.6896)	(9.0826)
Observations	372	516
Number of countries	15	25
R^2	0.802	0.748
Effects	Random	Random
Marginal effects of EDP	−0.4881*	−0.5579*
	(0.2379)	(0.2387)
Marginal effect of EDP for euro area countries	−0.4892*	−0.5742**
	(0.2478)	(0.2141)

Notes: Dependent variable: deficit/GDP. Robust standard errors in parentheses adjusted for country clusters. Average marginal effects computed for one year of oversight under the excessive deficit procedure. $^{**}p < 0.01$, $^{*}p < 0.05$, $^{\dagger}p < 0.1$.
[a]Since the indicator *Euro area* measures also expected membership, it enters the regression in its concurrent realization. Time period: 1994–2019.

given that such lagged deficits trigger oversight. In other words, some covariates are associated with both assignment and outcome.

To address this issue, we have extended the dataset to the period preceding the Treaty of Maastricht up to the early 1970s, using the data from Fortunato and Loftis (2018)[36] and Franzese (2002), and

[36] A caveat: although strongly correlated (0.937, p-value > 0.000), Fortunato and Loftis' (2018) OECD deficit estimates are not exactly the same as the European Commission's estimates used for oversight. In the online appendix, we list the small changes we have made to these datasets.

Table 8.3 *Average effects of oversight on potential deficit means of treated countries*

	Western Europe	Europe
Average treatment effects on the treated	-0.5471*	-0.5508*
	(0.2534)	(0.2341)
Observations	658	804
Number of countries	15	25

Notes: Difference-in-differences estimates adjusted for the covariates of the model in Table 8.2 and country fixed effects. Robust standard errors in parentheses adjusted for country clusters. *$p < 0.05$. Auxiliary results are reported in Table A8.3 in the online appendix.

estimated the difference-in-differences average treatment effects on the treated governments (i.e. under oversight). Table 8.3 indicates that the effect of oversight is an average reduction of 0.55 per cent of GDP over the mean deficit that would have been observed had governments not been subject to monitoring.

As mentioned earlier, we do not find evidence of anticipatory effects (i.e. procedural strategizing). Countries are exposed to repeated treatments, that is, they switch between being under surveillance and outside surveillance, and treatments occur at different times and for different durations.[37] Alternation in treatment status and variation in assignment time and duration, however, preclude the possibility of examining the appropriateness of the parallel trend assumption required for standard difference-in-differences estimates. To address this issue, at least partially, we employ the matching method for panel data recently developed by Imai, Kim, and Wang (2023). For the time being, this procedure works only for binary treatment indicators. Therefore, we consider treating a country that has been under oversight for an entire year, including the year when the Council terminated the procedure since it seems appropriate to account for some carryover effects due to uncertainty about such termination.[38]

37 See the treatment variation plot in Figure A8.2 in the online appendix.

38 While governments are preparing their budgets, they may be uncertain about whether the procedure will terminate this year and, if monitoring has ended early enough in the year, compliance is still quite plausible in the aftermath of oversight. On the other hand, treatment status is more uncertain at the onset

We have then matched each treated country in a given year to a set of control countries that have the same treatment history in the preceding two years. This procedure adjusts for time-specific unobserved confounders while, given the nature of the oversight, it allows for a reasonable balance between controlling for carryover effects, that is, the effects of the treatment history on the deficit, and limiting the number of unmatched treated units.[39] Following the applications by Imai, Kim, and Wang (2023), we have used all the lagged covariates of the model in Table 8.2 to refine the matched sets.[40] Figure 8.1 displays the estimated average effects on the deficit of the treated countries over a period of five years – one more than the average duration of the oversight spells. There is no contemporaneous effect of oversight, but governments rein in their deficits over time. After four to five years, euro area governments produce deficits that are on average between 1.72 and 2.81 per cent of GDP lower than that of governments with identical treatment histories and similar covariate distributions but which were not supervised in year *t*0.[41]

We assess now whether the impact of oversight on the public deficit is substantively comparable with that of other economic and political determinants included in the models in Table 8.2.

Tax-smoothing and transfer functions: Economic conditions have an unsurprisingly large impact on public finances. For spending shocks, a standard deviation increase in the concurrent rate of unemployment (between 4.1 per cent and 4.4 per cent) produces an increase in the deficit of between 1.91 and 2.13 per cent of GDP, which is almost twice as much as the size of the effect reported by

of an oversight spell. Council recommendations may have been issued after the national budgetary process has been set in motion.

39 Figure A8.3 displays the frequency distribution of the number of matched control units across treatment histories of one to three years.

40 In our circumstances, Mahalanobis distance matching, up to five matches, produces the best improvement of the covariance balance. Figure A8.4 compares such improvement across refinement methods and number of matches. Figure A8.5 illustrates the improved balance over the pre-treatment period and lends support to the parallel trend assumption.

41 If we forbid treatment reversal, that is, we match only treated countries that have been continuously under oversight in the lead window, the procedure leads to deficits in the fourth and fifth year that are on average 1.75 per cent and 5.40 per cent of GDP lower than those of untreated countries (see Figure A8.6). However, balance diagnostics requires dropping some covariates to assess the improvement across refinement methods.

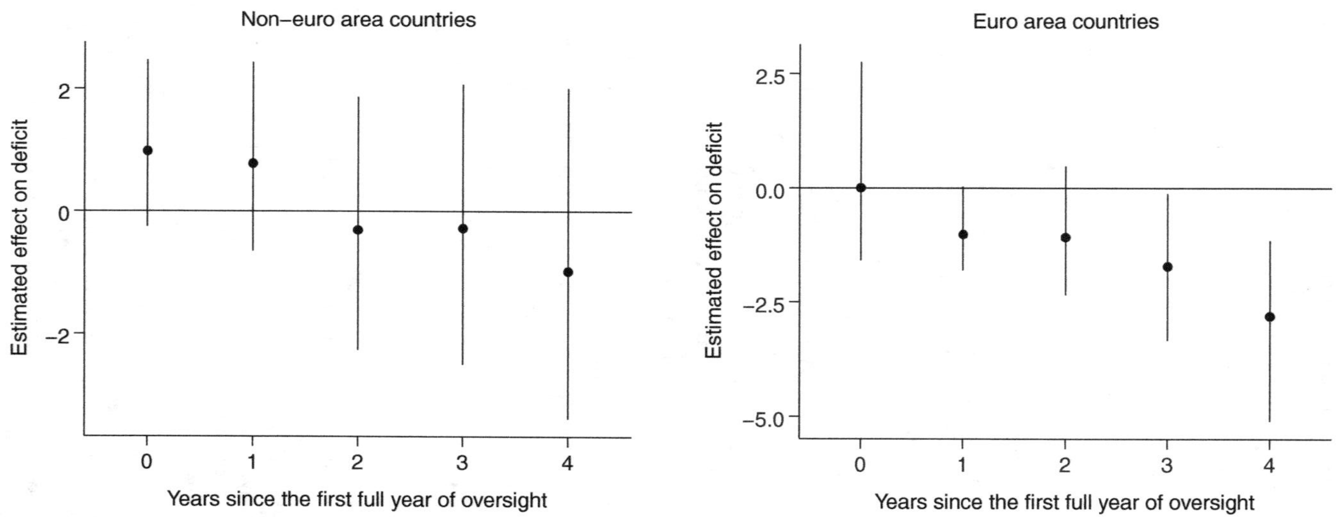

Figure 8.1 Estimated average effects of oversight on the deficits of the treated countries

Note: The estimates are percentages of GDP. They are based on the exact matching of the treatment histories during the two years preceding the first full year of oversight. Matched sets are refined with Mahalanobis distance matching up to five matches, using the lagged covariates of the model in Table 8.2. Treatment reversal is allowed. Vertical bars are the 95 per cent confidence intervals derived from a bootstrapping procedure of 500 iterations.

Source: Franchino (2024).

Franzese (2002: 188). Deficits have also been more sensitive to revenue shocks, at least in Western Europe. A similar increase in the rate of real GDP growth, around 2.14 per cent, leads to a drop in deficit of 0.67 per cent of GDP. Instead, we cannot reject the expectation that governments do not account for expected increases in debt-servicing costs when determining their fiscal policies.[42] On the other hand, improvements in the terms of trade have reduced deficits, except for very open economies (i.e. when openness exceeds 170 per cent of GDP), but the size of the effect reaches standard significance only in Western Europe. A standard deviation improvement (0.03) produces an average reduction in the deficit of 0.76 per cent of GDP.[43] Economic conditions however cover only half of the explanatory story, almost literally. If we use a model with only temporal effects, spatial effects, and lagged debt levels as a benchmark, the improvement in explaining the overall observed variation in deficit by including economic conditions exceeds only slightly the improvement one would obtain from adding political determinants.

There is also some evidence in support of both the inter- and the intragenerational transfer functions of debt, unlike Franzese (2002: 168) but, partially, in line with Fortunato and Loftis (2018). Considering the concurrent realizations, poorer and older countries tend to be associated with higher deficits in respectively the full and Western Europe samples, but these structural economic and demographic trends of course take a long time to display their effects.

Expected government duration and risk of parliamentary dissolution: Moving on to national political factors, electoral pressures operate as expected. As a government's expected time in office draws to a close, it begins to accumulate budget deficits. In the year it is

[42] Coefficients are in the expected direction, but substantively small. In the late 1990s and 2000s, historically high, albeit decreasing, nominal interest rates have been associated with debt consolidation, as expected. But the relation broke down during the 2008–2013 crises when increased nominal rates and lower inflationary and growth expectations generated doubts about the ability to repay, *but* deficits in some countries increased. Similarly, lower nominal rates and improved growth expectations improved the prospects to repay debt obligations in the post-crisis period, but consolidation has continued in some countries.

[43] In the full sample, more trade openness improves fiscal discipline, but only when the terms of trade worsen considerably (see Figure A8.7 in the online appendix).

expecting parliamentary dissolution, a national executive produces a deficit that is larger by, on average, between 0.32 and 0.45 per cent of GDP[44] than the deficit produced by a government expecting dissolution within two years (1.6 standard deviations). The figures are very close to the 0.42 per cent reported by Fortunato and Loftis (2018: 948). Note that the impact on the deficit of a two-year shortening of expected duration is fully offset by one year of supranational oversight during budget drafting.

Fractionalization and polarization of the executive and budgetary rules: The top two panels in Figure 8.2 display the marginal effects of government fractionalization on fiscal discipline, across levels of debt, replicating the analysis of Franzese (2002: 176, 179). *If* budgetary rules are relatively constraining, higher fractionalization leads as expected to higher deficits when a country is highly indebted. In these circumstances, the addition of a party to a coalition government produces an average increase in the deficit of 0.45 per cent of GDP in Western Europe and 0.29 per cent across all the countries. The size of the effects is lower than in the past (cf. Franzese 2002: 188) and it decreases as budgetary rules loosen. Moreover, the slope of the curve is contrary to expectations in the full sample (see top row left panel in Figure 8.2), so the effects become insignificant at further higher levels of debt. In other words, fractionalization does not appear to impede fiscal consolidation in Central and Eastern Europe.

On the other hand, more polarization (a larger *Government range*[45]) significantly *reduces* deficits at high levels of indebtedness (see the middle panel in Figure 8.2). At relatively high debt-to-GDP ratios (a standard deviation above the mean), a standard deviation

44 The difference is an indication that the effects of electoral cycles are attenuated in Central and Eastern Europe, which is coherent with the findings of Fabrizio and Mody (2006).

45 Franzese (2002: 156) finds this conception of government weakness based on veto players to encompass an alternative that operationalizes weakness with the effective number of government parties and the standard deviation of cabinet parties' positions (or similar measures of dispersion) (De Haan, Jong-A-Pin, and Mierau 2013; De Haan and Sturm 1997; Fabrizio and Mody 2006; Volkerink and De Haan 2001; Wehner 2010b). We do not reach the same conclusion. For Western Europe, *J*-tests indicate that the two alternatives reject each other, suggesting that both conceptualizations are informative. In the full sample, the veto-based conception only weakly rejects the alternative (p-value = 0.075), while it is rejected by it. The results about supranational oversight hold using this alternative concept of weakness.

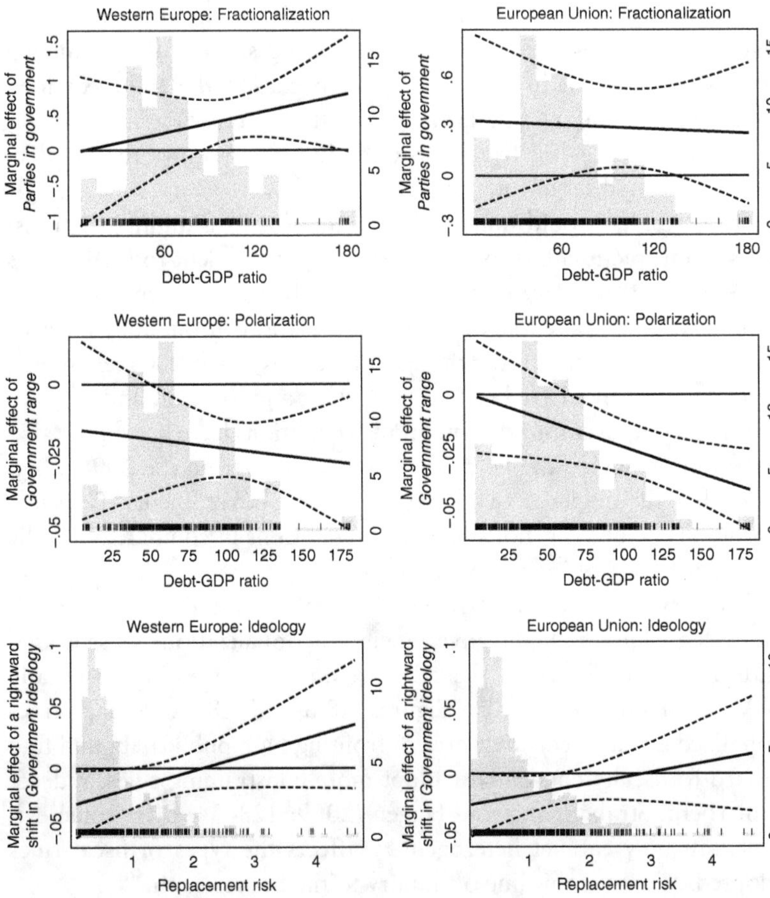

Figure 8.2 Marginal effects of fractionalization, polarization, and ideology
Note: In the top two panels, the budgetary constraint index is set at a standard deviation above its mean. Curves shift upward as constraints increase. Positive and significant effects occur at high debt ratios and budgetary constraints for Western Europe, but only at mid-high debt ratios in the full sample because of the downward sloping curve. One outlying observation is dropped from the bottom two panels. Histograms underlaid.
Source: Franchino (2024). Creative commons license: https://creativecommons.org/licenses/by/4.0/

increase in range, approximately the difference between the mean polarization of Belgian and Greek governments, leads to a deficit reduction of between 0.31 and 0.34 per cent of GDP. Thus, while fractionalization is still an impediment to fiscal consolidation, *more* heterogeneous governments have been *more* successful at reducing deficits. This is not in line with the expectation that more divided governments produce smaller policy shifts. As Franzese (2002: 178) conjectures, successful fiscal consolidation may require the involvement of a broad set of interests.

These results should not be surprising. Notwithstanding the pressures from fractionalization, from the heights of debt-to-GDP ratios exceeding 130 per cent in the mid-1990s, Belgian government coalitions have undertaken significant consolidation throughout most of this period, including after the euro area crisis, while Greek single-party governments have been accumulating a lot of debt, and they are still struggling to consolidate it. Finnish coalitions have been more successful in managing the fiscal challenges arising from the 2008–2013 crises than the single- or two-party Portuguese governments. The same is true for the heterogenous Slovakian coalitions in comparison to the more cohesive Slovenian governments.

Contrary to expectations, the historical record indicates that, if the indebtedness is high, government fractionalization is associated with *higher* deficits when the rules are *more* constraining (especially in Western Europe, see also Figures A8.8 and A8.9). Perhaps fractionalized governments that are confronting high public debt and find it hard to fiscally consolidate adopt more constraining rules. Indeed, Hallerberg, Strauch, and von Hagen (2009: 123–34) offer some evidence on how cabinet heterogeneity affects the types of fiscal rules adopted. We leave this line of inquiry to further research.[46]

Government ideology and risk of replacement: The bottom panels in Figure 8.2 display the marginal effects of a rightward shift in government ideology across levels of replacement risk. A higher risk does not engender a higher deficit,[47] but governments are more likely to follow their ideological inclinations when the risk of being replaced by ideologically different ones is low. Right-leaning governments tend

46 To test whether polarized governments that cannot avail themselves of suitable budgetary rules to offset spending demands run larger deficits (De Haan, Jong-A-Pin, and Mierau 2013; Hallerberg, Strauch, and Hagen 2009), we interact executive polarization with two indexes of budgetary rules produced by Hallerberg, Strauch, and von Hagen (2009). We do not find evidence corroborating this expectation; see Table A8.4 and Figure A8.10.

47 See also Figure A8.11 in the online appendix.

to reduce deficits, while left-leaning governments tend to increase them. If the risk of replacement rises, they are less likely to entertain these options. Unlike the findings of Franzese (2002: 181–83), this behaviour is in line with the theoretical expectations of Persson and Svensson (1989). When the risk of replacement is a standard deviation lower than the mean, a standard deviation rightward shift, the difference between the German Christian democrat-liberal coalition and the Christian democrat-social democrat coalition in the 2010s is associated with a reduction in the deficit by between 0.32 and 0.42 per cent of GDP.

Other interesting results concern, for instance, macroinstitutional features, such as effective semipresidentialism and electoral districting, and the simplicity of the tax structure, which may have discouraged the exploitation of voters' fiscal illusion. These factors account for some differences between Western European countries. We discuss these results in the online appendix to this chapter.

8.2.5 Extensions: Oversight, Electoral Pressures, and Policy Reforms

Before concluding, we explore how oversight and electoral pressures may have interacted and whether the impact of oversight has varied across reform periods.

Oversight and electoral pressures: The pressure to accrue support in the proximity of new elections is, as expected, one of the most important political drivers of deficit spending, but does it interact with the pressure from oversight? To explore this, we have added to the models in Table 8.2 a three-way interaction between *Expected duration*, *EDP*, and *Euro area*. Figure 8.3 illustrates the marginal effects of a two-year shortening of expected government duration across four scenarios. Electoral pressures do not dissipate for governments under oversight since these effects remain positive at similar levels. However, estimates are more uncertain, and this is not due to fewer observations but because some of these governments are less eager to entertain fiscal expansion. There is, therefore, some indication that being under surveillance may lower the electoral benefits of profligacy, perhaps because charges of fiscal irresponsibility are more persuasive in the presence of a supranationally determined excessive deficit. For instance, following oversight, the

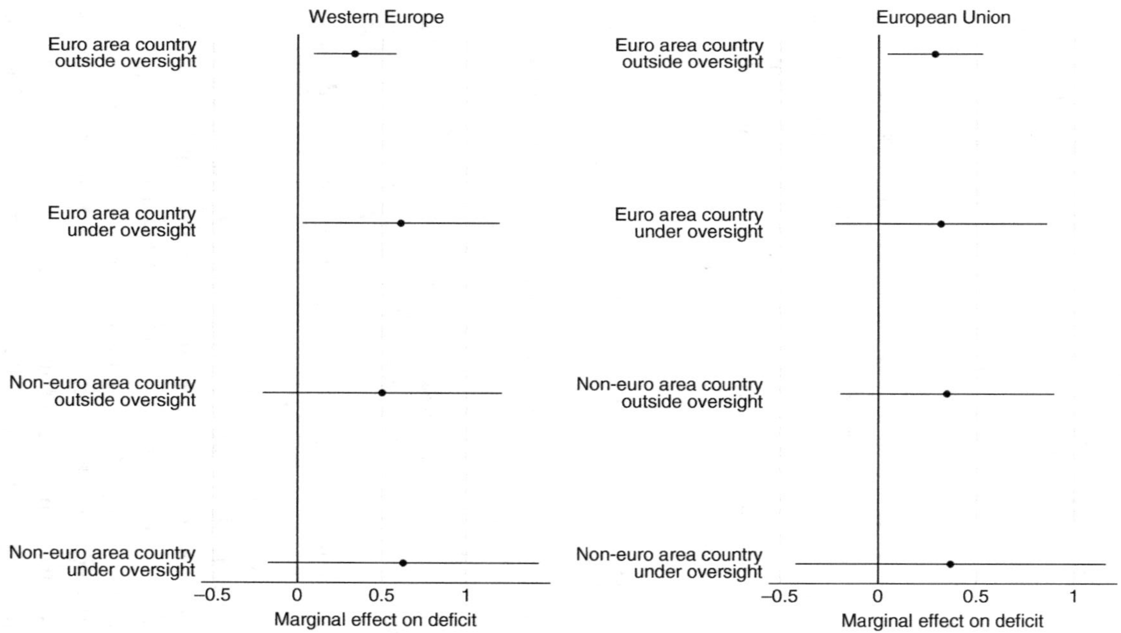

Figure 8.3 Marginal effects on deficit of a two-year shortening of expected duration
Note: Marginal effects of expected duration derived from models adding three-way interactions between *Expected duration*, *EDP*, and *Euro area* to the models in Table 8.2. For the oversight scenarios, they are computed for a full year (i.e. *EDP* = 1). Horizontal bars are the 95 per cent confidence intervals.
Source: Franchino (2024).

Table 8.4 ***Marginal effects of oversight across reform periods and euro area membership***

Periods	Euro area countries	Non-euro area countries
Maastricht	[a]	−0.707
		(1.063)
SGP	−0.353	−0.239
	(0.277)	(0.732)
SGP reform	−0.798*	0.237
	(0.372)	(0.584)
European Semester	−0.406	−1.262**
	(0.387)	(0.312)

Note: Periods: Maastricht 1994–1996; SGP (Stability and Growth Pact) 1997–2004; SGP reform 2005–2011; European Semester (Six Pack and Fiscal Compact) 2012–2019. [a]Not applicable. $N = 516$. $^{**}p < 0.01$, $^{*}p < 0.05$.

Swedish and German governments posted a budget surplus during their election years in 1998 and 2013, respectively. This topic surely deserves further research.

The impact of oversight across reforms: To address this question, we have added to the European Union model in Table 8.2 a three-way interaction between *EDP*, *Euro area*, and a one-year lagged period indicator. Table 8.4 reports the marginal effects of oversight across reform periods and euro area membership. The effects are negative across almost all circumstances and they do not differ significantly among themselves. There is thus limited evidence, especially for euro area countries, that oversight has been more effective in some periods. Monitored euro area governments consolidated more extensively after the SGP reform and this resonates with De Jong and Gilbert's (2020: 11, 19) findings about their better compliance record in the pre-crisis period. Several non-euro area governments were under oversight just prior to the institutionalization of the European Semester, which occurred in the midst of the crisis. This explains the only positive value. These governments then consolidated after this reform.[48]

[48] During the euro area crisis, several countries established or extended the mandates of domestic independent fiscal institutions, which eventually were mandated for euro area countries by the two-pack Regulation 473/2013.

8.3 Conclusion

Whether an excessive deficit procedure is launched or concluded is shaped mostly by supranational factors related to compliance and bargaining. Finance ministers pay attention primarily to a country's past fiscal performance to open a procedure and continue surveillance. Deficit forecasts for the relevant country, as well as for the EU as a whole, also influence duration. Perhaps more surprisingly, past or expected economic shocks have quite limited effects. Despite the development of ever more sophisticated economic performance indicators after every reform, it seems that finance ministers use rather simple compliance heuristics. More interestingly, we find evidence of supranational and national responsiveness. A rightward or leftward shift in the positions of the ministers within the Council or of the Economic affairs commissioner in the Commission produces the expected tightening or loosening of oversight. Pro-European executives and countries with a more pro-European public spend less time under oversight.

As for the consequences of oversight, surveillance has shaped national budgetary processes to a significant extent. Our results shine a light on the reasons for establishing such a policy, that is, to counterbalance the national pressures governments face when they set their fiscal policies. Besides the moderate transfer functions of debt, six are the main political processes that have been driving fiscal deficits. First, government fractionalization has produced higher deficits at high levels of indebtedness (and constraining fiscal rules).[49] Second, left-leaning governments have taken the opportunity to expand their fiscal policies when they were not facing high risks of replacement. Third, the expected proximity to an electoral contest has induced executives to relax their fiscal belts. Fourth and fifth, at least in Western Europe, electoral districting intensified expansionary pressures and higher tax structure complexity appears to have encouraged the exploitation of illusory effects.

On the other hand, we have shown that the impact of one year of supranational monitoring during budget drafting offsets that of

For the time being, the operation of these bodies is associated with higher deficits. We will have to see whether they will replace the supranational procedure in the future.

[49] This effect has been compensated by the successful fiscal consolidation carried out by broader coalitions.

a two-year shortening of expected duration, or the addition of one party to a government coalition when debt is high, or a leftward shift in government ideology when the risk of replacement is low. There is nothing normatively wrong with democratically elected executives trying to win elections, pursue their policy priorities, or cater to their constituencies. That governments have not given up their freedom to choose the timing and extent of their deficit spending, *if they have been fiscally disciplined*, is good news. But actual or expected membership of a monetary union has strings attached. Excessive fiscal profligacy normally leads financial markets to doubt a country's ability to meet its obligations. Eventually, governments will have to put their house in order or face the distressing prospect of default, if growth or inflation are not readily achievable. As we have extensively argued and the sovereign debt crisis has shown, the effects of profligacy and default and the vagaries of market behaviour reverberate more severely in a monetary union. Thus, the excessive deficit procedure has been designed to address the legitimate concerns of limiting these negative externalities. The effectiveness of this regime is, therefore, reassuring.

We conclude our book with a final chapter that summarizes the main findings of our investigation and assesses the overall effectiveness, fairness, and responsiveness of the policy.

9 Effectiveness, Fairness, and Responsiveness

By definition, a government has no conscience. Sometimes it has a policy, but nothing more.

Albert Camus on policy effectiveness

Life is never fair, and perhaps it is a good thing for most of us that it is not.

Oscar Wilde on fairness

Power has to be insecure to be responsive.

Ralph Nader on responsiveness

We normally teach our undergraduate students that the discipline of political science is divided between comparative politics, which focuses on political phenomena that occur predominantly within countries, and international politics, which investigates political phenomena that occur predominantly between countries (Clark, Golder, and Golder 2012: 5–7). And then we point out that this scientific typology, although logically exhaustive, is not mutually exclusive. The analysis of many contemporary political issues requires the researcher to take into account factors that occur both within and between countries.

Nothing is probably more emblematic than studying the economic policy of the European Union: an endeavour that requires taking into account the interaction between politics and economics and between national politics and supranational politics. In this book, we have argued that European politicians balance pressures arising from the economy, national politics, and supranational politics when they design and implement the policy. In Section 9.1, we summarize the key findings of this arduous balancing act. These results offer also the opportunity for drawing some tentative, yet interesting, insights about the effectiveness, fairness, and responsiveness of the policy. We address them in the second part of the chapter.

9.1 Main Findings

Table 9.1 summarizes the main findings. Let's review them.

Table 9.1 ***Research questions and key findings***

Research question	Key findings
Defining the policy problem	
Which economic *ideas* explain its design?	Standard short-and medium-run macroeconomic theories set the contour of the potential problems associated with monetary union.
Negotiating and designing economic governance	
What are the main *cleavages* and what are the *sources* of these controversies?	Key cleavages: (1) national discretion and (2) Council and Commission involvement in enforcement. Main economic pressures: economic crisis. Main national pressures: public support and left–right position. Main supranational pressures: risk of noncompliance, euro area membership, and voting power.
What explains the *outcomes* of the negotiations?	Outcomes are compromise positions based on the distribution of governmental preferences, salience, and voting power. Main supranational factors: costs of failure and legislative procedures.
What explains the *timing* and *direction* of the reforms?	Noncompliance and threats of exclusion are the main reform triggers. Noncompliance is partially associated with national tightening and Commission empowerment. Informational pressures (i.e. economic uncertainties) explain Council-centred enforcement.
Implementing economic governance	
What explains the *adoption* of the country-specific recommendations?	• Modification of recommendations Main economic pressures: worsening economic conditions. Main national pressures: left–right position of the addressed government.

Table 9.1 (*cont.*)

Research question	Key findings
	Main supranational pressures: noncompliance (high public debt), divisiveness within the Council, and extreme Commission position. • Strengthening of recommendations Main supranational pressures: noncompliance (high public debt), Council pivotal minister position, country voting power, and budgetary power.
What explains national *compliance* with the country-specific recommendations?	Main economic pressures: worsening economic conditions. Main national pressures: proximity to elections. Main supranational pressures: costs of noncompliance.
What explains corrective oversight and does it engender *fiscal discipline*?	• Use and duration of oversight Main economic pressures: economic size. Main national pressures: public support, anti–pro EU position, left–right position, and replacement risk. Main supranational pressures: past and expected noncompliance, Council pivotal minister position, and economic affairs commissioner position. • Consequences of oversight Oversight engenders lower deficits, especially in euro area countries. Main economic pressures: economic shocks. Main national pressures: fractionalized government, left–right position and replacement risk, and proximity to elections.

9.1.1 *What Is the Problem?*

The ideational pressures that underlie the EU economic policy are straightforward. Any undergraduate textbook in macroeconomics illustrates how fiscal and monetary policies are deeply interconnected and how the way they interact with each other matters greatly for the health of the economy. In a nutshell decentralized fiscal expansion in a monetary union may give rise to externalities that range from higher interest rates, higher average inflation (in the case of an accommodating central bank), currency appreciation, trade imbalances, and even default, financial contagion, and, in the long run, lower capital accumulation and output. It is this very basic understanding of how an economy operates, associated with, on the one side, the objective of price stability for the monetary union and, on the other, a track record of fiscal profligacy in some member states that laid the foundations for the policy. And there is no need to go much further than the first few chapters of the textbook to appreciate the contour of the problem. As we explain in Chapter 2, sophisticated extensions of macroeconomic theorizing, which, according to some scholars, underpin this presumably austerity-based policy, would actually recommend a much *looser* regime than the one we observe.

But ideas are only one set of factors that shaped this policy and, short of advocating a common fiscal policy, which is, at least for the time being, politically unattainable, macroeconomic theories offer limited insights into its design and implementation. At Maastricht, policymakers opted for a path of least resistance: a system of preventive surveillance of national economic policies and a procedure for correcting excessive deficits when prevention fails. How policymakers developed their views on how such a policy should operate, negotiated over its features, adopted laws and took decisions that produced policy outputs are the subjects of inquiry of the remainder of the book.

9.1.2 What Explains the Controversies During Policy Reforms?

The core contentious issues during the three major reforms of the policy concerned (1) the degree to which supranational surveillance should constrain national economic policies, and (2) the degree to which the Council and the Commission should be involved in enforcement. The examination of the causes of these conflicts in Chapter 3 illustrates neatly how the three sets of pressures operate.

As far as the first divide is concerned, left-leaning governments with a high risk of noncompliance have tended to prefer less intrusive provisions, but less so if their countries were members of the euro area or held the Council presidency during negotiations.[1] Unsurprisingly, the sovereign debt crisis has titled positions towards greater national tightening. For the second controversy, governments that have higher voting power within the Council have preferred greater involvement of this institution in enforcement as their noncompliance risk increased, but a right-leaning orientation of the executive attenuated these dynamics. Lower influence within the Council has not translated into a preference for the Commission, probably because ministers do not control this institution directly. Indeed, governments facing greater public Euroscepticism have been more reluctant to empower the supranational executive. And a reputation of being a harsh enforcer did not help: governments benefiting from financial assistance have strongly preferred the Council over the Commission.

9.1.3 How Were the Controversies Resolved?

Most of the time, these controversies have been resolved by finding a compromise resulting from the distribution of governmental preferences, issue salience, and countries' voting power, as we show in Chapter 4. Across time and issues, there is hardly any evidence that any one state has been systematically advantaged. Preference centrality is, therefore, core to bargaining success, but two additional factors need considering. First, since these reforms occurred in circumstances where the costs of failing to reach an agreement were large, the most conservative actors have been inevitably weakened. Second, procedural factors have not been irrelevant since governments with positions proximate to that of the European Parliament have been more successful when the supranational legislature was non-trivially involved in the negotiations.

9.1.4 What Explains the Timing and Direction of Policy Reforms?

Reforms have been triggered by serious noncompliance problems and credible threats of exclusion. As we explain in Chapter 5, the very real possibility of being excluded from the monetary union, for

[1] Anti-EU governmental positions and higher public Euroscepticism have also been associated with tightening positions, to some degree.

countries that did not comply with the Maastricht criteria, triggered the SGP negotiations. Yet, the most recalcitrant governments still relied on their veto power to curb the reform of the corrective procedure, which remained Council-centred. In 2005, noncompliance led to some tightening as well as empowerment of the Commission in data quality oversight. Overall, the outcome represented a compromise between, on the one side, looser rules for determining a deficit excess and greater emphasis on preventive surveillance and, on the other side, the resumption of the suspended procedure and stricter constraints once an excess had been determined. Last, in the face of a European sovereign debt crisis and widespread noncompliance, the major 2010 reform tried to secure commitments to both fiscal soundness and bailout in the context of prohibitive costs of exit from the euro area. This explains the further tightening of provisions and empowerment of the Commission, as well as the greater relevance assigned to the debt criterion in the corrective phase, over the objections of veto-holding recalcitrant governments.

Two important aspects need mentioning. First, the politicization of negotiations has hardly affected policy design. Policymakers have not loosened the national obligations or avoided pooling and delegation as the scope of conflict within national political systems expanded. Second, enforcement has remained predominantly Council-centred, despite the problems of compliance. This ministerial reluctance to empower the supranational executive is rooted in informational pressures (i.e. economic uncertainties), which translate into major difficulties in estimating government budget balances. Some policy parameters like the reference values are essentially arbitrary: they reflect supranational bargaining dynamics rather than economic theories. Other policy indicators, like the structural budget, which is based on the output gap – a cornerstone construct of medium-run macroeconomic theories –, are unobservable. These uncertainties play a major role in centring enforcement around the Council and away from the Commission.

9.1.5 How Is Preventive Surveillance Designed?

Country-specific recommendations, proposed by the Commission and adopted by the Council, are the cornerstone of preventive surveillance – the first pillar of the policy. The Council has modified about two-thirds of these proposed recommendations, primarily to strengthen policy actions. As shown in Chapter 6, these changes reflect the economic and supranational pressures facing Council ministers – the latter being primarily related to bargaining and compliance.

The Council has modified more extensively the proposals if the target country has reported higher public debt or worsening economic conditions, or if such conditions have worsened across the whole continent. Greater divisiveness within the Council and an extreme position of the Commission (compared to the ministerial preferences) have also been associated with more modifications. Before 2010, the Council seemed also to have paid more attention to the recommendations addressed to more left-leaning governments.

Interestingly, the Council has strengthened the proposed actions if the position of the government whose support within this institution is necessary for adoption – the so-called acceptance pivot – has shifted to the right, and if the addressee country has been highly indebted (i.e. noncompliant). Until 2010, governments of larger countries, which have greater voting power, and, later on, governments of EU budget net contributing countries have been slightly more successful at weakening the recommendations addressed to them.

9.1.6 What Explains Compliance with Preventive Recommendations?

After eight months of their adoption, about six in ten recommended measures have been either fully or partially implemented, but there has been considerable variation across countries and time, as we show in Chapter 7. Examining national compliance with recommendations is a mirror image of analyzing position-taking as it, too, offers a good illustration of how the three sets of pressures operate. Governments have been inclined to adopt those recommended preventive measures that were associated with a more institutionalized supranational sanctioning system, which increases noncompliance costs (a supranational pressure factor) and, usually, if the economic conditions in their countries have worsened. As for national pressures, governments have procrastinated implementation in the proximity to an electoral contest, since adopting these measures may have engendered costs for their supporters. Other national factors did not seem to matter.

9.1.7 *What Explains Corrective Oversight and What Are Its Consequences?*

If prevention fails and the fiscal position of a country worsens, the Council may decide to open an excessive deficit procedure (EDP) – the most intrusive oversight of the entire policy. Reassuringly, compliance-related factors play centre stage in its use, as we show in Chapter 8. The Council has more likely begun the procedure and it has maintained oversight for a longer period if a country's deficit–GDP ratio has worsened. The Council has also prolonged oversight if the *expected* fiscal deficit of either the country under surveillance or (more weakly) across the whole EU increased. More interestingly, supranational bargaining pressures display non-trivial effects. A rightward shift, at the beginning of and throughout a given year, of the position of the Council minister which is pivotal for initiating or continuing the procedure has been associated with more probable and longer oversight. A rightward shift of the position of the Economic affairs commissioner had produced similar effects.

Past and expected economic conditions instead did not appear to matter much, most probably because they have been already factored in the actual and expected fiscal performance. On the other hand, larger economies have been more likely subject to oversight. As for national political factors, more pro-EU governments and pro-European countries spent less time under oversight, but the size of these effects is small. So did more right-leaning governments if they faced a low risk of replacement.

Importantly, in Chapter 8, we also show that supranational oversight has been very effective in constraining fiscal deficits, especially if the country has adopted the single currency.[2] A euro area government under oversight during the year of budgetary drafting has reduced the deficit by 0.57 per cent of GDP on average – a substantial impact considering the 3 per cent deficit–GDP reference value. Fiscal consolidation takes root gradually over four to five years of surveillance.

In line with established scholarship, Chapter 8 also shows that several economic and political factors have shaped public deficits. Higher

[2] Regardless of whether governments have been negotiating or benefiting from assistance. As expected, these governments tended to reduce their deficits significantly.

unemployment and, in Western Europe, lower economic growth and worsening terms of trade (i.e. spending, revenue and open-economy shocks) are associated with higher deficits. The fiscal performance also reflects a world of policy-seeking and office-seeking politicians, and fiscally illuded voters: highly indebted and fractionalized governments, left-leaning governments facing low replacement risks and governments expecting proximate electoral contests have tended to post higher deficits.[3] Notably, supranational oversight provides an effective offsetting barrier to these national political pressures.

9.2 Is the EU Economic Policy Effective?

This latter result is encouraging but it also prompts us to assess, concisely, the overall effectiveness of the policy. Has the policy safeguarded the long-term fiscal sustainability of its member countries? Has it achieved the objectives of strong sustainable growth and employment creation that are also explicitly stated in the SGP? Has it achieved a current account balance, especially within the euro area, as the macroeconomic imbalance procedure prescribes?

9.2.1 Fiscal Sustainability

Indeed, the long-term trajectory of fiscal sustainability in the EU as a whole has been anything but reassuring. Yet, it has been better than that of other large advanced economies. Figure 9.1 compares the development of government debt over GDP in the EU and the euro area with that of the US. The ratio has increased by respectively 11 and 12 percentage points since the establishment of the monetary union. The euro area has systematically exceeded the EU average by about 5 percentage points, and the difference has increased to more than 6 percentage points as a result of the crises. Euro area countries have been accumulating more debt as a percentage of their GDP than non-euro area countries.[4] Additionally, the bottom panel of Figure 9.1 shows that dispersion has increased significantly after

[3] In Western Europe, a higher effective number of electoral districts and higher tax structure complexity are also associated with higher deficits, while effective semipresidentialism appears to engender lower deficits.

[4] The best- and worst-performing countries are shown in Figures A9.1 and A9.2 in the online appendix to this chapter.

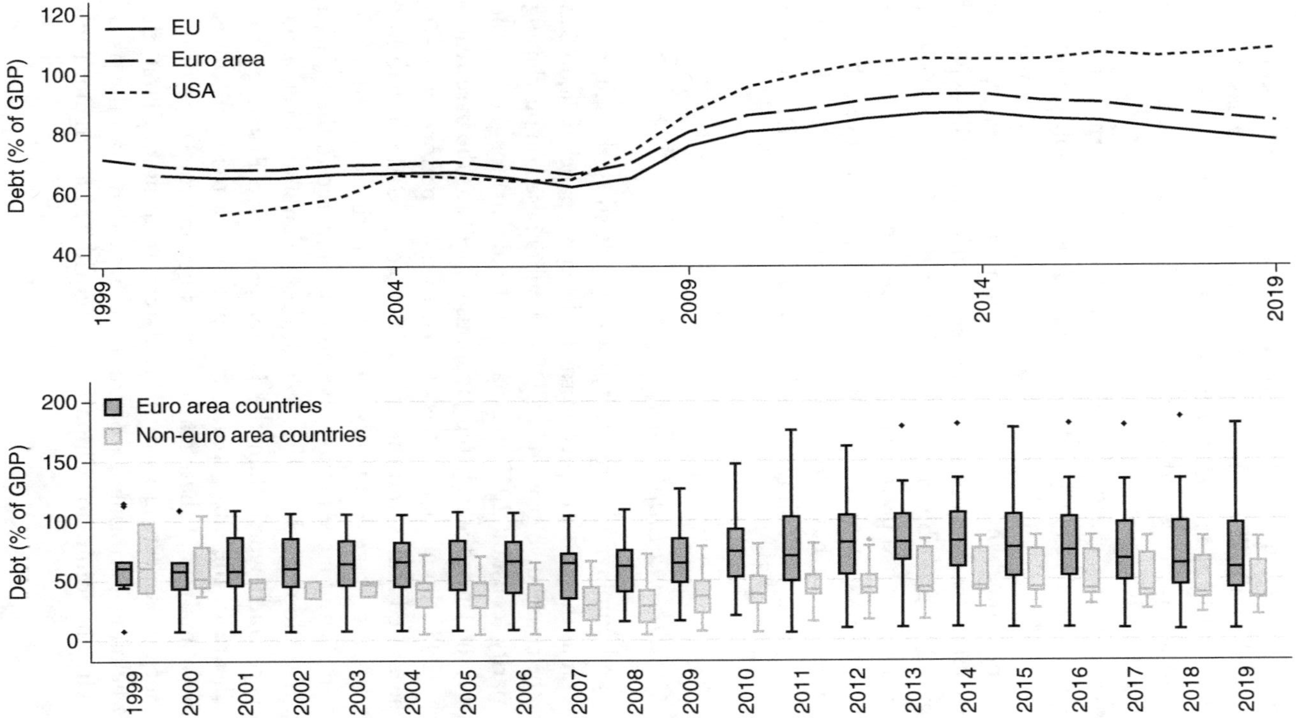

Figure 9.1 Debt as a percentage of GDP
Note: EDP measure of general government gross debt for EU countries. Data are from Eurostat and IMF.

the sovereign debt crisis, especially within the euro area, with Greece, Italy, and Portugal among the worst performers. Indeed, according to Koehler and König (2015), the adoption of the euro *per se* has engendered lower debt *than it would have otherwise been* for six northern European countries and higher debt for four southern European countries, plus Ireland.

If a comparison can be made, the policy has performed poorly as a preventive tool but reasonably as a corrective tool. Countries have, *on average*, failed to implement four out of six preventive recommendations, while the EDP has been used, *on average*, in the expected circumstances and it has delivered, *on average*, the expected outcomes. It is probably the combination of these two features that helps explain the bad performance in *absolute* terms and the acceptable performance in *relative* terms. On an aggregate level, the EU and the euro area have done indeed better than both the United States and Japan (not shown), which reached a debt–GDP ratio of 234 per cent in 2019.

9.2.2 Growth and Employment

Output and employment growth tell a different story though, especially as far as the euro area is concerned. The upper panel of Figure 9.2 reports the cumulative growth in GDP per capita based on purchasing power parity (constant 2017 international US dollar) for the EU, the euro area, the United States, and Japan, using 1994 as the base year.

Since 2003, the euro area has started to underperform vis-à-vis both the United States and the EU as a whole. By 2019, it had lost almost 10 percentage points in cumulative growth compared to the United States and more than twelve points compared to the EU as a whole. If we look at the entire period, the Italian and Greek economies performed worse than the Japanese. Twelve EU states, ten of which are in the euro area, have done worse than the United States.[5] An analysis of these trajectories is beyond the scope of our book, but two aspects are worth briefly commenting on. First, the underwhelming performance of the euro area is temporally associated with the joining of China to the World Trade Organization

[5] See Figures A9.3 and A9.4 in the online appendix to this chapter.

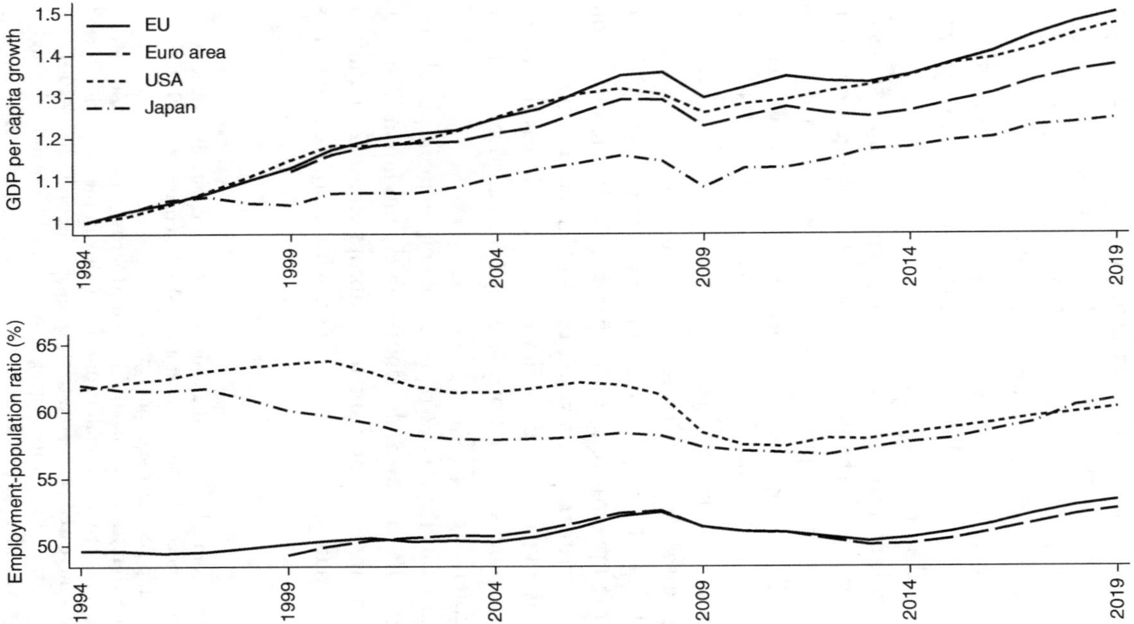

Figure 9.2 GDP per capita cumulative growth and employment-to-population ratio
Note: Upper panel: GDP at purchasing power parity per capita (constant 2017 international US dollar) calculated from the time series available from the World Development Indicators database. The base year is 1994. Lower panel: Employment to population ratio, for ages 15 to 64 (modelled ILO estimate). World Development Indicators database.

in December 2001[6] and the EU eastern enlargements of 2004 and 2007. The extant euro area economies appeared to have had a hard time dealing with the more intense continental and global competition. Surely, as a result of the enlargement, the EU included several poorer economies with higher growth prospects, accounting at least partially for the difference in performance between EU and euro area countries. Second, the sovereign debt crisis (and the poor management thereof, Stiglitz 2016) hampered the entire continent between 2011 and 2013 and engendered the largest gap in growth vis-à-vis both the United States and Japan.

A related issue is an increasing dispersion across member states of per capita income levels. The euro area is more heterogeneous than the EU because the per capita income of non-euro area countries is closer to the EU mean, but both sets of countries have become *more* heterogeneous over time.[7] Whether increased dispersion is bad depends on its causes. Enlargements to poorer countries increased dispersion, while the financial and sovereign debt crises reduced it because of their greater impact on higher-income countries.[8] More concerning is the upward trend in the per capita income dispersion in the euro area, primarily as a result of its enlargement, given that countries cannot take advantage of devaluation to address the asymmetric economic shocks that a more heterogeneous euro area is more likely to encounter.

The lower panel in Figure 9.2 reports the employment-population ratios for the EU, the euro area, the United States, and Japan. The slow upward trend in employment came to an abrupt end in 2008, and it has taken more than a decade to recover, with euro area countries

[6] Although starting from a low base, the Chinese GDP per capita experienced a seven-fold increase since 1994 and almost a four-fold increase since 2002.

[7] See Figures A9.5 and A9.6 in the online appendix.

[8] Especially within countries: Garcilazo, Moreno-Monroy, and Oliveira Martins (2021) report that regional income inequality in the post-crisis period (2008–2017) has increased compared to the pre-crisis period (2000–2007) within all EU countries, except for Portugal, Austria, and Finland. Although in most cases greater inequality was driven by better performances of the top-income regions, in others it was not. The dispersion was driven by either bottom regions becoming poorer (Greece), top regions becoming poorer (Portugal), or both (Italy). The bottom regions fared better in Finland, Belgium, and Austria.

underperforming compared to fellow EU members.[9] Structural differences in the labour markets tend to account for this enduring gap of approximately 10 percentage points between, on the one side, the European economy and, on the other side, the American and Japanese economies. Yet, solid evidence of employment creation across most European countries is missing.

9.2.3 *Current Account*

From an external perspective, the current account balance reinforces this story. The upper panel of Figure 9.3 reports the current account over GDP for the EU, the euro area, the US, China, and Japan. Since 2004, the EU balance has started to deteriorate considerably, despite remaining above the American balance. Certainly, the EU had to deal with the enlargement to Eastern and Central European countries, which began to have large deficits after opening up their markets to imports, during the 1990s, and integrating financially (Tang 2019). The financial crisis triggered sudden stops and reversals in imbalances within the EU as well as the euro area. Excess imbalances amplified between 2004 and 2009, but they were followed by a vigorous correction after 2010, except for the surpluses. In other words, excess deficits adjusted more forcefully than excess surpluses. Since 2014 both the EU and euro area current accounts have reached pre-crisis levels, performing as well as the Chinese balance and slightly less well than the Japanese one.

The lower panel of Figure 9.3 shows that dispersion has increased during the sovereign debt crisis, initially among non-euro area countries and then among the euro area countries. The German current account, for example, overperformed and is still overperforming even the Chinese one, while seventeen EU states, ten of which are in the euro area, have done worse than the EU average.[10]

In sum, the record of policy effectiveness is mixed. The long-term trends of overall fiscal sustainability, current account balance, and (EU-wide) economic growth appear reasonably reassuring, but these dynamics hide large cross-country differences that, rather worryingly, characterize mainly the euro area.

[9] Due especially to the significant improvement of eastern European countries, see Figures A9.7 and A9.8 in the online appendix.

[10] See Figures A9.9 and A9.10 in the online appendix to this chapter.

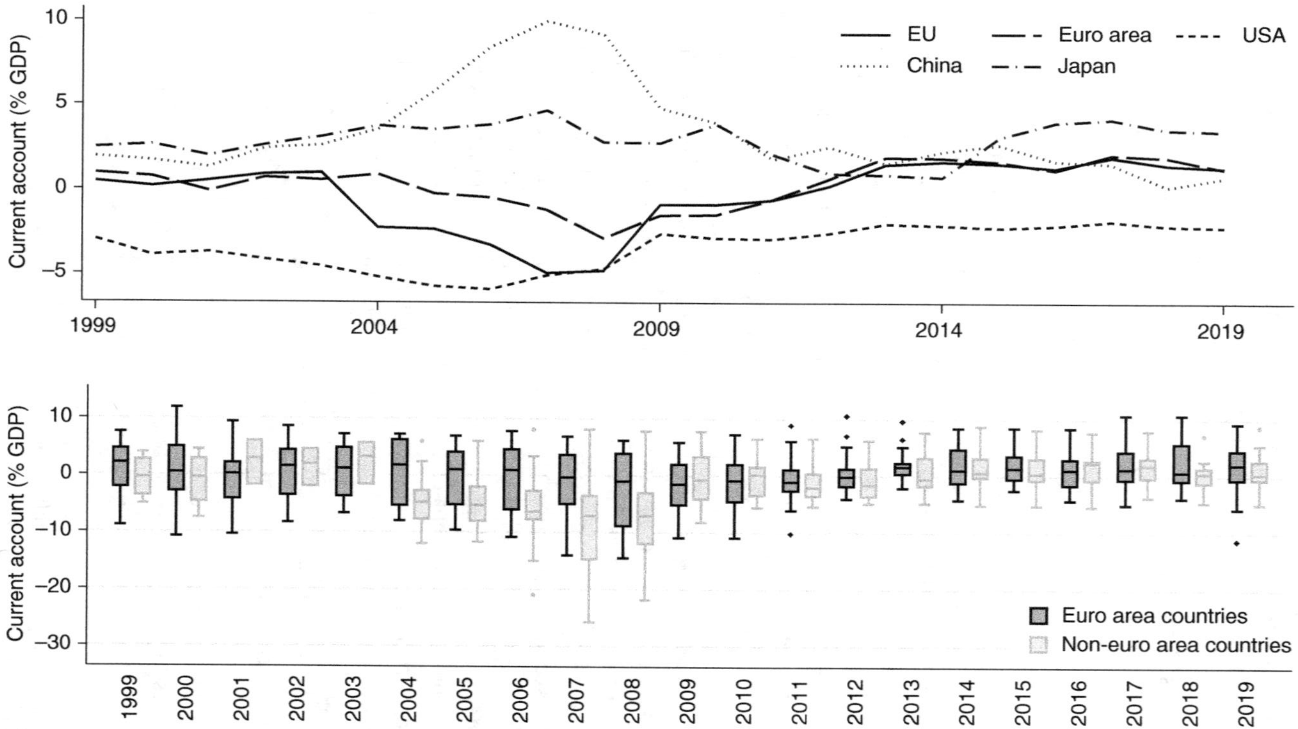

Figure 9.3 Current account as a percentage of GDP
Note: Data are from the World Development Indicators database.

9.3 Is the EU Economic Policy Fair?

Our results also point to some preliminary, yet intriguing, observations about fairness and responsiveness. Policy fairness can be assessed in relation to the design and the implementation. Consider policy design first. Do the negotiations produce fair outcomes? Do they abide by some normative principles of justice? There is no doubt of the hard bargaining and the intense pressures policymakers are subject to. Yet, in Chapter 4, we find the minimax solution, an approximation of the Rawlsian principle of justice, to outperform some bargaining and procedural models in terms of both mean absolute error and point predictive accuracy. Outcomes seem then to accommodate imperfectly, perhaps even inadvertently, some principles of justice. As a minimum, they are fairer than what we would obtain if we were to account for the conservative bias of the mere legal status quo ante of the issues under negotiations.

Fairness in implementation implies that governments should be subject to *similar* decisions if facing *similar* circumstances.[11] Issues of fairness concern the design of and compliance with surveillance recommendations and the use and consequences of the EDP. Are governments of more powerful countries, anti-EU governments, or governments facing public Euroscepticism treated differently? Early assessments have been disheartening. For instance, Jones (2013: 158) states that 'European institutions had little power to enforce the rules for smaller states, even when it made sense to do so, and little desire to enforce the rules for larger countries when it arguably made more sense to exercise discretion'. Later qualitative analyses emphasize how the rise of Euroscepticism and politicization have induced the Commission to exercise greater flexibility in enforcement (Miró 2021; van der Veer 2022).

In Chapter 6, we have seen that the Council has indeed weakened the recommendations addressed to larger or net-contributing countries before and after 2010, respectively. That these countries are treated more favourably raises fairness issues, but the sizes of these effects are admittedly rather small. Reassuringly, there is no evidence that the

[11] This implies that decisions should differ if circumstances are different. For instance, the 2011 reform of the corrective regulation mandated different adjustment benchmarks for countries with a debt–GDP ratio exceeding the reference value.

Council's treatment has varied as a function of Euroscepticism among the public at large. Prior to 2010, the Council had slightly strengthened the recommendations addressed to more Eurosceptic executives (and, after 2010, those addressed to more left-leaning ones), but these effects are also rather small. Similarly, the European orientation of the government is not associated with compliance with the recommendations, as we have shown in Chapter 7.[12] Mirroring the results in Chapter 6, countries with higher voting power were less compliant before 2010, but this effect disappeared with the establishment of the European Semester. Reassuringly, larger economies have been slightly *more* compliant from then on.

In Chapter 8, we find no evidence that the Council's use of the EDP is related to governmental or public Euroscepticism. The fact that more pro-EU governments and countries with a more pro-EU public spend less time under oversight has more to do with the greater political costs of being monitored than with fairness. And these results surely do not indicate that Euroscepticism engenders leniency. Moreover, larger countries are actually *more* likely to be put under the radar, probably because of the larger negative externalities associated with fiscal profligacy.

These conclusions are somewhat similar if we investigate the consequences of oversight. We have added to the European Union models in Table 8.2 three variables: *Economic size*, the *Anti–pro EU position* of a government, and *Public support* (their measurement is explained in Chapter 8). If included, with a one-year lag, separately or jointly in the model, these factors hardly affect the deficit. But results are more interesting if the variables are included separately in a three-way interaction with *Euro area* and *EDP*. Figure 9.4 displays the marginal effects of oversight across the size of the economy and the support for the EU in the government and among the public.

In line with the previous result, governments of larger economies consolidate *more* when under surveillance. A full year of oversight during budget drafting leads the government of an economy of the size of France or Italy to reduce the deficit by 1.2 per cent of GDP. Again, this is reassuring in terms of fairness. Larger economies do not use their clout to avoid compliance. Instead, because of the larger externalities of their excessive deficits, they consolidate more.

[12] The positive association between public Euroscepticism and compliance, during the European Semester period, appears to be a statistical quirk.

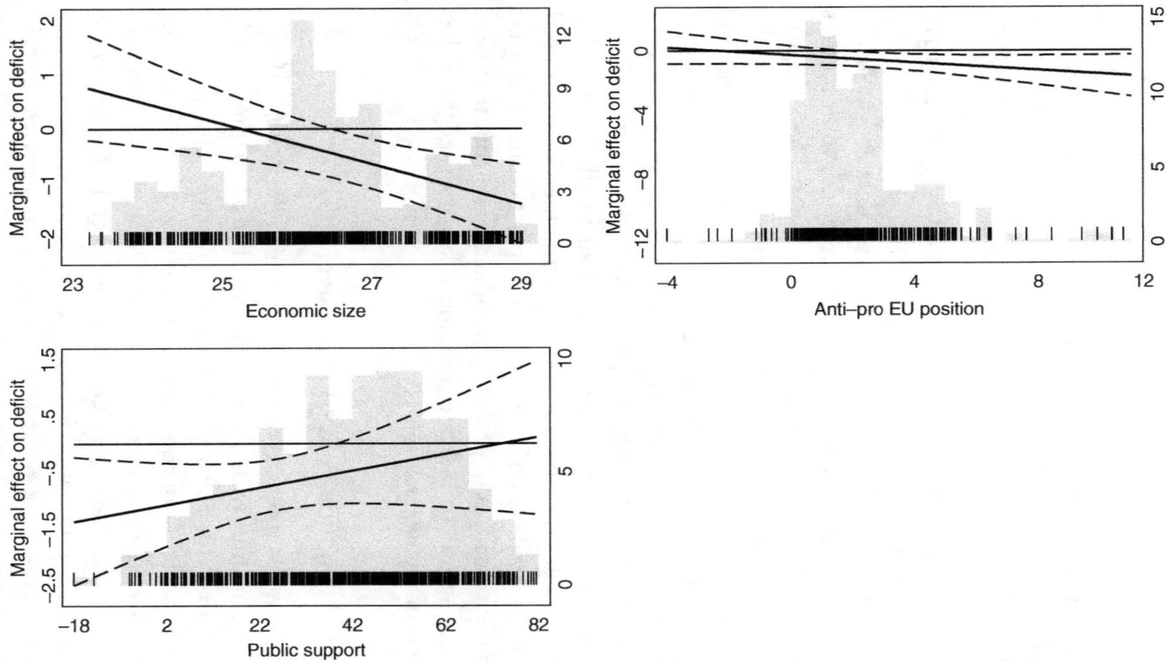

Figure 9.4 Marginal effects of oversight across economic size, government EU position, and public support
Note: Marginal effects derived from adding, separately, three-way interactions with *EDP* and *Euro area* to the European Union model in Table 8.2. Four outlying observations are dropped from the top right panel. Histograms underlaid.

Pro-European governments consolidate more than Eurosceptic ones (hence, they spend less time under oversight). A government with a pro-EU position a standard deviation above the mean, such as the socialist Lionel Jospin's government in France in 1998, would reduce the deficit by 0.95 per cent of GDP. On the other hand, countries with a more Eurosceptic public also consolidate more (by 0.80 per cent of GDP, if Euroscepticism is a standard deviation below the mean, like in Slovenia in 2014). Public Euroscepticism and executive Euroscepticism do not seem to produce similar outcomes then, and a Eurosceptic public opinion is surely not interpreted by governments as a license to loosen fiscal policy.

In sum, we cannot find glaring indications of unfairness. Surely, bargaining outcomes diverge from the Rawlsian ideal. Power matters in the negotiations over policy rules and instruments. The European orientation of the executive has not been entirely ignored by the Council in its recommendations, and larger countries were, initially, less compliant. But these effects have been either small or did not last. Notably, larger economies became over time *more* compliant with the recommendations. They have also been *more* likely subject to oversight and consolidated to a greater extent than smaller economies. In other words, concerns about negative externalities have trumped the influence of raw economic power in implementation. Moreover, the different performances of pro-EU governments and countries with pro-EU publics appear to indicate differing costs of oversight rather than problems of unfairness.

9.4 Is the EU Economic Policy Responsive?

Congruence normally refers to the extent to which the actions of representatives are in line with public opinion at a given time, while responsiveness has to do with how representatives change their behaviour to become more congruent with public opinion over time (Huber and Powell 1994; Page and Shapiro 1983). But we can take a broader view. For instance, we may wonder whether the actions of representatives are congruent with their ideological inclinations and whether policy outputs are congruent with and responsive to shifts in the political preferences of key representatives.

In the EU context, at least two types of actions have been objects of investigation: the positions governments take at the EU negotiating table and the policy outcomes.[13] A proper examination of this topic is beyond the objectives of this book, but we can draw some tentative conclusions from our findings. As far as national public opinion is concerned, we find evidence of responsiveness during preference formation and policy execution, but not policy design. As we have shown in Chapters 3 and 8, governments facing a pro-European public are keener to empower the Commission[14] and they are faster in exiting the EDP. On the other hand, the politicization of negotiations and national public opinion hardly appear to shape how legal provisions and executive instruments are designed.

As far as the congruence of actions with ideological inclinations is concerned, the association between left-leaning positions and a preference for greater national discretion and more Council involvement is coherent with an ideological aversion to the monitoring of national budgets, while pro-European positions associated with domestic loosening positions are harder to interpret in this light. The picture is also mixed if we look at policy implementation. We find, for instance, no association between governmental positions and compliance with recommendations. On the other hand, pro-EU and (if facing low replacement risks) right-leaning governments put more effort into exiting the EDP – a behaviour that is coherent with their inclinations.

Finally, consider policy outputs. We have repeatedly stated that legal provisions tend to reflect faithfully compromise positions, but it is also worth emphasizing that executive measures *respond* to changes in governmental and supranational positions. As we have reported in Chapters 6 and 8, for instance, a rightward shift of the position of the Council's pivotal government is associated with a strengthening of the recommendations, and with more probable and longer oversight. So does a rightward shift within the Commission, as far as oversight is concerned.

Surely, more research is needed. Following the recent works of Miró (2021) and van der Veer (2022), the responsiveness of the supranational

[13] Congruence and responsiveness have been assessed with regard to EU-wide and national public opinion (Hagemann, Hobolt, and Wratil 2017; Schneider 2018; Toshkov 2011; Wratil 2019) and to the positions of domestic support coalitions and parliaments (Franchino and Wratil 2019; Hagemann, Bailer, and Herzog 2019; Hobolt and Wratil 2020).

[14] The fact that they also tend to prefer greater national discretion is harder to interpret though.

executive should perhaps become a priority in future research, given its steady empowerment. Government responsiveness also deserves a more systematic analysis. These results, nevertheless, paint a picture of a policy that is not insensitive to changes in public opinion and governmental positions and of representatives that do not ignore their voters and that act on their inclinations whether that entails tabling negotiating positions, adopting executive measures, or complying with recommendations and decisions.

9.5 Conclusion: The Scope of the Theoretical Framework

Perhaps the main takeaway from the theoretical framework we have introduced is highlighting how the pressures we have identified cut across the entire policy cycle and how they resurface across time. The framework is built atop extraordinarily rich literature yet, because of the narrower focus of most of these scholarly works, we may fail to appreciate how these pressure patterns reverberate across the stages of the policy process – from design to implementation, and back – and how they reoccur over time.

In our view, this approach is likely to be useful for the study of many EU policies. Also in other circumstances, the combination of socioeconomic, national, and supranational pressures should help us explain the formation of preferences, the outcomes of negotiations over legislative and executive measures, the timing and direction of reforms, and the patterns of implementation and compliance. And the relative importance of these pressures is likely to vary across the policy cycle in predictable ways: more equally balanced during preference formation and compliance, whilst more dominated by supranational factors during negotiations.

Surely, the ideational foundations, the levels of uncertainty, and the socioeconomic aspects vary from policy to policy, but the need to win office and pursue policies is a recurrent feature of national democratic politics as much as bargaining and ensuring compliance and effective implementation are enduring characteristics of supranational politics. Controversies will vary across policies, but they will still probably reflect supranational, national, and socioeconomic pressures. If the triggers for reforms are powerful enough, compromise positions would still be likely to emerge victorious. The direction reforms would take would probably be shaped by policy uncertainties, patterns of noncompliance, problems of commitment, threats, and issue linkages. And although the specific implementation procedures would vary across policies, the key building blocks that characterize supranational negotiations would still be useful. Similarly, national compliance would not only reflect the socioeconomic conditions surrounding a policy but also the national and supranational constraints under which national politicians operate.

As for the development of EU economic policy, the reader may recall from Chapter 1 that the general escape clause was activated in March 2020 following the COVID-19 pandemic. The suspension has been further extended to 2023 after the Russian invasion of Ukraine. Soon thereafter, in the spring of 2024, the European Parliament and the governments agreed on a reform that tried to address some of the policy's problematic features. In addition, the recent expansion of the EU's limited fiscal capacity – a serious flaw of the monetary union according to several observers – has raised legitimate concerns about the waste of public resources that can only be assuaged by effective, fair, and responsive policymaking. An in-depth analysis of this latest reform and its implementation is premature, but what our research indicates is that they are unlikely to escape the competing pressures arising from the economy, national politics, and supranational politics.

References

Abbott, Kenneth W., Robert O. Keohane, Andrew Moravcsik, Anne-Marie Slaughter, and Duncan Snidal. 2000. 'The Concept of Legalization'. *International Organization* 54 (3): 401–19.

Achen, Christopher H. 2006a. 'Evaluating Political Decision-Making Models'. In *The European Union Decides*, edited by Robert Thomson, Frans N. Stokman, Christopher H. Achen, and Thomas König, 264–98. Cambridge: Cambridge University Press.

2006b. 'Institutional Realism and Bargaining Models'. In *The European Union Decides*, edited by Robert Thomson, Frans N. Stokman, Christopher H. Achen, and Thomas König, 86–123. Cambridge: Cambridge University Press.

Agence Europe. 1996. 'Europe Daily Bulletin n. 6851,' 12 November.

Agnello, Luca, Vitor Castro, João Tovar Jalles, and Ricardo M. Sousa. 2015. 'What Determines the Likelihood of Structural Reforms?' *European Journal of Political Economy* 37 (March): 129–45.

Aksoy, Deniz. 2012. 'Institutional Arrangements and Logrolling: Evidence from the European Union'. *American Journal of Political Science* 56 (3): 538–52.

Alesina, Alberto, Silvia Ardagna, and Jordi Galí. 1998. 'Tales of Fiscal Adjustment'. *Economic Policy* 13 (27): 489–545.

Alesina, Alberto, Carlo Favero, and Francesco Giavazzi. 2019. *Austerity: When It Works and When It Doesn't*. Princeton, NJ: Princeton University Press.

Alesina, Alberto, and Vittorio Grilli. 1994. 'The European Central Bank: Reshaping Monetary Politics in Europe'. In *Monetary and Fiscal Policy*, edited by Torsten Persson and Guido Tabellini, Volume 1: Credibility: 247–77. Cambridge, MA: The MIT Press.

Alesina, Alberto, and Roberto Perotti. 1995. 'Fiscal Expansions and Adjustments in OECD Countries'. *Economic Policy* 10 (21): 207–48.

Alesina, Alberto, Nouriel Roubini, and Gerald D. Cohen. 1997. *Political Cycles and the Macroeconomy*. Cambridge, MA: The MIT Press.

Alesina, Alberto, and Guido Tabellini. 1990. 'A Positive Theory of Fiscal Deficits and Government Debt'. *The Review of Economic Studies* 57 (3): 403–14.

Al-Kadi, Rayan, and Stefan Clauwaert. 2019. 'Socialising the European Semester? Measuring Member States' Implementation of Country-Specific Recommendations in the Social Policy Field'. *ETUI Working Paper* 08: 24.

Alt, James, David Dreyer Lassen, and Joachim Wehner. 2014. 'It Isn't Just about Greece: Domestic Politics, Transparency and Fiscal Gimmickry in Europe'. *British Journal of Political Science* 44 (4): 707–16.

Alter, Karen J. 2001. *Establishing Supremacy of European Law: The Making of an International Rule of Law in Europe*. Oxford: Oxford University Press.

Armingeon, Klaus, and Skyler Cranmer. 2018. 'Position-Taking in the Euro Crisis'. *Journal of European Public Policy* 25 (4): 546–66.

Arregui, Javier. 2016. 'Determinants of Bargaining Satisfaction across Policy Domains in the European Union Council of Ministers'. *Journal of Common Market Studies* 54 (5): 1105–22.

Arregui, Javier, Frans N. Stokman, and Robert Thomson. 2006. 'Compromise, Exchange and Challenge in the European Union'. In *The European Union Decides*, edited by Robert Thomson, Frans N. Stokman, Christopher H. Achen, and Thomas König, 124–52. Cambridge: Cambridge University Press.

Arregui, Javier, and Robert Thomson. 2009. 'States' Bargaining Success in the European Union'. *Journal of European Public Policy* 16 (5): 655–76.

Artis, Michael J., and Marco Buti. 2000. "'Close-to-Balance or in Surplus': A Policy-Maker's Guide to the Implementation of the Stability and Growth Pact'. *Journal of Common Market Studies* 38 (4): 563–91.

Baerg, Nicole, and Mark Hallerberg. 2022. 'Council Checks of the Commission under the European Semester: Does Member State Power and Euroscepticism Still Matter?'. *Journal of Common Market Studies* 60 (1): 58–80.

Baerg, Nicole Rae, and Mark Hallerberg. 2016. 'Explaining Instability in the Stability and Growth Pact: The Contribution of Member State Power and Euroskepticism to the Euro Crisis'. *Comparative Political Studies*, 49 (7): 968–1009.

Bailer, Stefanie. 2004. 'Bargaining Success in the European Union: The Impact of Exogenous and Endogenous Power Resources'. *European Union Politics* 5 (1): 99–123.

Bailer, Stefanie, Mikko Mattila, and Gerald Schneider. 2015. 'Money Makes the EU Go Round: The Objective Foundations of Conflict in the Council of Ministers'. *Journal of Common Market Studies* 53 (3): 437–56.

Bailer, Stefanie, and Gerald Schneider. 2006. 'Nash versus Schelling? The Importance of Constraints in Legislative Bargaining'. In *The European*

Union Decides, edited by Robert Thomson, Frans N. Stokman, Christopher H. Achen, and Thomas König, 153–77. Cambridge: Cambridge University Press.

Balassone, Fabrizio, and Raffaela Giordano. 2001. 'Budget Deficits and Coalition Governments'. *Public Choice* 106 (3): 327–49.

Baron, David P., and John A. Ferejohn. 1989. 'Bargaining in Legislatures'. *American Political Science Review* 83 (4): 1181–1206.

Barro, Robert J. 1974. 'Are Government Bonds Net Wealth?' *Journal of Political Economy* 82 (6): 1095–1117.

1979. 'On the Determination of the Public Debt'. *Journal of Political Economy* 87 (5, Part 1): 940–71.

Bauer, Michael W., and Stefan Becker. 2014. 'The Unexpected Winner of the Crisis: The European Commission's Strengthened Role in Economic Governance'. *Journal of European Integration* 36 (3): 213–29.

Bawn, Kathleen, and Frances Rosenbluth. 2006. 'Short versus Long Coalitions: Electoral Accountability and the Size of the Public Sector'. *American Journal of Political Science* 50 (2): 251–65.

Beetsma, Roel, and Massimo Giuliodori. 2009. 'Fiscal Adjustment to Cyclical Developments in the OECD: An Empirical Analysis Based on Real-Time Data'. *Oxford Economic Papers* 62 (3): 419–41.

2010. 'The Macroeconomic Costs and Benefits of the EMU and Other Monetary Unions: An Overview of Recent Research'. *Journal of Economic Literature* 48 (3): 603–41.

Beetsma, Roel, and Harald Uhlig. 1999. 'An Analysis of the Stability and Growth Pact'. *The Economic Journal* 109 (458): 546–71.

Beetsma, Roel M. W. J., and A. Lans Bovenberg. 1997a. 'Designing Fiscal and Monetary Institutions in a Second-Best World'. *European Journal of Political Economy* 13 (1): 53–79.

1997b. 'Central Bank Independence and Public Debt Policy'. *Journal of Economic Dynamics and Control* 21 (4–5): 873–94.

1998. 'Monetary Union without Fiscal Coordination May Discipline Policymakers'. *Journal of International Economics* 45 (2): 239–58.

Beetsma, Roel M. W. J., and A. Lans Bovenberg. 1999. 'Does Monetary Unification Lead to Excessive Debt Accumulation?' *Journal of Public Economics* 74 (3): 299–325.

Béland, Daniel, and Robert Henry Cox. 2010. *Ideas and Politics in Social Science Research. Ideas and Politics in Social Science Research*. Oxford: Oxford University Press.

Bergin, Paul R. 2000. 'Fiscal Solvency and Price Level Determination in a Monetary Union'. *Journal of Monetary Economics* 45 (1): 37–53.

Bernhard, William T., and David Leblang. 2016. 'Sovereign Debt, Migration Pressure, and Government Survival'. *Comparative Political Studies* 49 (7): 907–38.

Bickerton, Christopher J., Dermot Hodson, and Uwe Puetter. 2015. 'The New Intergovernmentalism: European Integration in the Post-Maastricht Era'. *Journal of Common Market Studies* 53 (4): 703–22.

Biermann, Felix, Nina Guérin, Stefan Jagdhuber, Berthold Rittberger, and Moritz Weiss. 2019. 'Political (Non-)Reform in the Euro Crisis and the Refugee Crisis: A Liberal Intergovernmentalist Explanation'. *Journal of European Public Policy* 26 (2): 246–66.

Birch, Sarah. 2001. 'Electoral Systems and Party Systems in Europe East and West'. *Perspectives on European Politics and Society* 2 (3): 355–77.

Blanchard, Olivier. 2019. 'AEA Presidential Address: Public Debt and Low Interest Rates'. *American Economic Review*, 109 (4): 1197–1229.

Blyth, Mark. 2013. *Austerity: The History of a Dangerous Idea.* Oxford, NY: Oxford University Press.

Bokhorst, David. 2022. 'The Influence of the European Semester: Case Study Analysis and Lessons for Its Post-Pandemic Transformation'. *Journal of Common Market Studies* 60 (1): 101–17.

Boranbay-Akan, Serra, Thomas König, and Moritz Osnabrügge. 2017. 'The Imperfect Agenda-Setter: Why Do Legislative Proposals Fail in the EU Decision-Making Process?' *European Union Politics* 18 (2): 168–87.

Börzel, Tanja A., Tobias Hofmann, and Diana Panke. 2012. 'Caving in or Sitting It out? Longitudinal Patterns of Non-Compliance in the European Union'. *Journal of European Public Policy* 19 (4): 454–71.

Börzel, Tanja A., Tobias Hofmann, Diana Panke, and Carina Sprungk. 2010. 'Obstinate and Inefficient: Why Member States Do Not Comply With European Law'. *Comparative Political Studies* 43 (11): 1363–90.

Börzel, Tanja A., and Thomas Risse. 2018. 'From the Euro to the Schengen Crises: European Integration Theories, Politicization, and Identity Politics'. *Journal of European Public Policy* 25 (1): 83–108.

Bräuninger, Thomas. 2005. 'A Partisan Model of Government Expenditure'. *Public Choice* 125 (3/4): 409–29.

Brender, Adi, and Allan Drazen. 2005. 'Political Budget Cycles in New versus Established Democracies'. *Journal of Monetary Economics* 52 (7): 1271–95.

Bressanelli, Edoardo, and Nicola Chelotti. 2016. 'The Shadow of the European Council. Understanding Legislation on Economic Governance'. *Journal of European Integration* 38 (5): 511–25.

2018. 'The European Parliament and Economic Governance: Explaining a Case of Limited Influence'. *The Journal of Legislative Studies* 24 (1): 72–89.

Buiter, Willem H. 1999. 'Alice in Euroland'. *Journal of Common Market Studies* 37 (2): 181–209.

2006. 'The 'Sense and Nonsense of Maastricht' Revisited: What Have We Learnt about Stabilization in EMU?' *Journal of Common Market Studies* 44 (4): 687–710.

Buiter, Willem H., Giancarlo Corsetti, Nouriel Roubini, Rafael Repullo, and Jeffrey Frankel. 1993. 'Excessive Deficits: Sense and Nonsense in the Treaty of Maastricht'. *Economic Policy* 8 (16): 57–100.

Burley, Anne-Marie, and Walter Mattli. 1993. 'Europe Before the Court: A Political Theory of Legal Integration'. *International Organization* 47 (1): 41–76.

Camisão, Isabel. 2015. 'Irrelevant Player? The Commission's Role during the Eurozone Crisis'. *Journal of Contemporary European Research* 11 (3): 268–86.

Canzoneri, Matthew B., Robert E. Cumby, and Behzad T. Diba. 2001. 'Fiscal Discipline and Exchange Rate Systems'. *The Economic Journal* 111 (474): 667–90.

Canzoneri, Matthew B., and Behzad T. Diba. 2001. 'The SGP: Delicate Balance or Albatross?' In *The Stability and Growth Pact: The Architecture of Fiscal Policy in EMU*, edited by Anne Brunila, Marco Buti, and Daniele Franco, 53–74. New York: Palgrave.

Caplin, Andrew, and Barry Nalebuff. 1991. 'Aggregation and Social Choice: A Mean Voter Theorem'. *Econometrica* 59 (1): 1–23.

Carrubba, Clifford J. 1997. 'Net Financial Transfers in the European Union: Who Gets What and Why?' *Journal of Politics* 59 (2): 469–96.

2005. 'Courts and Compliance in International Regulatory Regimes'. *Journal of Politics* 67 (3): 669–89.

Carrubba, Clifford J., Matthew Gabel, and Charles Hankla. 2008. 'Judicial Behavior under Political Constraints: Evidence from the European Court of Justice'. *American Political Science Review* 102 (04): 435–52.

Carstensen, Martin B., and Vivien A. Schmidt. 2018. 'Ideational Power and Pathways to Legitimation in the Euro Crisis'. *Review of International Political Economy* 25 (6): 753–78.

Caselli, Francesca G., and Philippe Wingender. 2018. 'Bunching at 3 Percent: The Maastricht Fiscal Criterion and Government Deficits'. *IMF Working Papers* 18 (182): 1–38.

Chari, Varadarajan V., and Patrick J. Kehoe. 2007. 'On the Need for Fiscal Constraints in a Monetary Union'. *Journal of Monetary Economics* 54 (8): 2399–2408.

Chayes, Abram, and Antonia Handler Chayes. 1995. *The New Sovereignty: Compliance with International Regulatory Agreements*. Cambridge, MA: Harvard University Press.

Cheruvu, Sivaram. 2022. 'When Does the European Commission Pursue Noncompliance?' *European Union Politics* 23 (3): 375–97.

Chiba, Daina, Lanny W. Martin, and Randolph T. Stevenson. 2015. 'A Copula Approach to the Problem of Selection Bias in Models of Government Survival'. *Political Analysis* 23 (1): 42–58.

Cimadomo, Jacopo. 2012. 'Fiscal Policy in Real Time'. *The Scandinavian Journal of Economics* 114 (2): 440–65.

Citi, Manuele, and Mogens K. Justesen. 2016. 'Institutional Constraints, Legislative Activism and Policy Change: The Case of the European Union'. *European Journal of Political Research* 55 (3): 609–25.

Claeys, Grégory, Zsolt Darvas, and Àlvaro Leandro. 2016. 'A Proposal to Revive the European Fiscal Framework'. *Bruegel Policy Contribution* 07: 20.

Clark, William Roberts. 2003. *Capitalism, Not Globalism: Capital Mobility, Central Bank Independence, and the Political Control of the Economy*. Ann Arbor, MI: University of Michigan Press.

Clark, William Roberts, Matt Golder, and Sona Nadenichek Golder. 2012. *Principles of Comparative Politics*. 2nd ed. Washington, D.C: Cq Pr.

Clarke, P. 2008. 'When Can Group Level Clustering Be Ignored? Multilevel Models versus Single-Level Models with Sparse Data'. *Journal of Epidemiology and Community Health* 62 (8): 752–58.

Copeland, Paul, and Mary Daly. 2018. 'The European Semester and EU Social Policy'. *Journal of Common Market Studies* 56 (5): 1001–18.

Copelovitch, Mark, Jeffry Frieden, and Stefanie Walter. 2016. 'The Political Economy of the Euro Crisis'. *Comparative Political Studies* 49 (7): 811–40.

Cova, Joshua. 2022. 'Reconsidering the Drivers of Country-Specific Recommendations: The Commission's Ideological Preferences on Wage Policies'. *European Union Politics* 23 (4): 639–61.

Crespy, Amandine, and Vivien Schmidt. 2014. 'The Clash of Titans: France, Germany and the Discursive Double Game of EMU Reform'. *Journal of European Public Policy* 21 (8): 1085–1101.

Crombez, Christophe. 1996. 'Legislative Procedures in the European Community'. *British Journal of Political Science* 26 (2): 199–218.

1997. 'The Co-decision Procedure in the European Union'. *Legislative Studies Quarterly* 22 (1): 97–119.

Crombez, Christophe, and Simon Hix. 2015. 'Legislative Activity and Gridlock in the European Union'. *British Journal of Political Science* 45 (3): 477–99.

Cross, James P. 2013. 'Everyone's a Winner (Almost): Bargaining Success in the Council of Ministers of the European Union'. *European Union Politics* 14 (1): 70–94.

Darvas, Zsolt, and Àlvaro Leandro. 2015. 'The Limitations of Policy Coordination in the Euro Area under the European Semester'. *Bruegel Policy Contribution* 2015/19: 29. www.bruegel.org/system/files/wp_attachments/pc_2015_194.pdf

Degner, Hanno, and Dirk Leuffen. 2019. 'Franco-German Cooperation and the Rescuing of the Eurozone'. *European Union Politics* 20 (1): 89–108.

De Grauwe, Paul, and Yuemei Ji. 2013a. 'From Panic-Driven Austerity to Symmetric Macroeconomic Policies in the Eurozone'. *Journal of Common Market Studies* 51 (S1): 31–41.

2013b. 'Self-Fulfilling Crises in the Eurozone: An Empirical Test'. *Journal of International Money and Finance* 34 (April): 15–36.

De Haan, Jakob, Helge Berger, and David-Jan Jansen. 2004. 'Why Has the Stability and Growth Pact Failed?' *International Finance* 7 (2): 235–60.

De Haan, Jakob, Richard Jong-A-Pin, and Jochen O. Mierau. 2013. 'Do Budgetary Institutions Mitigate the Common Pool Problem? New Empirical Evidence for the EU'. *Public Choice* 156 (3): 423–41.

De Haan, Jakob, and Jan-Egbert Sturm. 1994. 'Political and Institutional Determinants of Fiscal Policy in the European Community'. *Public Choice* 80 (1): 157–72.

1997. 'Political and Economic Determinants of OECD Budget Deficits and Government Expenditures: A Reinvestigation'. *European Journal of Political Economy* 13 (4): 739–50.

2000. 'Do Financial Markets and the Maastricht Treaty Discipline Governments? New Evidence'. *Applied Financial Economics* 10 (2): 221–26.

Dehousse, Renaud. 2016. 'Why Has EU Macroeconomic Governance Become More Supranational?' *Journal of European Integration* 38 (5): 617–31.

De Jong, Jasper F. M., and Niels D. Gilbert. 2020. 'Fiscal Discipline in EMU? Testing the Effectiveness of the Excessive Deficit Procedure'. *European Journal of Political Economy* 61: 101822.

D'Erman, Valerie, Jörg Haas, Daniel F. Schulz, and Amy Verdun. 2019. 'Measuring Economic Reform Recommendations under the European Semester: 'One Size Fits All' or Tailoring to Member States?' *Journal of Contemporary European Research* 15 (2): 194–211.

D'Erman, Valerie J., Daniel F. Schulz, Amy Verdun, and Dennis Zagermann. 2022. 'The European Semester in the North and in the South: Domestic Politics and the Salience of EU-Induced Wage Reform in Different Growth Models'. *Journal of Common Market Studies* 60 (1): 21–39.

Dias da Silva, Antonio, Audrey Givone, and David Sondermann. 2018. 'When Do Countries Implement Structural Reforms?' In *The Political Economy of Structural Reforms in Europe*, edited by Nauro F. Campos, Paul De Grauwe, and Yuemei Ji, 45–74. Oxford: Oxford University Press.

Di Mascio, Fabrizio, Alessandro Natalini, Edoardo Ongaro, and Francesco Stolfi. 2019. 'Influence of the European Semester on National Public

Sector Reforms under Conditions of Fiscal Consolidation: The Policy of Conditionality in Italy 2011–2015' *Public Policy and Administration* 35 (2): 201–23.

Dimitrova, Antoaneta, and Bernard Steunenberg. 2000. 'The Search for Convergence of National Policies in the European Union. An Impossible Quest?' *European Union Politics* 1 (2): 201–26.

Dixit, Avinash. 2001. 'Games of Monetary and Fiscal Interactions in the EMU'. *European Economic Review* 45 (4–6): 589–613.

Dixit, Avinash, and Luisa Lambertini. 2001. 'Monetary–Fiscal Policy Interactions and Commitment versus Discretion in a Monetary Union'. *European Economic Review* 45 (4–6): 977–87.

2003. 'Symbiosis of Monetary and Fiscal Policies in a Monetary Union'. *Journal of International Economics* 60 (2): 235–47.

Döring, Holger, and Philip Manow. 2019. '*Parliaments and Governments Database (ParlGov): Information on Parties, Elections and Cabinets in Modern Democracies*'. *Development Version*. Technical report.

2021. 'Parliaments and Governments Database (ParlGov): Information on Parties, Elections and Cabinets in Modern Democracies'. Development Version. Technical report.

Downs, George W., David M. Rocke, and Peter N. Barsoom. 1996. 'Is the Good News about Compliance Good News about Cooperation?' *International Organization* 50 (3): 379–406.

Drazen, Allan, and William Easterly. 2001. 'Do Crises Induce Reform? Simple Empirical Tests of Conventional Wisdom'. *Economics & Politics* 13 (2): 129–57.

Drazen, Allan, and Vittorio Grilli. 1993. 'The Benefit of Crises for Economic Reforms'. *American Economic Review* 83 (3): 598–607.

Dyson, Kenneth, and Kevin Featherstone. 1996. 'Italy and EMU as a 'Vincolo Esterno': Empowering the Technocrats, Transforming the State'. *South European Society and Politics* 1 (2): 272–99.

Dyson, Kenneth, and Ivo Maes, eds. 2016. *Architects of the Euro: Intellectuals in the Making of European Monetary Union*. Oxford: Oxford University Press.

Efstathiou, Konstantinos, and Guntram Wolff. 2019. 'What Drives National Implementation of EU Policy Recommendations?' *Bruegel Working Paper* 04: 28.

Eichengreen, Barry, and Ugo Panizza. 2014. 'A Surplus of Ambition: Can Europe Rely on Large Primary Surpluses to Solve Its Debt Problem?' *National Bureau of Economic Research* Working Paper 20316.

Eichengreen, Barry, and Charles Wyplosz. 1998. 'The Stability Pact: More than a Minor Nuisance?' *Economic Policy* 13 (26): 65–113.

Eihmanis, Edgars. 2018. 'Cherry-Picking External Constraints: Latvia and EU Economic Governance, 2008–2014'. *Journal of European Public Policy* 25 (2): 231–49.

Einaudi, Luigi. 2004. *Lezioni di politica sociale*. Torino: Einaudi.

Elgie, Robert. 2011. *Semi-Presidentialism: Sub-Types and Democratic Performance*. Oxford: Oxford University Press.

European Commission. 2009. *European Union Budget 2008: Financial Report*. Luxembourg: European Communities.

2019. 'Assessment of the 2019 Stability Programme for Italy'. Brussels: European Commission.

European Court of Auditors. 2018. 'Audit of the Macroeconomic Imbalance Procedure (MIP)'. 3. Luxembourg: European Court of Auditors.

2020. 'The European Semester – Country Specific Recommendations Address Important Issues but Need Better Implementation'. 16. Special Report. Luxembourg: European Court of Auditors.

European Parliament. 2013. 'Country Specific Recommendations 2012 and 2013: Comparison and Overview of Implementation'. PE 497.731. Brussels: European Parliament.

Fabbrini, Sergio. 2013. 'Intergovernmentalism and Its Limits Assessing the European Union's Answer to the Euro Crisis'. *Comparative Political Studies* 46 (9): 1003–29.

2016. 'From Consensus to Domination: The Intergovernmental Union in a Crisis Situation'. *Journal of European Integration* 38 (5): 587–99.

Fabbrini, Sergio, and Uwe Puetter. 2016. 'Integration without Supranationalisation: Studying the Lead Roles of the European Council and the Council in Post-Lisbon EU Politics'. *Journal of European Integration* 38 (5): 481–95.

Fabrizio, Stefania, and Ashoka Mody. 2006. 'Can Budget Institutions Counteract Political Indiscipline?' *Economic Policy* 21 (48): 690–739.

Faini, Riccardo, Gilles Duranton, and Harald Hau. 2006. 'Fiscal Policy and Interest Rates in Europe'. *Economic Policy* 21 (47): 443–89.

Falkner, Gerda, Oliver Treib, Miriam Hartlapp, and Simone Leiber. 2005. *Complying with Europe*. New York: Cambridge University Press.

Fatás, Antonio, and Ilian Mihov. 2010. 'The Euro and Fiscal Policy'. In *Europe and the Euro*, edited by Alberto Alesina and Francesco Giavazzi, 287–326. Chicago: University of Chicago Press.

Fearon, James D. 1998. 'Bargaining, Enforcement, and International Cooperation'. *International Organization* 52 (2): 269–305.

Finke, Daniel, and Stefanie Bailer. 2019. 'Crisis Bargaining in the European Union: Formal Rules or Market Pressure?' *European Union Politics* 20 (1): 109–33.

Fjelstul, Joshua C., and Clifford J. Carrubba. 2018. 'The Politics of International Oversight: Strategic Monitoring and Legal Compliance in the European Union'. *American Political Science Review* 112 (3): 429–45.
Fortunato, David, and Matt W. Loftis. 2018. 'Cabinet Durability and Fiscal Discipline'. *American Political Science Review* 112 (4): 939–53.
Franchino, Fabio. 2007. *The Powers of the Union: Delegation in the EU*. Cambridge: Cambridge University Press.
2020. 'In Search of the Ideational Foundations of EU Fiscal Governance: Standard Ideas, Imperfect Rules'. *Journal of European Integration* 42 (2): 179–94.
2024. 'International Oversight of Fiscal Discipline'. *European Journal of Political Research* 63 (1): 281–302.
Franchino, Fabio, and Camilla Mariotto. 2020. 'Politicisation and Economic Governance Design'. *Journal of European Public Policy* 27 (3): 460–80.
2021. 'Noncompliance Risk, Asymmetric Power and the Design of Enforcement of the European Economic Governance'. *European Union Politics* 22 (4): 591–610.
2022. 'Bargaining Outcomes and Success in EU Economic Governance Reforms'. *Political Science Research and Methods* 10 (2): 227–42.
Franchino, Fabio, and Christopher Wratil. 2019. 'Representing the Compromise: How Institutions Serve Government Support Coalitions in European Union Policy Making'. *European Journal of Political Research* 58 (4): 1129–51.
Frankel, Jeffrey, and Jesse Schreger. 2013. 'Over-Optimistic Official Forecasts and Fiscal Rules in the Eurozone'. *Review of World Economics* 149 (2): 247–72.
Franzese, Robert J. Jr. 2002. *Macroeconomic Policies in Developed Democracies*. Cambridge: Cambridge University Press.
Galbács, Peter. 2015. 'Fiscal Policy and New Classical Macroeconomics'. In *The Theory of New Classical Macroeconomics: A Positive Critique*, edited by Peter Galbács, 221–81. Contributions to Economics. Cham: Springer International Publishing.
Gamble, Andrew. 2013. 'Neo-Liberalism and Fiscal Conservatism'. In *Resilient Liberalism in Europe's Political Economy*, edited by Vivien A. Schmidt and Mark Thatcher. Cambridge: Cambridge University Press.
Garcilazo, Enrique, Ana I. Moreno-Monroy, and Joaquim Oliveira Martins. 2021. 'Regional Inequalities and Contributions to Aggregate Growth in the 2000s: An EU vs US Comparison Based on Functional Regions'. *Oxford Review of Economic Policy* 37 (1): 70–96.

Garrett, Geoffrey, and George Tsebelis. 1996. 'An Institutional Critique of Intergovernmentalism'. *International Organization* 50 (2): 269–99.

Genschel, Philipp. 2013. *Beyond the Regulatory Polity?: The European Integration of Core State Powers*. Oxford: Oxford University Press.

Genschel, Philipp, and Markus Jachtenfuchs. 2016. 'More Integration, Less Federation: The European Integration of Core State Powers'. *Journal of European Public Policy* 23 (1): 42–59.

2018. 'From Market Integration to Core State Powers: The Eurozone Crisis, the Refugee Crisis and Integration Theory'. *Journal of Common Market Studies* 56 (1): 178–96.

Giavazzi, Francesco, and Marco Pagano. 1990. 'Can Severe Fiscal Contractions Be Expansionary? Tales of Two Small European Countries'. In *NBER Macroeconomics Annual 1990*, Volume 5, edited by Olivier J. Blanchard and Stanley Fischer, 75–122. Cambridge, MA: The MIT Press.

Golder, Matt. 2005. 'Democratic Electoral Systems around the World, 1946–2000'. *Electoral Studies* 24 (1): 103–21.

Golub, Jonathan. 2012. 'How the European Union Does Not Work: National Bargaining Success in the Council of Ministers'. *Journal of European Public Policy* 19 (9): 1294–1315.

Guardiancich, Igor, and Mattia Guidi. 2020. 'The Political Economy of Pension Reforms in Europe under Financial Stress'. *Socio-Economic Review*, no. 20 (2): 817–40.

Guidi, Mattia, and Igor Guardiancich. 2018. 'Intergovernmental or Supranational Integration? A Quantitative Analysis of Pension Recommendations in the European Semester'. *European Union Politics* 19 (4): 684–706.

Haas, Jörg S., Valerie J. D'Erman, Daniel F. Schulz, and Amy Verdun. 2020. 'Economic and Fiscal Policy Coordination after the Crisis: Is the European Semester Promoting More or Less State Intervention?' *Journal of European Integration* 42 (3): 327–44.

Haftel, Yoram Z. 2013. 'Commerce and Institutions: Trade, Scope, and the Design of Regional Economic Organizations'. *The Review of International Organizations* 8 (3): 389–414.

Hagemann, Sara, Stefanie Bailer, and Alexander Herzog. 2019. 'Signals to Their Parliaments? Governments' Use of Votes and Policy Statements in the EU Council'. *Journal of Common Market Studies* 57 (3): 634–50.

Hagemann, Sara, Sara B. Hobolt, and Christopher Wratil. 2017. 'Government Responsiveness in the European Union: Evidence From Council Voting'. *Comparative Political Studies* 50 (6): 850–76.

Hagemann, Sara, and Bjørn Høyland. 2008. 'Parties in the Council?' *Journal of European Public Policy* 15 (8): 1205–21.

Hall, Peter A. 1989. *The Political Power of Economic Ideas: Keynesianism Across Nations*. Princeton, NJ: Princeton University Press.

Hallerberg, Mark, Rolf Rainer Strauch, and Jürgen von Hagen. 2009. *Fiscal Governance in Europe*. Cambridge: Cambridge University Press.

Hansen, Michael A. 2015. 'Explaining Deviations from the Stability and Growth Pact: Power, Ideology, Economic Need or Diffusion?' *Journal of Public Policy* 35 (3): 477–504.

Harrinvirta, Markku, and Mikko Mattila. 2001. 'The Hard Business of Balancing Budgets: A Study of Public Finances in Seventeen OECD Countries'. *British Journal of Political Science* 31 (3): 497–521.

Hartlapp, Miriam, Julia Metz, and Christian Rauh. 2014. *Which Policy for Europe?: Power and Conflict inside the European Commission*. Oxford: Oxford University Press.

Heipertz, Martin, and Amy Verdun. 2005. 'The Stability and Growth Pact – Theorizing a Case in European Integration'. *Journal of Common Market Studies* 43 (5): 985–1008.

2010. *Ruling Europe: The Politics of the Stability and Growth Pact*. Cambridge: Cambridge University Press.

Hellwig, Martin, Manfred J. M. Neumann, Roland Vaubel, and Marcus Miller. 1987. 'Economic Policy in Germany: Was There a Turnaround?' *Economic Policy* 2 (5): 105–45.

Hennis, Marjoleine. 2022. 'Par Le Haut Ou Par Les Pays-Bas? French and Dutch Approaches to European Social Policy Coordination Compared'. *Journal of Common Market Studies* 60 (1): 136–51.

Hix, Simon, and Bjørn Høyland. 2022. *The Political System of the European Union*. 4th ed. London: Bloomsbury Academic.

Hobolt, Sara B., Jae-Jae Spoon, and James Tilley. 2009. 'A Vote Against Europe? Explaining Defection at the 1999 and 2004 European Parliament Elections'. *British Journal of Political Science* 39 (01): 93–115.

Hobolt, Sara B., and Christopher Wratil. 2020. 'Contestation and Responsiveness in EU Council Deliberations'. *Journal of European Public Policy* 27 (3): 362–81.

Hodson, Dermot. 2013. 'The Little Engine That Wouldn't: Supranational Entrepreneurship and the Barroso Commission'. *Journal of European Integration* 35 (3): 301–14.

Hofmann, Tobias. 2018. 'How Long to Compliance? Escalating Infringement Proceedings and the Diminishing Power of Special Interests'. *Journal of European Integration* 40 (6): 785–801.

Hooghe, Liesbet, Jeanine Bezuijen, Svet Derderyan, and Emanuel Coman. 2013. 'Designing Third Party Dispute Settlement for International Organizations'. In *Proceedings of International Studies Association Annual Convention*, 50. San Francisco.

Hooghe, Liesbet, and Gary Marks. 2009. 'A Postfunctionalist Theory of European Integration: From Permissive Consensus to Constraining Dissensus'. *British Journal of Political Science* 39 (1): 1–23.

2015. 'Delegation and Pooling in International Organizations'. *The Review of International Organizations* 10 (3): 305–28.

Howlett, Michael. 2000. 'Managing the 'Hollow State': Procedural Policy Instruments and Modern Governance'. *Canadian Public Administration* 43 (4): 412–31.

Hox, J. J., Mirjam Moerbeek, and Rens van de Schoot. 2017. *Multilevel Analysis: Techniques and Applications*. 3rd ed. Quantitative Methodology Series. New York, NY: Routledge.

Huber, John D., and G. Bingham Powell. 1994. 'Congruence between Citizens and Policymakers in Two Visions of Liberal Democracy'. *World Politics* 46 (3): 291–326.

Hübscher, Evelyne, and Thomas Sattler. 2017. 'Fiscal Consolidation under Electoral Risk'. *European Journal of Political Research* 56 (1): 151–68.

Hutter, Swen, Edgar Grande, and Hanspeter Kriesi. 2016. *Politicising Europe: Integration and Mass Politics*. Cambridge: Cambridge University Press.

Imai, Kosuke, In Song Kim, and Erik H. Wang. 2023. 'Matching Methods for Causal Inference with Time-Series Cross-Sectional Data'. *American Journal of Political Science* 67 (3): 587–605.

Inglehart, Ronald. 1970a. 'Cognitive Mobilization and European Identity'. *Comparative Politics* 3 (1): 45–70.

1970b. 'Public Opinion and Regional Integration'. *International Organization* 24 (4): 764–95.

International Monetary Fund. 2012. 'Euro Area Policies: 2012 Article IV Consultation—Selected Issues Paper'. Country Report No. 12/182. Washington, D.C.: IMF.

Ioannou, Demosthenes, and Livio Stracca. 2014. 'Have the Euro Area and EU Governance Worked? Just the Facts'. *European Journal of Political Economy* 34: 1–17.

Jabko, Nicolas. 2019. 'Contested Governance: The New Repertoire of the Eurozone Crisis'. *Governance* 32 (3): 493–509.

Jensen, Christian B. 2007. 'Implementing Europe: A Question of Oversight'. *European Union Politics* 8 (4): 451–77.

Jevons, William Stanley. 1871. *The Theory of Political Economy*. London: Macmillan.

Jones, Erik. 2013. 'The Collapse of the Brussels–Frankfurt Consensus and the Future of the Euro'. In *Resilient Liberalism in Europe's Political Economy*, edited by Mark Thatcher and Vivien A. Schmidt, 145–70. Cambridge: Cambridge University Press.

Jonung, Lars, Martin Larch, Carlo A. Favero, and Philippe Martin. 2006. 'Improving Fiscal Policy in the EU: The Case for Independent Forecasts'. *Economic Policy* 21 (47): 491–534.

Junge, Dirk, and Thomas König. 2007. 'What's Wrong With Eu Spatial Analysis?: The Accuracy and Robustness of Empirical Applications To the Interpretation of the Legislative Process and the Specification of Preferences'. *Journal of Theoretical Politics* 19 (4): 465–87.

Junge, Dirk, Thomas König, and Bernd Luig. 2015. 'Legislative Gridlock and Bureaucratic Politics in the European Union'. *British Journal of Political Science* 45 (4): 777–97.

Kaeding, Michael. 2008. 'Lost in Translation or Full Steam Ahead: The Transposition of EU Transport Directives across Member States'. *European Union Politics* 9 (1): 115–43.

Kelemen, R. Daniel, and Terence K. Teo. 2014. 'Law, Focal Points, and Fiscal Discipline in the United States and the European Union'. *American Political Science Review* 108 (2): 355–70.

Keohane, Robert O. 1984. *After Hegemony: Cooperation and Discord in the World Political Economy*. Princeton: Princeton University Press.

Key, V.O., Jr. 1966. *The Responsible Electorate: Rationality in Presidential Voting 1936–1960*. Cambridge, MA: Harvard University Press.

Keynes, John Maynard. 1936. *The General Theory of Employment, Interest and Money: With The Economic Consequences of the Peace*. Ware: Wordsworth Editions.

Koehler, Sebastian, and Thomas König. 2015. 'Fiscal Governance in the Eurozone: How Effectively Does the Stability and Growth Pact Limit Governmental Debt in the Euro Countries?' *Political Science Research and Methods* 3 (2): 329–51.

König, Thomas, and Lars Mäder. 2014. 'The Strategic Nature of Compliance: An Empirical Evaluation of Law Implementation in the Central Monitoring System of the European Union'. *American Journal of Political Science* 58 (1): 246–63.

König, Thomas, and Sven-Oliver Proksch. 2006. 'A Procedural Exchange Model of EU Legislative Politics'. In *The European Union Decides*, edited by Robert Thomson, Frans N. Stokman, Christopher H. Achen, and Thomas König, 211–38. Cambridge: Cambridge University Press.

Koremenos, Barbara. 2008. 'When, What, and Why Do States Choose to Delegate?' *Law and Contemporary Problems* 71 (1): 151–92.

Koremenos, Barbara, Charles Lipson, and Duncan Snidal. 2001. 'The Rational Design of International Institutions'. *International Organization* 55 (4): 761–99.

Kreppel, Amie, and Buket Oztas. 2017. 'Leading the Band or Just Playing the Tune? Reassessing the Agenda-Setting Powers of the European Commission'. *Comparative Political Studies* 50 (8): 1118–50.

Kriesi, Hanspeter, and Edgar Grande. 2016. 'The Euro Crisis: A Boost to the Politicisation of European Integration?' In *Politicising Europe: Integration and Mass Politics*, edited by Swen Hutter, Edgar Grande, and Hanspeter Kriesi, 240–76. Cambridge: Cambridge University Press.

Laakso, Markku, and Rein Taagepera. 1979. 'Effective Number of Parties: A Measure with Application to West Europe'. *Comparative Political Studies* 12 (1): 3–27.

Lasswell, Harold Dwight. 1956. *The Decision Process: Seven Categories of Functional Analysis*. College Park, MD: University of Maryland Press.

Leblond, Patrick. 2006. 'The Political Stability and Growth Pact Is Dead: Long Live the Economic Stability and Growth Pact'. *Journal of Common Market Studies* 44 (5): 969–90.

Lehner, Thomas, and Fabio Wasserfallen. 2019. 'Political Conflict in the Reform of the Eurozone'. *European Union Politics* 20 (1): 45–64.

Levenshtein, Vladimir I. 1966. 'Binary Codes Capable of Correcting Deletions, Insertions and Reversals'. *Soviet Physics Doklady* 10 (8): 707–10.

Levine, Paul, and Andrew Brociner. 1994. 'Fiscal Policy Coordination and EMU: A Dynamic Game Approach'. *Journal of Economic Dynamics and Control* 18 (3–4): 699–729.

Lodge, David, and Marta Rodriguez-Vives. 2013. 'How Long Can Austerity Persist? The Factors That Sustain Fiscal Consolidations'. *European Journal of Government and Economics* 2 (1): 5–24.

Long, J. Scott, and Jeremy Freese. 2014. *Regression Models for Categorical Dependent Variables Using Stata*. 3rd ed. College Station, TX: Stata Press Publication.

Lucas, Robert E. Jr. 1972. 'Expectations and the Neutrality of Money'. *Journal of Economic Theory* 4 (2): 103–24.

Lundgren, Magnus, Stefanie Bailer, Lisa M Dellmuth, Jonas Tallberg, and Silvana Târlea. 2019. 'Bargaining Success in the Reform of the Eurozone'. *European Union Politics* 20 (1): 65–88.

Mabbett, Deborah, and Waltraud Schelkle. 2016. 'Searching Under the Lamppost: The Evolution of Fiscal Surveillance'. In *The Political and Economic Dynamics of the Eurozone Crisis*, edited by James A. Caporaso and Martin Rhodes, 122–44. Oxford: Oxford University Press.

Mansbridge, Jane. 2003. 'Rethinking Representation'. *American Political Science Review* 97 (4): 515–28.

Mariotto, Camilla. 2019. 'Negotiating Implementation of EU Fiscal Governance'. *Journal of European Integration* 41 (4): 465–86.

2022. 'The Implementation of Economic Rules: From the Stability and Growth Pact to the European Semester'. *Journal of Common Market Studies* 60 (1): 40–57.

Mariotto, Camilla, and Fabio Franchino. 2020. 'Implementation of the Specific Recommendations to Italy between 2002 and 2018'. *Rivista Italiana di Politiche Pubbliche*, no. 2/2020: 159–186.

Marks, Gary, Liesbet Hooghe, and Arjan H Schakel. 2008. 'Patterns of Regional Authority'. *Regional & Federal Studies* 18 (2): 167–81.

Martin, Lanny W., and Georg Vanberg. 2013. 'Multiparty Government, Fiscal Institutions, and Public Spending'. *Journal of Politics* 75 (4): 953–67.

Matthijs, Matthias. 2016. 'Powerful Rules Governing the Euro: The Perverse Logic of German Ideas'. *Journal of European Public Policy* 23 (3): 375–91.

Matthijs, Matthias, and Mark Blyth. 2018. 'When Is It Rational to Learn the Wrong Lessons? Technocratic Authority, Social Learning, and Euro Fragility'. *Perspectives on Politics* 16 (1): 110–26.

Mattila, Mikko. 2004. 'Contested Decisions: Empirical Analysis of Voting in the European Union Council of Ministers'. *European Journal of Political Research* 43 (1): 29–50.

Mbaye, Heather A. D. 2001. 'Why National States Comply with Supranational Law: Explaining Implementation Infringements in the European Union'. *European Union Politics* 2 (3): 259–81.

McCall Smith, James. 2000. 'The Politics of Dispute Settlement Design: Explaining Legalism in Regional Trade Pacts'. *International Organization* 54 (Winter 1): 137–80.

McElroy, Gail, and Kenneth Benoit. 2012. 'Policy Positioning in the European Parliament'. *European Union Politics* 13 (1): 150–67.

McNamara, Kathleen R. 1998. *The Currency of Ideas: Monetary Politics in the European Union*. Ithaca, NY: Cornell University Press.

Meissner, Thomas, and Davud Rostam-Afschar. 2014. 'Do Tax Cuts Increase Consumption? An Experimental Test of Ricardian Equivalence'. *Discussion Paper 2014/16*. School of Business & Economics, Free University Berlin.

Mérand, Frédéric. 2022. 'Political Work in the Stability and Growth Pact'. *Journal of European Public Policy* 29 (6): 846–64.

Mink, Mark, and Jakob De Haan. 2006. 'Are There Political Budget Cycles in the Euro Area?' *European Union Politics* 7 (2): 191–211.

Miró, Joan. 2021. 'Austerity's Failures and Policy Learning: Mapping European Commission Officials' Beliefs on Fiscal Governance in the Post-Crisis EU'. *Review of International Political Economy* 28 (5): 1224–48.

Mody, Ashoka. 2018. *Eurotragedy: A Drama in Nine Acts*. New York, NY: Oxford University Press.

Moravcsik, Andrew. 1998. *The Choice for Europe: Social Purpose and State Power from Messina to Maastricht*. Ithaca, NY: Cornell University Press.

Moschella, Manuela. 2017. 'Italy and the Fiscal Compact: Why Does a Country Commit to Permanent Austerity?' *Italian Political Science Review* 47 (2): 205–25.

Mourlon-Druol, Emmanuel. 2014. 'Don't Blame the Euro: Historical Reflections on the Roots of the Eurozone Crisis'. *West European Politics* 37 (6): 1282–96.

2020. 'History of an Incomplete EMU'. In *The EU Law of Economic and Monetary Union*, edited by Fabian Amtenbrink and Christoph Herrmann, 13–36. Oxford: Oxford University Press.

Müller, Wofgang C, and Kaare Strøm, eds. 1999. *Policy, Office, or Votes? How Political Parties in Western Europe Make Hard Decisions*. Cambridge: Cambridge University Press.

Neumayer, Eric, and Thomas Plümper. 2017. *Robustness Tests for Quantitative Research*. Cambridge: Cambridge University Press.

Niemann, Arne, and Demosthenes Ioannou. 2015. 'European Economic Integration in Times of Crisis: A Case of Neofunctionalism?' *Journal of European Public Policy* 22 (2): 196–218.

Nugent, Neill, and Mark Rhinard. 2005. *The European Commission*. 2nd ed. New York: Palgrave.

Page, Benjamin I., and Robert Y. Shapiro. 1983. 'Effects of Public Opinion on Policy'. *American Political Science Review* 77 (1): 175–90.

Pan, Wen, Madeleine O. Hosli, and Michaël Lantmeeters. 2023. 'Historical Institutionalism and Policy Coordination: Origins of the European Semester'. *Evolutionary and Institutional Economics Review*, 20 (1): 141–67.

Pasinetti, Luigi L. 1998. 'The Myth (or Folly) of the 3% Deficit/GDP Maastricht "Parameter"'. *Cambridge Journal of Economics* 22 (1): 103–16.

Perotti, Roberto, and Yianos Kontopoulos. 2002. 'Fragmented Fiscal Policy'. *Journal of Public Economics* 86 (2): 191–222.

Persson, Torsten, Gerard Roland, and Guido Tabellini. 2007. 'Electoral Rules and Government Spending in Parliamentary Democracies'. *Quarterly Journal of Political Science* 2 (2): 155–88.

Persson, Torsten, and Lars E. O. Svensson. 1989. 'Why a Stubborn Conservative Would Run a Deficit: Policy with Time- Inconsistent Preferences'. *The Quarterly Journal of Economics* 104 (2): 325–45.

Pierson, Paul. 1996. 'The Path to European Integration. A Historical Institutionalist Analysis'. *Comparative Political Studies* 29 (2): 123–63.

Piketty, Thomas. 2017. *Capital in the Twenty-First Century*. Translated by Arthur Goldhammer. Reprint edition. Cambridge, MA: Belknap Press [An Imprint of Harvard University Press].

Pircher, Brigitte, and Karl Loxbo. 2020. 'Compliance with EU Law in Times of Disintegration: Exploring Changes in Transposition and Enforcement in the EU Member States between 1997 and 2016'. *Journal of Common Market Studies* 58 (5): 1270–87.

Polk, Jonathan, Jan Rovny, Ryan Bakker, Erica Edwards, Liesbet Hooghe, Seth Jolly, Jelle Koedem, Filip Kostelka, Gary Marks, Gijs Schumacher, Marco Steenbergen, Milada Vachudova, and Marko Zilovic. 2017. 'Explaining the Salience of Anti-Elitism and Reducing Political Corruption for Political Parties in Europe with the 2014 Chapel Hill Expert Survey Data'. *Research & Politics* 4 (1): 1–9.

Poterba, James M., and Lawrence H. Summers. 1987. 'Finite Lifetimes and the Effects of Budget Deficits on National Saving'. *Journal of Monetary Economics* 20 (2): 369–91.

Predtetchinski, Arkadi. 2011. 'One-Dimensional Bargaining'. *Games and Economic Behavior* 72 (2): 526–43.

Princen, Sebastiaan, and Femke van Esch. 2016. 'Paradigm Formation and Paradigm Change in the EU's Stability and Growth Pact'. *European Political Science Review* 8 (03): 355–75.

Puetter, Uwe. 2012. 'Europe's Deliberative Intergovernmentalism: The Role of the Council and European Council in EU Economic Governance'. *Journal of European Public Policy* 19 (2): 161–78.

2016. 'The Centrality of Consensus and Deliberation in Contemporary EU Politics and the New Intergovernmentalism'. *Journal of European Integration* 38 (5): 601–15.

Quaglia, Lucia. 2004. 'Italy's Policy towards European Monetary Integration: Bringing Ideas Back In?' *Journal of European Public Policy* 11 (6): 1096–1111.

2005. 'Civil Servants, Economic Ideas, and Economic Policies: Lessons from Italy'. *Governance* 18 (4): 545–66.

Raustiala, Kal, and Anne-Marie Slaughter. 2002. 'International Law and Compliance'. In *Handbook of International Relations*, edited by Walter Carlsnaes, Thomas Risse, and Beth A. Simmons, 538–58. London: Sage Publications.

Ray, Leonard. 1999. 'Measuring Party Orientations towards European Integration: Results from an Expert Survey'. *European Journal of Political Research* 36 (2): 283–306.

Rehn, Olli. 2013. *Letter to ECOFIN Ministers, 13 February*. Ares (2013) 185796. Brussels: European Commission.

Ricardo, David. 1820. *Essay on the Funding System*. London: Timeless Book Edition.

Roper, Steven D. 2002. 'Are All Semipresidential Regimes the Same? A Comparison of Premier-Presidential Regimes'. *Comparative Politics* 34 (3): 253–72.

Rosendorff, B. Peter. 2005. 'Stability and Rigidity: Politics and Design of the WTO's Dispute Settlement Procedure'. *American Political Science Review* 99 (3): 389–400.

Rosendorff, B. Peter, and Helen V. Milner. 2001. 'The Optimal Design of International Trade Institutions: Uncertainty and Escape'. *International Organization* 55 (4): 829–57.

Roubini, Nouriel, and Jeffrey D. Sachs. 1989. 'Political and Economic Determinants of Budget Deficits in the Industrial Democracies'. *European Economic Review* 33 (5): 903–33.

Sacchi, Stefano. 2015. 'Conditionality by Other Means: EU Involvement in Italy's Structural Reforms in the Sovereign Debt Crisis'. *Comparative European Politics* 13 (1): 77–92.

Sacher, Martin. 2021. 'Avoiding the Inappropriate: The European Commission and Sanctions under the Stability and Growth Pact'. *Politics and Governance* 9 (2): 163–72.

Savage, James D., and David Howarth. 2018. 'Enforcing the European Semester: The Politics of Asymmetric Information in the Excessive Deficit and Macroeconomic Imbalance Procedures'. *Journal of European Public Policy* 25 (2): 212–30.

Savage, James D., and Amy Verdun. 2016. 'Strengthening the European Commission's Budgetary and Economic Surveillance Capacity since Greece and the Euro Area Crisis: A Study of Five Directorates-General'. *Journal of European Public Policy* 23 (1): 101–18.

Sbragia, Alberta. 2001. 'Italy Pays for Europe: Political Leadership, Political Choice and Institutional Adaptation'. In *Transforming Europe: Europeanization and Domestic Change*, edited by James Caporaso, Maria Green Cowles, and Thomas Risse, 79–96. Ithaca, NY: Cornell University Press.

Schild, Joachim. 2013. 'Leadership in Hard Times: Germany, France, and the Management of the Eurozone Crisis'. *German Politics & Society* 31 (1): 24–47.

2020. 'EMU's Asymmetries and Asymmetries in German and French Influence on EMU Governance Reforms'. *Journal of European Integration* 42 (3): 449–64.

Schimmelfennig, Frank. 2014. 'European Integration in the Euro Crisis: The Limits of Postfunctionalism'. *Journal of European Integration* 36 (3): 321–37.

2015. 'Liberal Intergovernmentalism and the Euro Area Crisis'. *Journal of European Public Policy* 22 (2): 177–95.

Schmidt, Vivien A. 2016a. 'EU Leaders' Ideas and Discourse in the Eurozone Crisis: A Discursive Institutionalist Analysis'. In *EU Foreign Policy through the Lens of Discourse Analysis: Making Sense of Diversity*, edited by Caterina Carta and Jean-Frederic Morin, 245–64. London: Routledge.

2016b. 'Reinterpreting the Rules 'by Stealth' in Times of Crisis: A Discursive Institutionalist Analysis of the European Central Bank and the European Commission'. *West European Politics* 39 (5): 1032–52.

2017. 'The Resilience of 'Bad Ideas' in Eurozone Crisis Discourse, Even as Rival Ideas Inform Changing Practices'. *TLI Think!* Paper 52/2017: 23.

2020. *Europe's Crisis of Legitimacy: Governing by Rules and Ruling by Numbers in the Eurozone*. Oxford, NY: Oxford University Press.

Schmidt, Vivien A., and Mark Thatcher. 2013. 'Theorizing Ideational Continuity: The Resilience of Neo-Liberal Ideas in Europe'. In *Resilient Liberalism in Europe's Political Economy*, edited by Vivien A. Schmidt and Mark Thatcher, 1–50. Cambridge: Cambridge University Press.

Schneider, Christina J. 2018. *The Responsive Union: National Elections and European Governance*. New York: Cambridge University Press.

Schneider, Gerald, Daniel Finke, and Stefanie Bailer. 2010. 'Bargaining Power in the European Union: An Evaluation of Competing Game-Theoretic Models'. *Political Studies* 58 (1): 85–103.

Schoeller, Magnus G. 2017. 'Providing Political Leadership? Three Case Studies on Germany's Ambiguous Role in the Eurozone Crisis'. *Journal of European Public Policy* 24 (1): 1–20.

Schure, Paul, and Amy Verdun. 2008. 'Legislative Bargaining in the European Union: The Divide between Large and Small Member States'. *European Union Politics* 9 (4): 459–86.

Schütze, Robert. 2018. *European Constitutional Law*. 2nd ed. Cambridge Cambridge University Press.

Sczepanski, Ronja, and Tanja A. Börzel. 2023. 'Two Sides of the Same Coin? The Effect of Differentiation on Noncompliance with European Union Law'. *European Union Politics* 24 (1): 63–80.

Segers, Mathieu, and Femke van Esch. 2007. 'Behind the Veil of Budgetary Discipline: The Political Logic of the Budgetary Rules in EMU and the SGP'. *Journal of Common Market Studies* 45 (5): 1089–109.

Seikel, Daniel. 2016. 'Flexible Austerity and Supranational Autonomy. The Reformed Excessive Deficit Procedure and the Asymmetry between Liberalization and Social Regulation in the EU'. *Journal of Common Market Studies* 54 (6): 1398–416.

Simmons, Beth A. 2010. 'Treaty Compliance and Violation'. *Annual Review of Political Science* 13 (1): 273–96.

Slapin, Jonathan B. 2014. 'Measurement, Model Testing, and Legislative Influence in the European Union'. *European Union Politics* 15 (1): 24–42.

Smithers, Andrew. 2022. *The Economics of the Stock Market*. Oxford, NY: Oxford University Press.

Spendzharova, Aneta, and Esther Versluis. 2013. 'Issue Salience in the European Policy Process: What Impact on Transposition?' *Journal of European Public Policy* 20 (10): 1499–516.

Steinberg, Federico, and Mattias Vermeiren. 2016. 'Germany's Institutional Power and the EMU Regime after the Crisis: Towards a Germanized Euro Area?' *Journal of Common Market Studies* 54 (2): 388–407.

Steunenberg, Bernard. 1994. 'Decision Making under Different Institutional Arrangements: Legislation by the European Community'. *Journal of Institutional and Theoretical Economics* 150 (4): 642–69.

Steunenberg, Bernard, and Torsten J. Selck. 2006. 'Testing Procedural Models of EU Legislative Decision-Making'. In *The European Union Decides*, edited by Robert Thomson, Frans N. Stokman, Christopher H. Achen, and Thomas König, 54–85. Cambridge: Cambridge University Press.

Stiglitz, Joseph E. 2016. *The Euro: How a Common Currency Threatens the Future of Europe*. 1st ed. New York: W. W. Norton & Company.

Stone Sweet, Alec, and Thomas L. Brunell. 1998. 'Constructing a Supranational Constitution: Dispute Resolution and Governance in the European Community'. *American Political Science Review* 92 (1, March): 63–81.

Swinkels, Marij. 2020. 'How Ideas Matter in Public Policy: A Review of Concepts, Mechanisms, and Methods'. *International Review of Public Policy* 2 (2:3): 281–316.

Tallberg, Jonas. 2002. 'Paths to Compliance: Enforcement, Management, and the European Union'. *International Organization* 56 (3): 609–43.

2006. *Leadership and Negotiation in the European Union*. Cambridge: Cambridge University Press.

Tallberg, Jonas, and James McCall Smith. 2014. 'Dispute Settlement in World Politics: States, Supranational Prosecutors, and Compliance'. *European Journal of International Relations* 20 (1): 118–44.

Tang, Donny. 2019. 'Determinants of the Current Account Balances among Central and Eastern European Countries in the European Union'. *European Review* 27 (2): 220–45.

Târlea, Silvana, Stefanie Bailer, Hanno Degner, Lisa M Dellmuth, Dirk Leuffen, Magnus Lundgren, Jonas Tallberg, and Fabio Wasserfallen. 2019. 'Explaining Governmental Preferences on Economic and Monetary Union Reform'. *European Union Politics* 20 (1): 24–44.

Thomson, Robert. 2008. 'National Actors in International Organizations: The Case of the European Commission'. *Comparative Political Studies* 41 (2): 169–92.

2011. *Resolving Controversy in the European Union: Legislative Decision-Making Before and After Enlargement*. Cambridge: Cambridge University Press.

Thomson, Robert, Jovanka Boerefijn, and Frans Stokman. 2004. 'Actor Alignments in European Union Decision Making'. *European Journal of Political Research* 43 (2): 237–61.

Thomson, Robert, Frans N. Stokman, Christopher H. Achen, and Thomas König, eds. 2006. *The European Union Decides*. Cambridge: Cambridge University Press.

Toshkov, Dimiter. 2007. 'Transposition of EU Social Policy in the New Member States'. *Journal of European Social Policy* 17 (4): 335–48.

2008. 'Embracing European Law Compliance with EU Directives in Central and Eastern Europe'. *European Union Politics* 9 (3): 379–402.

2011. 'Public Opinion and Policy Output in the European Union: A Lost Relationship'. *European Union Politics* 12 (2): 169–91.

Tsebelis, George. 1994. 'The Power of the European Parliament as a Conditional Agenda Setter'. *American Political Science Review* 88 (1): 128–42.

Tsebelis, George, and Geoffrey Garrett. 2000. 'Legislative Politics in the European Union'. *European Union Politics* 1 (1): 9–36.

van Aarle, Bas, A. Lans Bovenberg, and Matthias G. Raith. 1997. 'Is There a Tragedy of a Common Central Bank? A Dynamic Analysis'. *Journal of Economic Dynamics and Control* 21 (2–3): 417–47.

Van den Bos, Jan M. M. 1991. *Dutch EC Policy Making: A Model-Guided Approach to Coordination and Negotiation*. Amsterdam: Thesis Publishers.

van der Veer, Reinout Arthur, and Markus Haverland. 2018. 'Bread and Butter or Bread and Circuses? Politicisation and the European Commission in the European Semester'. *European Union Politics* 19 (3): 524–45.

van der Veer, Reinout Arthur. 2022. 'Walking the Tightrope: Politicization and the Commission's Enforcement of the SGP'. *Journal of Common Market Studies* 60 (1): 81–100.

Vanheuverzwijn, Pierre. 2017. 'How the Commission Fills in the Blanks of the European Semester'. *Politique Europeenne* 55 (1): 8–35.

Verdun, Amy. 2015. 'A Historical Institutionalist Explanation of the EU's Responses to the Euro Area Financial Crisis'. *Journal of European Public Policy* 22 (2): 219–37.

Vilpišauskas, Ramūnas. 2013. 'Eurozone Crisis and European Integration: Functional Spillover, Political Spillback?' *Journal of European Integration* 35 (3): 361–73.

Viti de Marco, Antonio de. 1893. 'La Pressione Tributaria Dell'imposta e Del Prestito'. *Giornale Degli Economisti* 6 (1): 38–67.

Volkens, Andrea, Werner Krause, Pola Lehmann, Theres Matthieß, Sven Regel, Bernhard Weßels, Tobias Burst, Nicolas Merz, and Lisa Zehnter.

2020. 'The Manifesto Data Collection. Manifesto Project (MRG/CMP/MARPOR)'. *Technical Report Version 2020a*. Wissenschaftszentrum Berlin für Sozialforschung (WZB).

Volkerink, Bjørn, and Jakob De Haan. 2001. 'Fragmented Government Effects on Fiscal Policy: New Evidence'. *Public Choice* 109 (3): 221–42.

von Hagen, Jürgen. 2010. 'Sticking to Fiscal Plans: The Role of Institutions'. *Public Choice* 144 (3/4): 487–503.

von Hagen, Jürgen, and Ian J. Harden. 1995. 'Budget Processes and Commitment to Fiscal Discipline'. *European Economic Review* 39 (3): 771–79.

von Hagen, Jürgen, and Guntram B. Wolff. 2006. 'What Do Deficits Tell Us about Debt? Empirical Evidence on Creative Accounting with Fiscal Rules in the EU'. *Journal of Banking & Finance* 30 (12): 3259–79.

Walter, Stefanie, Ari Ray, and Nils Redeker. 2020. *The Politics of Bad Options: Why the Eurozone's Problems Have Been So Hard to Resolve*. Oxford: Oxford University Press.

Warntjen, Andreas. 2008. 'The Council Presidency: Power Broker or Burden? An Empirical Analysis'. *European Union Politics* 9 (3): 315–38.

Warren, Thomas. 2018. 'The European Parliament and the Eurozone Crisis: An Exceptional Actor?' *The British Journal of Politics and International Relations* 20 (3): 632–51.

Warwick, Paul V., and James N. Druckman. 2001. 'Portfolio Salience and the Proportionality of Payoffs in Coalition Governments'. *British Journal of Political Science* 31: 627–49.

Wasserfallen, Fabio, Dirk Leuffen, Zdenek Kudrna, and Hanno Degner. 2019. 'Analysing European Union Decision-Making during the Eurozone Crisis with New Data'. *European Union Politics* 20 (1): 3–23.

Wehner, Joachim. 2010a. 'Cabinet Structure and Fiscal Policy Outcomes'. *European Journal of Political Research* 49 (5): 631–53.

2010b. 'Institutional Constraints on Profligate Politicians: The Conditional Effect of Partisan Fragmentation on Budget Deficits'. *Comparative Political Studies* 43 (2): 208–29.

Williams, Christopher J. 2018. 'Responding through Transposition: Public Euroskepticism and European Policy Implementation'. *European Political Science Review* 10 (1): 51–70.

Wolf, Martin. 2014. *The Shifts and the Shocks: What We've Learned-and Have Still to Learn-from the Financial Crisis*. New York: Penguin Press.

Wratil, Christopher. 2019. 'Territorial Representation and the Opinion–Policy Linkage: Evidence from the European Union'. *American Journal of Political Science* 63 (1): 197–211.

Wray, L. Randall. 2015. *Why Minsky Matters: An Introduction to the Work of a Maverick Economist*. Princeton, NJ: Princeton University Press.

Zeitlin, Jonathan, and Bart Vanhercke. 2018. 'Socializing the European Semester: EU Social and Economic Policy Co-Ordination in Crisis and Beyond'. *Journal of European Public Policy* 25 (2): 149–74.

Zimmer, Christina, Gerald Schneider, and Michael Dobbins. 2005. 'The Contested Council: Conflict Dimensions of an Intergovernmental EU Institution'. *Political Studies* 53 (2): 403–22.

Index

Note: Page numbers in *italic* refers to figures

www.ingramcontent.com/pod-product-compliance
Lightning Source LLC
LaVergne TN
LVHW011811200926
848484LV00005B/1145

* 9 7 8 1 0 0 9 5 9 5 8 1 0 *